ESOTERIC PSYCHOLOGY
AND THE SCIENCE OF THE
RAYS AND CHAKRAS OF GOD:
A COMPILATION

ESOTERIC PSYCHOLOGY AND THE SCIENCE OF THE RAYS AND CHAKRAS OF GOD: A COMPILATION

VOLUME II

Dr. Joshua David Stone

Writers Club Press
San Jose New York Lincoln Shanghai

Esoteric Psychology and the Science of
the Rays and Chakras of God: A Compilation
Volume II

Writers Club Press
an imprint of iUniverse.com, Inc.

For information address:
iUniverse.com, Inc.
5220 S 16th, Ste. 200
Lincoln, NE 68512
www.iuniverse.com

ISBN: 0-595-19834-1

Printed in the United States of America

Contents

Introduction

My Beloved Readers,

This is a most wonderful compilation-type of book of the best chapters in my 40 volume Ascension Book Series on the Rays and Chakras. Spirit and the Masters have guided me, since I have so many books in this Spiritual Encyclopedia and not everyone has read all the books, to have a number of what I call "compilation-type books"! Compilation-type books are selected chapters on a specific subject. Since the study of the Rays and Chakras is such an important subject and this is such cutting-edge and revolutionary information, I have provided my readers with all this information in one book!

It is hard to believe that the study of the Rays in the field of psychology is almost an unknown science. The irony of this is that it is probably the single most important understanding in the entire field of psychology! In essence, God's Personality is made up of the Seven Great Rays! Since we are made in the image of God, it is the configuration of our personality as well!

The influence of the Rays is even more powerful than Astrology. The study of the Rays is of absolutely astronomical importance to all Spiritual Seekers! Within it you will find the basic personality structure of how God created each one of us in a specific sense and in terms of a general integrated ideal that we all need to strive for! I would go so far as to say that the full understanding of Spiritual Psychology literally cannot be understood without understanding the Science of the Rays!

The intensive study of this subject will literally revolutionize your consciousness! It is one of the foundational understandings of Spiritual and Soul Psychology! Enjoy!

Warmest Regards and Love!

Dr Joshua David Stone

1

The Personality of GOD

We have here one of the age old questions from the beginning of time, which is what is the Personality of GOD? If we could understand what the Personality of GOD was then we could really have a Golden Key to how to Realize GOD on Earth. By the Grace of GOD and the inner plane Ascended Masters, I will share with you just this in this chapter.

GOD's Personality is divided into three parts and seven parts. This is part of why the numbers three and seven are considered some of the holiest numbers. GOD is first divided into the Trinity of GOD, which, of course, is GOD, Christ, and the Holy Spirit. GOD being the Creator. The Christ being the Eternal Self we as the Sons and Daughters of GOD are, in truth, but are in the process of Realizing. The Holy Spirit, which is the Voice of GOD and the "still, small voice within," which speaks for the Atonement or the At-One-Ment. The Holy Spirit is GOD's answer to every question and ever problem. For every miscreation of the negative ego/fear-based/separative mind, the Holy Spirit is the antidote. The Holy Spirit speaks for the Christ/Buddha Consciousness, which of course is the opposite of the negative ego/fear-based consciousness. The Holy Spirit speaks for the Atonement, which is the undoing of all problems, which come from separative thinking. It can help undo everything in your personality that is not of GOD. Most people, and even lightworkers, do not take advantage of the incredible powers of the Holy Spirit.

Now, we are made in GOD's Image, as the Bible says, so we are a Trinity as well. We are a Trinity made up of the Superconscious, conscious and subconscious minds. Part of our lesson is to become as integrated as GOD is in His Triune nature. This is our first clue into the Personality of GOD.

The second clue into the Nature of the Personality of GOD is to understand GOD's seven-fold nature. GOD's Body is made up of Seven Cosmic Dimensions, with each Dimension made up of Seven subplanes or subdimensions in each of these Cosmic Dimensions. These Dimensions are called the Cosmic Physical, Cosmic Astral, Cosmic Mental, Cosmic Buddhic, Cosmic Atmic, Cosmic Monadic, and Cosmic Logoic. The Cosmic Physical Plane is made up of seven subplanes by the same names, but are the subplanes of the Cosmic Physical Plane.

This, however, explains the nature and structure of GOD's Body but does not explain GOD's Personality. GOD's Personality is divined into seven parts as well. These are the great and Holy Rays of GOD. GOD's Personality is divided into Power, Love/Wisdom, Active Intelligence, Harmony and Beauty, New Age Science, Devotion, Freedom/Transmutation/Alchemy and Divine Structure. GOD's Personality is the Perfect Balanced and Integrated Synthesis of these Seven Attributes. This understanding is a Divine and Sanctified Gift and Map from GOD and the Masters to help us understand the proper way to balance and integrate our own personalities and psychological selves.

GOD's Personality is first made up of Power. This is the Power to be the First Cause and Creator of the Infinite Universe. It is the Power to completely cause His reality. It is also the Power and Will of GOD, rather than the will of the negative ego, lower self, fear based, separative mind. So my Beloved Readers, GOD owns His Power, and is the Embodiment of the Will of GOD and not the will of the negative ego fear-based thought system. This is the First Great Ray of GOD and Creation.

The second aspect of GOD's Personality is Love/Wisdom. GOD is Unconditionally Loving at all times towards self and His Creation and manifests and demonstrates this Unconditional Love with great Psychological Wisdom. This is the Second Great Ray of GOD and Creation.

The Third aspect of GOD's Personality is Active Intelligence. This again is a form of Wisdom, but it is not Wisdom of the Heart, or Wisdom in a Psychological Sense, as a different kind of Wisdom, that is "Wisdom to put GOD's Consciousness into Action." Without this Third Aspect of GOD's Personality, nothing would ever get done in GOD's Plan. We would have Personality/Power and Love/Wisdom; however, without this third aspect of GOD's Personality, the Power and Love would never manifest on the Material Plane of GOD's reality. This is the Third Great Ray of GOD and Creation!

The Fourth Aspect of GOD's Personality is Harmony and Beauty. GOD is not only Powerful, Loving, Psychologically Wise/Wise in Action in Material Creation but GOD is Harmonious and completely attuned to Beauty in every aspect of Creation, in the way GOD manifests his reality on the Material Plane of Creation. This is the Fourth Great Ray of GOD and Creation.

The Fifth aspect of GOD's Personality is New Age Science. GOD is not only Power, Unconditional Love/Psychologically wise, Wise in Action, Attuned to Harmony and Beauty, but GOD is very Scientific in how He has Created the Infinite Universe. Everything in GOD's Universe is governed by Laws and is very much in Divine Order. It is possible to understand and Master these Laws and hence understand the Nature of GOD on His various levels. This is why, in truth, Religion and Science blend perfectly together if properly understood. This is the Fifth Great Ray of GOD and Creation.

The Sixth Aspect of GOD's Personality is Devotion. God is not only All-Powerful, All-Loving, All-Wise, All-Wise in Action on the Material plane, Attuned to Harmony and Beauty, Totally Scientific; but is also filled with Devotion and Love for His Sons and Daughters of GOD and His entire Creation. GOD is the perfect balance of Masculine and Feminine, for GOD is totally scientific yet filled with Love and Devotion for His Sons and Daughters and all Sentient Beings. This is the Sixth Great Ray of GOD and Creation.

The Seventh aspect of GOD's Personality is Freedom, Transmutation, Alchemy, Ceremonial Order and Magic. GOD is not only Powerful, Unconditionally Loving, Psychologically Wise, Wise in Action, Attuned to Harmony and Beauty, Scientific, Filled with Devotion, He is also the Embodiment of Freedom and is Divinely Structured in the process to achieve this Freedom. GOD is skilled in the process of how to Transmute and Transform energy from Fear into Love. From lower-self into Higher Self, from Separation into Oneness, from negative ego into Christ/Buddha/God consciousness. This Seventh Aspect of GOD's Personality is very skilled at setting up Structures and Systems to help His Creation achieve Freedom. Freedom from what? Freedom from glamour, illusion, maya, and negative ego thinking. As Sai Baba has said, "The mind creates bondage and the mind creates liberation." GOD is Total Freedom from limitation and from the negative ego fear based thought system. GOD knows how to set up structures to help lead His Creation back to Freedom.

There is now one last aspect to GOD's Personality and that is GOD's Personality is not just the embodiment of these Seven Great Attributes, but is also the "Perfect Synthesis, Balance and Integration" of these Seven Great GOD Qualities and Rays. My beloved readers, listen very closely to my following words: we are made in the "Image and Likeness of GOD." We too are made up of these Seven Great Rays. For the micro-cosm is like the macrocosm. "As within, so without. As above, so below." If we want to fully Realize GOD, then we too must become the perfect integration and balance of these Seven Great Rays. We must fully own our personal power, and surrender to GOD's Will and not the negative ego's will. We must learn to be unconditionally loving at all times to self and others. We must develop Active Intelligence to be wise inn learning how to manifest our conscious-ness onto the Earthly plane, and manifest our Spiritual Mission on Earth not just in our minds. We must learn to strive to be Harmonious, and Attuned to Beauty and Aesthetics in all that we do. We must learn to be very Spiritually Scientific in all that we do, and learn to understand the Laws that make up GOD's Infinite Universe. We must not only understand these laws, but we must use these Great Laws to help our selves and others. We must cultivate Devotion to GOD, to the Masters, to our fellow Brothers and Sisters in GOD, and to all GOD's Kingdoms without giving up our personal power, yet still retain the total unconditional love. We must learn to set up Divine Structure in our life and in the design of our society and world, which will ultimately lead to Freedom for all. We must learn the process of Divine Alchemy, Transmutation, Transformation, and Spiritual Magic to change our selves and our world from just seeing ourselves as people to our true reality as Sons and Daughters of GOD living in physical bodies. Lastly, we must learn to perfectly balance and integrate these Seven Great Attributes of GOD within ourselves and develop each of them to our highest potential. In this way, we will become the living embodiment of the Mighty I Am Presence on Earth. In this way we will become full-fledged Ascended Masters on Earth.

In conclusion, I just wanted to point out that we are all aware of the Three-Fold Nature of GOD, which has also been called the Three-Fold Flame of GOD. This has been called the Love/Wisdom/Power of GOD. My beloved readers, do you not see that this embodies these First Three Rays and attributes of GOD? It contains the First Ray of Power, The Second Ray of Love/Wisdom, and the Third Ray of Wisdom. Wisdom here has two meanings. The Psychological Wisdom of knowing how to Unconditionally Love, and the Wisdom of how to manifest GOD's Power and Unconditional love on the Material Plane. These Three Divine Attributes are the Three Key Qualities that need to be perfectly integrated to Realize GOD. I bring this up for many have not noticed the relationship of the Three-Fold Flame of GOD to the First Three Rays of GOD, and I felt it was important here to make this Relationship and Tie. Add to the Three-Fold Flame of GOD, the Four Remaining Attributes of GOD, and you have the Seven-Fold Nature of GOD and of your self as an Incarnation of God. If you truly want a map of how to demonstrate GOD on Earth, my beloved readers, let this be your Guide and Divine Road Map for how you Create, Manifest, and Demonstrate your own Divine Personality on Earth!

2

The Glory and the Corruption of the Seven Great Rays of GOD

We have already established that the perfect integration and balance of the Seven Rays is the Personality of GOD. It is essential to understand as with all things that the Seven Rays have a higher and lower aspect. This is because the Rays although created by GOD, can be misused and corrupted by the negative ego/fear-based/separative thought system. In this chapter I would like to go through each of these aspects of GOD's Personality and clearly explain the glory and the corruption that can take place when they are used purely and when they are corrupted by the negative ego thought system.

The glory of the First Ray is when a person owns their personal power 100% in total service of GOD and Unconditional Love. It is also the glory of surrendering to GOD's Will and not the ego's self-centered, negatively selfish will. The corruption of the First Ray is when a person owns their personal power to control, hurt, and manipulate others for self-centered, narcissistic, selfish gain; not recognizing their Brother and Sister or themselves as an incarnation of GOD. The Corruption of the First Ray is also not surrendering to GOD's Will in all things and instead unconsciously or consciously following the will of the negative ego, lower-self, and self-centered mind. The glory of the First Ray is its ability to own one's personal power at all times, but be able to surrender to GOD's Will simultaneously. The negative ego/fear-based thought system completely corrupts this understanding by having the person either own their personal power and not surrender, or has them surrender to GOD's Will and not own their personal power. Both are a corruption of the negative ego/separative/lower self thought system. Hitler, Mussolini, Stalin were classic examples of historical figures who misused and misunderstood the First Ray. In the Spiritual Movement those who are on a trip of self-aggrandizement, being better than everyone else is, power trips over being a perceived Guru, and or people who are constantly angry and attacking others are classic examples.

The glory of the Second Ray is its ability to Unconditionally Love self and others at all times, and the Psychological wisdom it brings to help one do this in all situations and with all people. The corruption of the Second Ray is first off, the negative ego/fear based thought systems distortion of having the person manifest conditional love rather than Unconditional Love. The negative ego thought system has one love under certain conditions and requirements. The second main danger and corruption is becoming overly flowery, sentimental, and loving, and not having a backbone, so to speak. This might stem from not having enough of Rays One, Three and Five, which are a little more mental in nature, embodying power, intelligence, and science. The third corruption could be becoming overidentified with the teacher or guru role, and not being able to step out of it. Being a know-it-all, since the Second Ray is that of education. In the First Ray the danger would be being too political, and not speaking one's truth enough. In the case of overidentification with the Second Ray it would be speaking one's truth too much, and not knowing how to be self-controlled, tactful, Spiritually discerning, and attuned to timing. I am also reminded of a book called *Women Who Love Too Much*. This would also be an example of the imbalance of the Second Ray. A person can become obsessed, addicted and co-dependent in relationship to love, and this is in truth a negative ego thought system distortion of the true Second Ray Unconditional Love, GOD would have us learn.

The glory of the Third Ray is the Active Intelligence or Wisdom to put our God Consciousness into demonstration and action on and in the Material/Earthly world, and not just on the Spiritual, mental and emotional plane. The corruption of the Third Ray could be an over intellectual nature and lack of proper integration of one's feelings and emotions. It could also be being run by the mind, instead of being the Master of one's mind, and learning how to quiet the mind when needed. It could also be over planning and over thinking about one's mission, but never doing it. It could also be a preoccupation and overi-dentification on making money and business pursuits to the neglect of one's Spiritual Life, because the Third Ray is associated with business. It could also be a corruption of negative ego business practices based on negative ego competition instead of Spiritual cooperation. It would be the negative ego controlling one's business practices which is to make a buck at any price, and it doesn't matter who you hurt in the process. This could be summed up, "So what that you gain the whole world and lose your own Soul."

The glory of the Fourth Ray is the creation of harmony, unity, and oneness at all times with self, relationship to others and one's world. It is also the creation of the Arts in the glorification and sanctification of GOD. This could come in the form of beautiful Spiritual Paintings, beautiful Spiritual Music, Spiritual Architecture, Spiritual Poetry, Spiritual Dance, Spiritual Opera, Play, and Theatre, to name just a few. It could also be Spiritual Movies, Feng Shui, and Aesthetics in daily living. The corruption of the Fourth Ray on a psychological level would be the negative ego/fear-based thought system creating disharmony and conflict within self because of lack of proper integration and negative ego contamination. This Conflict within self then would manifest in conflict with others, and lack of harmony with others. The Spiritual ideal of the Fourth Ray would be to create love, harmony, oneness and peace at all times and not disharmony, conflict, separation, attack and fear. On a professional level, the corruption of the Fourth Ray would be the lower-self, carnal self, and negative ego control the creation and flow of the Fourth Ray. This would manifest as maybe a great deal of the rock music these days, with very negative and dark lyrics. It could be the creation of art with images that do not Spiritually uplift, but do the opposite. Instead of Music of the Spheres and music that Spiritually inspires, it would be music that appeals to the lower-self and carnal-self. I do not think that this needs much explanation to my readers. It would be movies that appeal to violence, pornography, and horror films; instead of the use of the film or multimedia for uplifting Spiritual inspiration. We all see how many movies are playing in movie theatres that we can't even imagine that anyone would ever want to go see. These moviemakers appeal to those individuals run by the lower self, negative ego, and lower nature. When the consciousness of the masses rises enough to a more Spiritual/Christ/Buddha state, there will be no one who would even pay money to see these movies. Any form of art that is created from, and panders to the lower self and lower nature, and does not inspire and sanctify GOD by its beauty, is a corruption of the Fourth Ray of GOD.

The glory of the Fifth Ray of GOD is its focus on Spiritual New Age Science. On a Psychological level, it is the use of the mind in a scientific way; for healing all aspects of a person and our society. The proper use of this Fifth Ray leads to cutting-edge scientific breakthroughs in Medicine, Psychology, Law, Gardening, Ecology, Social Work, Religion, Business, to just name a few. In truth, the list is endless. Everything in GOD's Universe is made up of laws and by understanding and mastering these laws we can use them to help other people our world and ourselves. The corruption of the Fifth Ray could again be an over intellectual nature, that cuts off the feeling and intuitive nature if corrupted by the negative ego/fear-based thought system. It could also be a worship of

science and the rejection of religion and Spirituality thinking that
everything in life has to be proven by a scientific study. Or believing that
nothing is real except what can be proven by scientific means. Or that
nothing is real except that which can be sensed with one's five physical
senses. This is a complete perversion of Spiritual Science. This is the
negative ego controlling science and is not the Science of GOD. Another
corruption might be the imbalanced view that Science and Religion or
Spirituality do not blend and integrate perfectly together. Contrary to
popular opinion, GOD is totally scientific and understandable, if one
will also allow oneself to use ones intuitive mind and not just their logical mind. Another corruption of the Fifth Ray is a focus to much on
what I would call the concrete mind, and not allowing oneself to tap
into the abstract mind, the Higher Mind, and the Intuitive right-brain
mind. When the Fifth Ray is properly understood and utilized, enormous
scientific ideas and inspiration will come also not only from logical
thinking, which is fantastic when used properly, but also from telepathic Sources of Knowledge on the inner plane. Cures for Aids, Cancer,
and all the ills of our Society can come. There is not one field or
endeavor of life that the Fifth Ray Scientific mind can not prove useful.
There is in truth a Science for everything. Even a Science for how to run
an effective business, office or home. The danger and corruption of the
Fifth Ray can come in being overly scientific in an intellectual dry sense
and living too much in the mental body and scientific focus and not
smelling the roses, enjoying and experiencing life, and not just thinking
about it. Every Ray has this danger within its focus and lens; it is not
just the Fifth Ray. Each Ray of GOD can be a blinder in a sense, if not
balanced with the other Rays. The corruption of the Fifth Ray in a professional sense is Scientists doing animal experiments with no consideration or feeling for the animals they are experimenting upon. This is one
example. Another example might be the focus on only third dimensional
traditional methods as in Western medicine, and the inability to open
up to the vast Spiritual Technologies that are not so invasive and poisonous

to the physical body. In Psychology it is a science only focused on traditional Psychology, that does not even recognize or believe in GOD or the reality of the Soul. With no judgement intended, these people call themselves Scientists and they are seeing life through one seventh of reality and calling it science. It is a science based on seeing life through blinders. True Spiritual Science sees life through a Full Spectrum Prism lens utilizing all one's senses, not just the physical ones. Those are five of about fifty or one hundred we actually possess. For more information on this read my books *The Complete Ascension Manual, Integrated Ascension* and the *Golden Book of Melchizedek*. There are many more examples I could give of the corruption of science on a professional level; however, I think I have made my point here. You, my beloved readers, can extrapolate how this process carries over to all fields of study. I would also highly recommend that you read my book *Manual for Planetary Leadership* for a great deal of this book is an in-depth explanation of just this topic, and how this process has infiltrated all fields and aspects of our Society and Civilization. It is quite fascinating reading if you would like to see how this process carries on in other areas of Earth life as well!

The glory of the Sixth Ray is Devotion. This is embodied in the Master Jesus' commandment to "Love the Lord thy GOD, with all your heart and soul and mind and might, and to Love your neighbor as you Love yourself." The glory of the Sixth Ray is that it brings an enthusiastic unconditional love and Spiritual passion to one's relationship to GOD, the Masters, to family, friends, people, and life itself. It is essential in life to fully embrace the emotional body, and have total Spiritual passion, enthusiasm, and joy. The Sixth Ray brings this total devotion and idealism. The glory of the Sixth Ray is that it makes us strive also for the highest within us, and pursue excellence at all times. The corruption of the Sixth Ray is becoming overly emotional and letting one's emotions run away with you and becoming victimized by them. It is also giving your personal power away to GOD, the Masters, a Guru, and other people.

Another corruption and glamour of the Sixth Ray is putting Masters, Spiritual Teachers, and other people on pedestals. Another corruption of the negative ego fear based thought system that distorts the pure Sixth Ray is being to idealistic to the point of being a negative perfectionist. One can become so idealistic that they can become almost dysfunctional or impractical. The other great danger and corruption of the Sixth Ray is lack of Spiritual discernment. These are the main things to watch out for in how the negative ego/fear-based thought system can distort the Sixth Ray of Devotion and Spiritual Idealism. The corruption of the Sixth Ray professionally is in the Field of Religion where Ministers of all faiths are taken over by faulty negative ego concepts and beliefs and the true religious doctrine becomes contaminated. We have seen this take place in all the major religions where their doctrine is preaching negative ego based concepts and theology that has no relationship to what GOD, the Masters and Angels really believe. This is why so many people have left their Religion, which is unfortunate, but they had no choice. This is why more people have been killed in the name of GOD than for any other reason I believe. It is also why different religions compete with each other and why most religions but not all of them state that theirs is the only way to GOD, which of course is total illusion. It is also why there are so many false prophets, cults, and religious leaders being caught in scandal, as the negative ego and corruption ultimately becomes exposed.

The glory of the Seventh Ray is its emphasis on freedom and its ability to set up divine structures and systems within self and society to help lead towards even greater freedom within self and within our Society. The glory of the Seventh Ray is also the ability to use Spiritual magic in the form of transmutation and alchemy to transform misqualified energies into the purity and substance of GOD. The corruption of the Seventh Ray can come in many forms. It can come from the negative ego/fear based minds misguided understanding of what true freedom is. Many people think they are free, but, in truth, they are not. As His

Holiness the Lord Sai Baba has said, "The mind creates bondage and the mind creates liberation." Many people think they are free, but, in truth, they are being very much run by the negative ego, the emotional body, their mental body, the inner child, lower-self desire, and their subconscious mind. Another aspect of the corruption of the Seventh Ray by the negative ego/separative thought system is a misuse of structure. Either first not having enough, or on the other side of the coin having too much, where a certain amount of spontaneity and free flow can not take place. There is a proper balance to find here. Another corruption and glamour is setting up structures for the wrong purpose and goals which are really of the negative ego and not of the Divine Plan. Another corruption and glamour of the Seventh Ray is the use of magic without Spirituality. This is very common, and is one of the first signs of a cult. Slick fast talking teachers, who have some magic or alchemical abilities, however, their motivation, in truth, is totally governed by the personality, negative ego and lower-self. They are more interested in gaining power, fame, money and having sex with their followers, than in truly doing Spiritual magic to be of service. Lightworkers beware, for there are millions of teachers out there who fit into this category. A great many lightworkers are very naïve and Spiritually undiscerning, and are to easily impressed by magic that is motivated by impure motivations. The freedom is not giving free reign to one's negative ego, lower-self, inner child, and emotional body. This is not freedom, but being a victim. True freedom stems from total self-mastery of one's energies in service of GOD, unconditional love, and a balanced, integrated ideal. The corruption of the Seventh Ray in a professional sense comes in the form of the misuse of money. Money is, in truth, a Divine substance of GOD that is meant to be used as a means of helping self and others. The corruption of money comes in many ways. It can come in the form of greed and miserliness. It can also come in the form of spending it too freely and wasting it on lower-self, frivolous purposes. The corruption can come in not valuing money, using it for a Spiritual Purpose in life and not saving it in the appropriate balance. It can also come from not giving it away for needy purposes in a balanced appropriate manner when the time is right. Money is the energy we use to make changes in the Physical/Earthly world. One of the reasons the Earthly/Material world doesn't change as fast as it could is that most lightworkers do not have as much money as they would like. This is part of the development of the Seventh Ray. The ability to have prosperity consciousness and not poverty consciousness. To not be afraid of money. To see the making of large amounts of money as part of your Spiritual path. Money is not the root of all evil, as some would suggest. Money in and of itself is neutral. The negative ego/fear-based thought system is the root of all evil. It is when the negative ego/lower-self/separative mind controls money, that problems occur. It is every Son and Daughters of GOD to have as much money as they can imagine. It is part of their lesson to learn how to make money. The key point here being, the more money you have the more you can serve others. If you do not have money, then you become dependent on others to give you money. There are periods of time, of course, that this is okay and totally appropriate in everyone's life. In the long haul, so to speak, the ideal would be that each person be responsible for themselves and be able to make as much money as they can, for the more you have the more you can give. The great corruption of the Seventh Ray professionally is the enormous number of people in our Society who have money and greedily hold on to it. They do not help others or society, and they also use their money to hurt others and prevent others from gaining. Be aware of this my Beloved Readers, that the law of karma exists, and every "jot and tittle of the law is fulfilled." Those that misuse their money will ultimately lose their money. For the law of karma also extends over past and future lives. Part of the movement into this New Millennium and the Seventh Golden Age is the understanding that our Planet as a whole is now moving into a Seventh Ray Cycle from a previous Sixth Ray Cycle. Part of the energies of this Seventh Ray Cycle is to also now ground our Spirituality on Earth. For too long our Spirituality has been floating around on the Spiritual, mental, and emotional planes. In this New Millennium and Seventh Golden Age it is now time to create Heaven on Earth. It is now time to fully ground our Ascension in our physical bodies, into, and onto Earth life. It is now time for each person to fully ground their Spiritual mission on the physical Earthly plane. It is now time for lightworkers to become the Masters of money on all levels and to help use and allocate the money in our Government and economy to create the utopian Ascended Master Society that is its destiny build in this Seventh Golden Age. The proper use of the Seventh Ray both personally and collectively holds a great key to the transmutation and transformation that now needs to occur along with all the other Rays as well.

The final glory of the Seven Rays of GOD which form the true Personality of GOD which is extremely important to understand is how these Seven Rays in GOD's Personality work perfectly together in perfect synthesis and integration. In a true full-fledged Ascended Master this is also the case for the microcosm is like the Macrocosm.

The true Glory of GOD is seeing how these Seven Rays work together in perfect harmony and balance with self and within Society. In truth, we have yet to see this take place within our society. In my next book, I am going to endeavor to explain how this can take place, and I have been guided to call this "The Divine Plan for the New Millennium and Seventh Golden Age." For our purposes here, suffice it to say that, in truth, there are not that many even on a personal level who have learned to fully develop all Seven Rays and to also integrate and balance them in daily living. This is one of the great signs of a true full-fledged Spiritual Master on Earth. For this is the Personality of GOD. More and more, however, are beginning to realize this ideal. Many in the Spiritual Movement are focusing on the Spiritual or Heavenly level, and gaining initiations and building their light quotient and light bodies, as well as communicating and working in the Celestial Realms, and this is good. However, my beloved readers, if the Seven Great Rays are not balanced properly on the Psychological level, true God Realization will not have taken place, no matter what your level of initiation is. True God Realization must be done on the Spiritual, Psychological and Physical/Earthly level. All three levels must be realized, not just the Spiritual level. If the Seven Great Rays are not developed and balanced within self and the lower aspects, and/or corruption of these Rays are not transcended, then enormous corruption of the Spiritual work people are doing will take place. There are many who will not like to hear this, however, if you are truly a true lover of GOD then listen very closely to what I have to say. If the Psychological level of God Consciousness is not developed properly, and there is negative ego/fear-based distortion and corruption of these Rays, then this will color and affect all Channeling, Spiritual Teaching, Clairvoyant work, your Spiritual Vision, and all your Relationships. For as I have said many times in my writings, the single most important relationship in your life is your relationship to your self. If you are not right with self, this will skew all other relationships including your relationship to GOD, the Masters, and the Angels. This is because your thoughts create your reality. You can not have faulty thinking within self, and within your own personality and psychology and expect this not to affect all the Spiritual Channeling, Teaching and Healing work you are doing. Your relationship to your self, your relationship to your personality, your relationship to your psychology, your relationship to your own subconscious mind affects everything. It is the foundation of your Spiritual House. How can the first floor of one's house be corrupt and the second floor be working fine. The second floor works through the first floor. It is not separate from the first floor. It flows through the first floor. All Channeling, Spiritual Teaching and Spiritual Vision flows through one's subconscious mind, psychology, belief system, interpretations, perceptions, philosophy, and Spiritual Psychology. You cannot separate them. My beloved readers, this is why it is essential to learn to balance these Seven Great Rays within your own personality and psychology. This is a weak spot among a great many lightworkers. These Seven Great Rays of

GOD serve as a "Lens." It is also incredibly easy to get stuck in the lens of power, or love, or wisdom, or action, or art, or science, or devotion, or freedom, structure and magic. Even if your Monad and/or Soul is under the influence of a particular Ray as incarnating Sons and Daughters of God are, it is absolutely essential that you learn to see from a Full Spectrum Prism Consciousness through all Seven Rays in a balanced and integrated manner and not through just one or a few. This takes great psychological work and focus on your part. We all know people who are too stuck in power, or are too stuck in addicted love, or too stuck in the teacher know-it-all role, or too stuck in art and can't function in life. We all know people who are too stuck in science and the intellect, or in devotion and idealism to a Guru and are blinded. We all know a people who are too stuck in structure or lack of structure, can't deal with money, misuse magic, and do not know what their Spiritual Freedom is. These are the same great pitfalls and traps of the Spiritual Path. These are not all of them, but some of the main ones. Develop yourself most important in your personal power and surrendering to GOD's Will, Love/Wisdom, Active Intelligence, Harmony and Beauty, Science, Devotion and Idealism, Ceremonial Order and Magic. It is essential we develop our selves in these Seven Great Rays not only psychologically but also in the professional aspects of these Rays. I am not speaking here in the sense of taking on these professions, but being developed in them. Develop your political side, the Spiritual teacher side, your business side, your artistic side, your scientist side, your Spiritual leadership side, and your economic mastery side. Not only develop all these aspects, but also learn to not get stuck in each of their "Lenses." This is easier said than done, for it takes great psychological introspection and vigilance to not allow oneself to fall into these "Lenses." This is especially true because of the fact that each person's Monad and/or Soul is under the influence of one of these Rays. I am not saying here that one should deny how GOD created them and should not fulfill one's Spiritual Mission under that theme, so to speak.

However, be balanced and integrated in all Seven Rays while under the influence of that theme.

Most of all, my beloved readers, be aware of the negative ego/fear-based/separative/lower-self thought system and how it corrupts and creates glamour, illusion and maya in everything it touches if you allow it into your mind. Only allow yourself to think with your Spiritual/Christ/Buddha mind and not your negative ego/fear-based mind. Think with your Love Mind, my beloved readers, and not your Fear Mind. There are only two ways of thinking in the world and everything stems from Love or from fear. Everything stems from the negative ego thought system or the Spiritual/Christ/Buddha thought system. It is the negative ego/fear-based thought system that creates the distortion and corruption of the Seven Great Rays. Ever be joyously vigilant against the negative ego. This, my beloved readers, is the "Road Map" to achieve true God Consciousness. There is no work more important on your Spiritual Path than learning to properly master, develop, balance and integrate the Seven Great Rays in your psychology and personality, and to not allow the negative ego/fear-based thought system to enter your consciousness and corrupt your proper understanding of these Rays. Also to not get stuck in the "lens" of any one of these Rays, or this will become a negative ego distortion as well. This is the "Great Work" of the Spiritual Path. Continue the work on the Spiritual plane you are doing but do your Psychological and Personality level homework, for it is equally as important and, in truth, even more important, for the Psychological level is your Spiritual vision that colors your perception of the Spiritual level. To be a clear channel for Spirit you must be a clear and balanced psychological channel as well. Once you have mastered these do not forget to also put equal attention to doing your homework on the Physical/Earthly level as well; for GOD is as much in your physical body and in the Material/Earthly world as he is in the Heavenly realms, mental realm, emotional realm or psychic realm. There are Four Faces of GOD, Spiritual, Mental, Emotional and Physical. To truly realize

GOD, all four must be mastered and equally honored. To not master, honor and sanctify the Material face of GOD is to also disown the Divine Mother, the Earth Mother, and the Goddess energies. For the Goddess energies are also intimately connected to the Material Face of GOD. Our true Spiritual mission is to become our Mighty I Am Presence on Earth in a very grounded and balanced manner. Our true Purpose is to manifest our Spiritual mission on Earth and to get involved with Earth life. Our true Spiritual mission on Earth is to transform our Civilization and Society into an Ascended Master Society and to create Heaven on Earth, not to achieve liberation and leave the Earth as soon as we can. We are all the Light/Love/Power bearers for the New Millennium and Seventh Golden Age. Let us each now take on the "Full Mantle of the Christ/Buddha/God Consciousness" in a balanced and integrated manner and be about the business of fully transforming our selves and our world into the true Glory of GOD!

3

An Expanded Understanding and View of the 22 Great Cosmic Rays of GOD

My Beloved Readers, the following chart I have put together on the Seven Rays, the 12 Planetary Rays and the 22 Great Cosmic Rays of GOD is the most in-depth chart on the Rays ever put together in any book! The understanding of the 22 Cosmic Rays of GOD is one of the great Esoteric Secrets of the Universe. The understanding of the Seven Rays of GOD is the key to understanding the Personality of God, and understanding Spiritual Psychology! The understanding of the Seven Rays of God is one of the single most important Spiritual Practices on the Spiritual Path. I would like to acknowledge that the information used in this chart, which was gathered from the two Alice Bailey books on Esoteric Psychology, especially in the part of the chart dealing with the Seven Rays. Besides being a Spiritual Teacher and Channel, I am also a Psychologist, and I cannot emphasize enough the importance of studying the Rays. It is the key, in truth, to psychological health!

I have also included in this chart not only the Rays for this Planet, but also what I am calling here the Rays from a Universal Perspective. For as the Cosmic Rays are stepped down from GOD through the different dimensions of reality, their purpose, color and function sometimes change form. For example, the Third Ray deals with the activity of

Grounding Spirit into Matter. There is no need for this function on Cosmic Levels since there is no physical matter there. Hence, the Rays at that Level sometimes have a different Quality and Color. For your enjoyment and edification, I have given the Universal Qualities of the Seven Rays as well, as seen from a Higher Plane. This also reconciles some of the confusion by some lightworkers on the difference in teachings on the Rays from the Theosophical Movement, Alice Bailey books, my books, and the *I AM Discourses* of Saint Germain. In truth, all four of these Dispensations of Ascended Master Teachings are teaching the exact same thing about the Rays. Some are just using a different lens. The explanation I have just given above is why there is a seeming discrepancy, but, in truth, is not a discrepancy. The information in all of these books is, in truth, correct about the Rays. It is just a matter if we are looking through a Planetary lens or a Universal lens. Do not make the mistake of thinking one is true and one is not, for this would be a step into illusion. Both are 100% true! One is true on a Planetary level of understanding the Rays, and the other is true from the Universal Perspective or lens. It is only in acknowledging the truth of both the Planetary and Universal Perspectives on the Rays that a "Full Spectrum Prism Perspective" can be had and understood. To disregard either one would be to create a "Blind Spot" in your vision! For this reason, I have added both lenses to this chart, which adds even another dimension to the completeness of this chart! This is a chart you can meditate on and study for months! It is also a key to developing an "Immaculate and Flawless Character" which is essential in the process of achieving God Realization! On this note, I bring you, my Beloved Readers, "An Expanded Understanding and View of the 22 Great Cosmic Rays of GOD"!

First Ray

Planetary Level:
Color: Red
Personal Power, Will
Additional Qualities: singleness of purpose, dynamic power, detachment, courage, steadfastness, truthfulness arising from absolute fearlessness, power of ruling, clear vision, strength, courage, determination, leadership, dignity, independence, majesty, daring, executive ability, sense of time, solitariness, love, divine, capacity to grasp great questions in a large-minded way, and the handling of people and measures.

Vices of Ray: Pride, ambition, willfulness, hardness, arrogance, desire to control others, obstinacy and anger.

Virtues to be acquired: tenderness, humility, sympathy, tolerance, patience

Glamour: love of power and authority, pride, selfish ambition, impatience and irritation, self-centeredness, separateness and aloofness

Specific Glamours to be Avoided:

The glamour of physical strength.

The glamour of personal magnetism.

The glamour of self-centeredness and personal potency.

The glamour of "the one at the center".

The glamour of selfish personal ambition.

The glamour of rulership, of dictatorship, and wide control.

The glamour of messiah complex in political arena.

The glamour of destruction.

The glamour of isolation, of aloneness or aloofness.

Examples: Luther, Carlyle, Walt Whitman, Napoleon

Professions: Government, Politics, International Relations, Natural Ruler, Leader, Statesmen, Empire Builder, Colonizer, Soldier, Explorer, Pioneer, Executives

Higher and Lower Methods of Teaching Truth:
Higher Expression: The Science of Statesmanship and of Government
Lower Expression: Modern Diplomacy and Partisan Politics

Type of Person: Power Type—Full of will and governing capacity.
Methods of Development: Raja Yoga

Correlates with Crown Chakra
Planetary Connection: Vulcan
Plane of Operation: Divinity
Planetary Operation: Not in Manifestion
Type of Government: Dictatorship

Universal Level:
Blue Ray, Power, GOD's Will, Protection, Faith, Initiative
Manu and Chohan and Lord of the Ray: Allah Gobi and El Morya
Archangels: Michael and Faith
Elohim: Hercules and Amazonia

Second Ray

Planetary Level:
Color: Blue
Love/Wisdom
Additional Qualities: radiance, attraction, expansion, inclusiveness, the power to save, intuition, insight, philanthropy, unity, compassion, loyalty, generosity, universal love, calm, patience and endurance, love of truth, faithfulness, clear intelligence and serene temper.

Vices: Over absorption in study, coldness, indifference to others, contempt of mental limitations in others.

Virtues to be acquired: love, compassion, earnest Spiritual study, unselfishness, energy.

Glamours: Fear, necessity, a sense of inferiority or inadequacy, depression, constant anxiety, self-pity, excessive self-effacement, inertia and ineffectiveness, negativity.

Specific Glamours to be Avoided:

The glamour of being loved.

The glamour of popularity.

The glamour of personal wisdom.

The glamour of selfish responsibility.

The glamour of too complete an understanding, which negates right action.

The glamour of self-pity, a basic glamour of this ray.

The glamour of the messiah complex in the world of Spirituality or religion.

The glamour of fear, based on undue sensitivity.

The glamour of self-sacrifice.

The glamour of self-satisfaction.

The glamour of selfish service.

Professions: Spiritual Education and Teaching, Writing, Speaking, Television and Radio, Sage, Philanthropist, Reformer, Teacher, Inspirer, Healer, Servant to mankind, Ambassador, Head of College, Students.

Higher and Lower Methods of Teaching Truth:

The Higher Expression: The Process of Initiation and Ascension as taught by the Ascended Masters

The Lower Expression: Religion

Type of Person: The Love Type—Full of Love and Fusing Power

Methods of Development: Raja Yoga

Correlates with the Heart Chakra

Planetary Connection: Jupiter

Plane of Operation: Plane of the Monad

Planetary Operation: In Manifestation from 1575 A.D.

Type of Government: Democracy

Universal Level: Illumination, Wisdom, and Perception

Planetary Christ, Secondary Ray Chohan and Lord of Ray, Future Chohan, Inner Plane Synthesis Ashram Leader: Lord Maitreya, Master Kuthumi, Master Lanto, Ascended Master Djwhal Khul

Archangels: Jophiel and Christine
Elohim: Apollo and Lumina

Third Ray

Planetary Level:
Color: Yellow
Active Intelligence, Creative Intelligence, Physical Action
Additional Qualities: power of manifestation, power to evolve, mental illumination, perseverance, philosophical bent, clear mindedness, perfectionism, comprehension of fundamental principles, understanding, deeply penetrating and interpretive mind, adaptability, recognition of the power and value of silence, capacity for creative ideation, power to produce, synthesis on the physical plane.

Vices: intellectual pride, coldness, isolation, inaccuracy of details, absent minded, obstinacy, selfishness, overly critical of others, seeing too many details may paralyze action

Virtues to be acquired: compassion, tolerance, devotion, accuracy, energy and common sense.

Glamours: Glamour of always being busy, materialism, preoccupation with detail, efficiency and self-importance through being the one who knows, scheming and manipulation of others, deviousness, and self-interest

Specific Glamours to be avoided:

The glamour of being too busy.

The glamour of cooperation with the plan in a selfish or individual way, not a group way.

The glamour of active scheming.
The glamour of creative work without true motive.
The glamour of good intentions, which are basically selfish.
The glamour of self-importance.
The glamour of efficiency

Professions: Finance, Trade, Business and Economics, Arbiters and Peacemakers, Philosophers, Organizers, Diplomats, Strategists, Tacticians, Scholars, Economists, Bankers, Chess Players, Judges, Allegorists, Interpreters and Cartoonists, Mathematics.

The Higher and Lower Methods of Teaching Truth:
Higher Expression: means of communication or interaction: phone, fax, email, Internet, television, radio and transportation.
Lower Expression: the use and spread of money and gold

Methods of Development: exactitude in thought, higher mathematics, philosophy, wise view on all abstract questions, sincerity of purpose, capacity for concentration on philosophic studies, patience, caution, absence of tendency to worry over trivial things.
Type of Person: The Active Type—Full of action and manipulation of energy and matter.

Correlates with Throat Chakra

Universal Level: Divine love, tolerance, gratitude, adoration, exaltation, reverence, charity.

Planetary Connection: Saturn
Plane of Operation: Atmic Plane
Planetary Operation: In Manifestation from 1425 A. D.

Mahachohan and Chohan or Lord of the Ray: Saint Germain and Serapis Bey
Archangels: Chamuel and Charity
Elohim: Heros and Amora

Fourth Ray

Planetary Level:

Color: Green

Harmony, Beauty

Additional Qualities: Purity, Artistic Development, Creative Ideation, balance, rhythm, the special faculty to perceive and portray through the arts and through life, the principle of beauty in all things, aesthetics, strong sense of form, symmetry, equilibrium, artistry, the power to reveal the path, the power to express Divinity and growth, the harmony of the spheres, the synthesis of true beauty, strong affections, compassion, physical courage, generosity, quickness of intellect and perception.

Vices: Self-centeredness, worrying, inaccuracy, lack of moral courage

Virtues to be acquired: serenity, confidence, self-control, purity, unselfishness, accuracy, mental and moral balance.

Glamours: Diffusion of interest and energy, Impracticality and the glamour of imagination, Changeableness, fickleness, vagueness and lack of objectivity. Constant inner and outer conflict causing argument and acrimony. Dissatisfaction because of sensitive response to beauty and that which is higher and better, manic/depressive, need to gain equilibrium on all levels, need for self-control.

Specific Glamours to be avoided:

The glamour of harmony, aiming at self-centered personal comfort and satisfaction.

The glamour of war.

The glamour of conflict with the objective of imposing righteousness and peace.

The glamour of vague artistic perception.

The glamour of psychic perception instead of intuition.

The glamour of musical perception.

The glamour of the pairs of opposites, in the higher sense.

Professions: The Arts, Sociology, Race and Culture Cooperation and Conciliation, Artists and Musicians.

Higher and Lower Expressions of Seeking the Truth:
Higher Expression: City Planning based on Blueprints of the Ascended Masters.
Lower Expression: Modern City Planning

Type of Person: The Artistic Type—Full of the Sense of Beauty and Creative Aspiration

Correlates with the First Chakra

Universal Level: Perfection, Resurrection, Purity, Hope, Artistic Development

Planetary Connection: Earth
Plane of Operation: Buddhic Plane or Plane of Intuition
Planetary Operation: Comes into operation in 2025 A. D.
Type of Government: Socialism

Chohan and Lord of the Ray: Paul the Venetian
Archangels: Gabriel and Hope
Elohim: Purity and Astrea

Fifth Ray

Planetary Level:
Color: Orange
Concrete Science or Knowledge
Additional Qualities: Research, Keen Intellect, Attention to Detail, Truthfulness, analytical, deductive, formal mind, the acquirement and dissemination of factual knowledge, unwavering patience and extreme thoroughness and method-particularly in the repeated examination and classification of intricate and minute details, emergence into and out of form, the power to make the voice of silence heard, the power to

initiate activity, revelation of the way, purification with fire, the manifestation of the Great White Light, strictly accurate statements, justice, perseverance, common sense, uprightness, independence, punctual.

Vices: harsh criticism, narrowness, arrogance, unforgiving temper, lack of compassion and reverence, prejudice

Virtues to be acquired: reverence, devotion, compassion, love and open-mindedness.

Glamours: Constant analysis and splitting of hairs, criticism, overemphasis of form, cold mental assessment and disparagement of feeling, intellectual pride reason and need to prove are sacrosanct.

Specific Glamours to be avoided:

The glamour of materiality, or over emphasis of form.

The glamour of the intellect.

The glamour of knowledge and of definition.

The glamour of assurance, based on a narrow point of view.

The glamour of the form which hides reality.

The glamour of organization.

The glamour of the outer, which hides the inner.

Professions: New Age Science, Medicine, Psychology, Scientist, Mathematician, Lawyer, Detective, Physical Scientist or Occult and Metaphysical Scientist, Chemist, Engineer, Surgeon. Doctors, and Inventors.

Higher and Lower Methods of Teaching Truth;
Higher Expression: The Science of the Soul and Spirit, Spiritual Psychology Lower Expression: Modern Education System

Methods of Development: Exactitude in Action

Type of Person: The Scientific Type—Full of the idea of cause and results; mathematical

Correlates with Sixth Chakra

Universal Level: Consecration, Truth, Dedication, Concentration, Healing Love, Scientific Development

Planetary Connection: Venus
Plane of Operation: Mental Plane
Planetary Operation: In Manifestation since 1775 A. D.

Chohan and Lord of the Ray: Master Hilarion
Archangels: Mother Mary and Raphael
Elohim: Cyclopia and Virginia

Sixth Ray

Planetary Level:
Devotion, Spiritual Idealism, Abstract Idealism
Additional Qualities: Spirituality, religious fervor, sacrificial love, burning enthusiasm for a cause, fiery ardor, one-pointedness, single-minded, selfless devotion, adoration, intense sympathy for the suffering of others, idealism expressed as practical service and loyalty, the power to transcend desire, the spurning of that which is not desired, endurance and fearlessness, the power to detach oneself, the overcoming of the waters of the emotional nature, tenderness, intuition, reverence, religious instinct.

Vices: Selfish and jealous love, over-leaning on others, partiality, self-deception, sectarianism, superstition, prejudice, overly rapid conclusions, fiery anger.

Virtues to be acquired: Strength, self-sacrifice, purity, truth, tolerance, serenity, balance and common sense.

Glamours: Fanaticism, possessiveness and over-devotion.
Specific Glamours to be avoided:
The glamour of devotion.
The glamour of adherence to forms and persons.
The glamour of idealism.

The glamour of loyalties and creeds.
The glamour of emotional response.
The glamour of sentimentality.
The glamour of interference.
The glamour of the lower pairs of opposites.
The glamour of World Saviors and Teachers.
The glamour of narrow vision.
The glamour of fanaticism.
Narrow-mindedness, love of the past and existing forms, reluctance to change, rigidity, too much intense feeling, everything is either perfect or intolerable.

Profession: Religion, Philosophy, Ideology, Mystic, Devotee, Saint, Philanthropist, Martyr, Evangelist, Missionary, Reformer, Priest, Minister and Healer

The Higher and Lower Methods of Teaching Truth:
Higher Expression: The Ascension Movement and New Age Movement guided by the Ascended Masters
Lower Expression: Churches and religious organizations

Methods of Development Bhakti Yoga, Necessity for an Object
Type of Person: The Devotee Type—Full of Idealism

Correlates with the Third Chakra

Universal Level: Peace, Ministration, Mercy, Spiritual Idealism, Devotional Worship, Forgiving Love, Grace

Planetary Connection: Neptune
Plane of Operation: Astral Plane
Planetary Operation: Began to pass out of Manifestation in 1625 A. D.

Chohan and Lord and Lady of the Sixth Ray: Sananda and Lady Nada
Archangels: Uriel and Aurora
Elohim: Peace and Aloha

Seventh Ray

Planetary Level:
Ceremonial Order and Magic, Freedom, Ritual, Organization, Transmutation, Divine Structure, Structuring of Society Spiritual Grounding, Alchemy, Violet Flame, Invocation, Sacred Living, Transfiguration, Ritual Ceremony, Spiritual Tradition, Spiritual Protocol.

Additional Qualities: nobility, chivalry of character and conduct, splendor of estate and person, ordered activity, precision, skill, grace, dignity, diplomacy, tact, discipline, ceremonial pageantry, discovery, control and release of the hidden forces of nature, order in conduct of life, exactness of appointments, the power to create, the power to cooperate, the power to think, mental power, the power to vivify, courtesy, self-reliance

Vices: formalism, bigotry, pride, narrowness, superficial judgements, self-opinion, overindulgence

Virtues to be acquired: realization of unity, open-mindedness, tolerance, humility, gentleness, and love

Glamours: rigid adherence to law and order, overemphasis of organization and for love of the secret and the mysterious, psychism, the glamour of ceremonial order, ritual superstitions, deep interest in omens.

Specific Glamours to be avoided:
The glamour of magical work.
The glamour of the relation of the opposites.
The glamour of the subterranean powers.
The glamour of that which brings together.
The glamour of the physical body.
The glamour of the mysterious and secret.
The glamour of sexuality.
The glamour of the emerging manifested forms.

Profession: Business and Economics, Diplomats, Mystics, and Structuring of Society, Stage Director, Pageant Master, Ritualist, Magician, Occults and Priest in Ceremonial Order, Born Organizer, Doctor or Nurse, Sculptor, Military Parades, Naval Reviews, Genealogical Trees.

Higher and Lower Expressions of Teaching Truth:
Higher Expression: All forms of Ascension Teachings and Ascended Master Teachings
Lower Expression: Psychism, Fragmented and Nonintegrated Wisdom Teachings

Profession: The Structuring of Society, Ordering of power through Ceremony, Protocol and Ritual

Methods of Development: Ceremony, Observances
Type of Person: The Business Type–Full of organization, power; given to Ritualistic Ceremony

Correlates with the Second Chakra

Universal Level: Purification, Transformation, Ordered Service, Culture, Refinement, Diplomacy, Invocation, Control over Forces of Nature

Planetary Connection: Uranus
Plane of Operation: Physical Plane
Planetary Operation: In Manifestation since 1675 A. D.

Chohan and Lord and Lady of Seventh Ray: Lady Portia and Saint Germain
Archangels: Zadkiel and Amethyst
Elohim: Arcturus and Victoria

Eighth Ray

Color: Seafoam Green
Quality: The Higher Cleansing Ray

Ninth Ray

Color: Blue/Green
Quality: Joy, Attraction of the Body of Light

Tenth Ray

Color: Pearlescent
Quality: The Anchoring of the Body of Light, Inviting the Soul Merge and Monadic Merge

Eleventh Ray

Color: Pink-Orange
Quality: The Bridge to the New Age

Twelfth Ray

Color: Gold
Quality: The Anchoring of the New Age and Christ Consciousness

The Cosmic Rays

The Ray of Godhead
Quality: Clear Light, Translucent and Invisible

The Twelve Cosmic Rays
Quality: The Twelve Cosmic Ray Masters of the 12 Cosmic Rays; All Twelve Clear Light, Translucent, and Invisible

The Synthesis Ray
Quality: The Mahatma or Avatar of Synthesis containing all 352 Levels of Divinity, Rainbow

The Multi-Universal Ray
Quality: Archangel Metatron and The Platinum Ray

The Universal Ray
Quality: Melchizedek, our Universal Logos, and the Purest and most Refined Gold in the Universe

The Galactic Ray
Quality: Melchior, our Galactic Logos, and the Lord and Lady of Sirius in the Great White Lodge bring forth the Gold/Silver Ray

The Solar Ray
Quality: Helios and Vesta bring forth the Copper/Gold Ray

The Planetary Ray
Quality: Sanat Kumara and Lord Buddha bring forth the Shamballa Ray of White Light

The Twelve Planetary Rays
Quality: These are the Twelve Rays I began this chapter discussing!

The Ascension Seats of God

For your further enjoyment and edification I have also added here the Ascension Seats of GOD!

Cosmic Ascension Seats
Type: The GOD Ascension Seat

The Universal Ascension Seat
Type: The Golden Chamber of Melchizedek Ascension Seat under the guidance of Lord Melchizedek, our Universal Logos

The Galactic Ascension Seats

Type: The Galactic Core Ascension Seat under the direction of Melchior

Type: The Ascension Seat in the Great White Lodge of Sirius under the guidance of the Lord of Sirius

Type: The Arcturian Ascension Seat under guidance of the Lord of Arcturus and the Arcturians

Type: Lenduce Ascension Seat under the Guidance of Lenduce and Vywamus

The Solar Ascension Seats

Type: The Solar Core Ascension Seat under the Guidance of Helios and Vesta

Type: The Shamballa Ascension Seat under the Guidance of Lord Buddha

The Planetary Ascension Seats

Type: The Ascension Seat in the Planetary Ashram of El Morya

Type: The Ascension Seat in the Planetary Synthesis Ashram of the Ascended Master Djwhal Khul

Type: The Ascension Seat in the Planetary Ashram of Serapis Bey

Type: The Ascension Seat in the Planetary Ashram of Paul the Venetian

Type: The Ascension Seat in the Planetary Ashram of Master Hilarion

Type: The Ascension Seat in the Planetary Ashram of Sananda and Lady Nada

Type: The Ascension Seat in the Planetary Ashram of Portia and Saint Germain

Type: The Ascension Seat in the Mothership of Commander Ashtar and the Ashtar Command

Type: The Ascension Seat in Atomic Accelerator in Table Mountain under the Guidance of Saint Germain

Type: The Ascension Seat in Telos, a mile or two below Mount Shasta under the Guidance of Adama

Type: The Mt. Shasta Ascension Seat under the Guidance of Saint Germain

Type: The Ascension Seat in the Great Pyramid of Giza under the Guidance of Isis

Type: The Ascension Seat on Venus under the Guidance of Lady Venus and Sanat Kumara

4

Esoteric Psychology and the Science of the Rays

The seven rays are the first differentiation of God in manifestation and they provide the entire field of His expression in manifested form. The seven rays are embodiments of seven types of force which demonstrate seven qualities of God. These seven qualities have a sevenfold effect upon matter and form in all parts of God's infinite universe. The seven great rays are embodiments of seven great beings. These are:

1. The Lord of Power or Will
2. The Lord of Love/Wisdom
3. The Lord of Active Intelligence
4. The Lord of Harmony, Beauty, and Art
5. The Lord of Concrete Knowledge and Science
6. The Lord of Devotion and Idealism
7. The Lord of Ceremonial Order or Magic

The rays are, in truth, quite a complex subject and there are many ways of and frames of reference for understanding them. The study of the rays is almost an unknown science in our world. I am a serious student of the field and have been involved with just about every religion and mystery school on the planet, but it was only when I read the Alice

Bailey books on esoteric psychology that the profound significance of the rays came to my awareness. The rays are even more important than astrology, yet what I am going to share with you in this chapter is not talked about by those involved in 99.99% of the spiritual paths on Earth. The understanding of the rays may be the single most important spiritual science for understanding oneself and the world as a whole. It is these rays that govern all of creation.

The Rays of Aspect and the Rays of Attribute

Djwhal Khul, in his writings, has divided the seven great rays into two categories called the rays of aspect and the rays of attribute.

Rays of Aspect:
Ist ray of Power, Will or Purpose
2nd ray of Love/Wisdom
3rd ray of Active, Creative Intelligence
Rays of Attribute:
4th ray of Harmony through Conflict, Beauty, or Art
5th ray of Concrete Science or Knowledge
6th ray of Abstract Idealism or Devotion
7th ray of Ceremonial Order, Magic, Ritual, or Organization

The Ray of Structure of Every Incarnated Human Being

Every soul extension that incarnates onto the Earth plane is made up of six rays. Everyone has a separate ray for the monad, soul, personality, mind, emotions, and physical body.

The monadic ray and soul ray are basically the same throughout all of the person's incarnations. The rest of the rays can change from lifetime to lifetime. Every incarnated personality is found upon one of these seven rays. Soul extensions with soul rays found upon the fourth, fifth, sixth, and seventh rays must blend with the first three major rays after they pass the third initiation. However, the monadic ray of every incarnated personality is one of the first three rays.

In the unevolved person, the rays of the physical, emotional, and mental bodies dominate. As the person develops a more self-actualized personality, then the personality ray becomes dominant and the three body rays become subordinated to it.

As the person continues to evolve he begins to become polarized in the soul. A battle occurs between the lower self and the higher self, or between personality ray and the soul ray. As the soul ray begins to dominate and win this battle, and the disciple begins to gain self-mastery over the personality, then the personality ray becomes subordinate to the soul ray.

The process continues until, after the third initiation, the monadic ray begins to pour in. As the disciple learns to become polarized in the monad, the soul ray becomes subordinate to the monadic ray.

Now each of the seven groups of souls is responsive to the ray of the Planetary Logos (Sanat Kumara) who is on the third ray. In truth, we are all on a subray of his ray, just as he is on a subray of the Solar Logos (Helios) who is on the second ray. Helios is on a subray of the Galactic Logos, and the Galactic Logos is on a subray of the Universal Logos (Melchizedek). This process continues all the way back to the Godhead. All of Creation is on a subray of the Godhead. Each level is stepped down in hierarchical fashion.

People who are on the same ray tend to see things in a similar fashion. This can change, however, depending on which ray and initiation they are identified with. Two people during college may both have fourth ray personalities and hence have a lot in common. This could change as they open to their soul rays if they are on different soul rays. This is not to say that people of different rays don't get along. There are a lot of factors that play into this. The rays do have a great effect and influence, however.

People who have a two, four, or six ray structure usually tend to be more introverted and spiritually focused. People with a one, three, five, or seven ray structure tend to be more extroverted and focused on form and the concrete world level. When a soul extension is two-thirds along his or her spiritual path, the soul ray begins to govern the personality. It is to the benefit of every aspirant and disciple to try to come to an understanding of the six rays that make up his spiritual constitution.

The personality ray finds its major activity in the physical body. The soul ray finds its specific influence in the astral body. The monadic ray finds its specific influence in the mental body. The personality ray causes the attitude of separateness. The soul ray facilitates the attitude of group consciousness and detachment from the form side of life. The monadic ray can be felt only after the third initiation and brings in the will aspect of the Creator.

These rays have an incredibly powerful effect on every human being's life. The physical body ray greatly determines the features of the physical body. The rays determine the quality of the emotional body and greatly affect the nature of the mind.

The rays predispose every person to certain strengths and certain weaknesses. Certain attitudes of mind are easy for one ray type and extremely difficult for another. This is why the incarnating personality changes ray structure from life to life until all qualities are developed and demonstrated.

Given these facts, a knowledge of the rays is absolutely essential to knowing thyself, and such knowledge is also essential to the entire field of psychology. What is absolutely mind-blowing is that in the field of psychology on the Earth today, there is absolutely no understanding of the rays. That is one of the many reasons psychology is not very effective at this time.

The reason the rays are not understood is that there is almost no understanding of the soul. Of all the forms of psychology taught in schools and practiced by licensed professionals, 98% are separated and cut off from soul and monadic levels of consciousness. The new wave of the future will be the study of transpersonal, or spiritual, psychology. (I would recommend reading my book on this subject called *Soul Psychology*.)

It is not only people who have rays. Countries, cities, groups, and organizations also have rays. Usually, however, these are limited to just a soul ray and a personality ray. Most of the countries on Earth, for example, are still operating out of their personality rays.

When the soul ray is able to focus fully through an individual then the disciple is ready to take the third initiation. The personality ray is then occultly extinguished. The dweller on the threshold has been subjugated and mastered. It is the soul that chooses the rays for incarnated soul extensions, or personalities, each lifetime.

Each ray works primarily through one chakra. A knowledge of ray structure provides great insight in one's character, strengths, and weaknesses, in the same way an accurate astrological horoscope can. The study of esoteric psychology and the science of the twelve rays is as important as the study of astrology. In truth, it may even be more important, given the fact that the rays, on a more cosmic level, even affect, influence, and predate the creation of stars and constellations throughout God's infinite universe.

It is important to understand that a person can utilize all the rays whether he has them in his ray structure or not. One can call forth any of the twelve rays and their qualities for personal and planetary service.

An Analysis of the Twelve Rays
The First Ray of Will or Power

The first ray is an energy of will, power, and drive. It is connected with vitality, initiative, thrust. It breaks down the old and makes way for the new. It is a very dynamic energy. The color of this ray is red. Those upon this ray have a strong personal power that can be used for good or evil.

The first ray people will always come to the front in whatever line they are working upon. They will be at the head of their professions. They are born leaders. The first ray people who are not tempered by the love/wisdom of the second ray can be extremely cruel and hard.

The literary works of first ray people would be strong and powerful, but these people often care little for style or finish in their works. Examples of this type of person would be Luther, Carlyle, and Walt Whitman. The approach to the spiritual path is through sheer force of will.

The first ray people make excellent commanders and chiefs. Examples are Napoleon, Winston Churchill, General George Patton, General Douglas MacArthur, Indira Gandhi, Christopher Columbus (Saint Germain).

Many outstanding sports figures are of this type. Usually after the first ray makes its thrust, the other rays then take over. The first ray, in a sense, is connected with the energy of Aries. The first ray person begins the projects and then has other things to do.

The first ray is helpful when one is traumatized by his emotions; he can use the will energy to pull himself out of it. Wearing clothing of red can attune one to this energy. This is a very powerful ray and must be used with caution and in the appropriate amount.

Most people need a much smaller amount of first ray invocation than that of the other rays. The color red will intensify whatever condition already exists. The first ray will create an almost instant effect. All one usually needs is a little bit.

The negative manifestations of the first ray would be seen in the example of wars on the planet. The first and second rays would form a good team to counteract such negative manifestations. A person with a first ray mind would be very direct and intensely focused. A first ray emotional body would be very powerful, with intense emotional reactions.

A first ray body tends to be tall, strongly built, and large-boned. Military men and policemen are often first ray. A first ray body wills its way through anything. He would make a good football player. A first ray personality might be a little harsh.

Other famous people who were of the first ray were Hercules, Rama, Mao Tse-tung, Abraham Lincoln, and Janet McClure (founder of The Tibetan Foundation).

The special virtues of the first ray are strength, courage, steadfastness, truthfulness, fearlessness, powerful ruling, capacity to grasp great questions in a large-minded way, and ability to handle people. The vices of this ray are pride, ambition, willfulness, hardness, arrogance, desire to control others, obstinacy, and anger. The virtues to be acquired are tenderness, humility, sympathy, tolerance, and patience.

The Second Ray of Love/Wisdom

This ray embodies the Divine quality of love and desire for pure knowledge and absolute truth. The color it embodies is a deep intense blue. People on this ray are very loving, allowing, considerate, friendly, and responsible.

The second ray soul is usually a teacher or possibly an architect because of this ray's strong conceptual ability. This type of person has great tact and foresight. He would make an excellent ambassador, schoolteacher, or head of a college. This type of person has the ability to impress the true view of things on other people and make them see things as he does.

The second ray type would make an excellent artist as long as he would seek to teach art. This ray type is highly intuitive. He is not rash or impulsive. If anything, he might be slow to act.

The method of approach to the path would come through close and earnest study of the teachings until they become so much a part of the person that they are no longer intellectual knowledge but rather a rule of spiritual living.

A second ray mind would be very receptive. This type is not that common, however. A second ray emotional body would be very peaceful, stable, and mature. A second ray physical body is rather unusual, although more will be incarnating in the future. These types of physical bodies are usually small and delicately made. They are very refined and sensitive.

Every ray type has a higher and lower aspect. The lower type of second ray person would be trying to acquire knowledge for selfish purposes, and not for selfless service of humankind. The lower self would lead them into suspicion, coldness, and hardness. They are often over-absorbed in study and have contempt for the mental limitations of others.

Their special virtues are calmness, strength, patience, endurance, love of truth, faithfulness, intuition, clear intelligence, and serene temper. Their virtues to be acquired are love, compassion, unselfishness, and energy.

It is also to be remembered that all souls incarnated on this planet are connected with the second ray because we live in a second ray solar system. The second ray is the ray our Solar Logos, Helios, operates on. Other solar systems are on different rays. All the other rays are subrays of this great cosmic second ray.

The Lord Maitreya and the Buddha were both on the second ray, as were most of the great world teachers. Djwhal Khul is a second ray teacher as is his teacher, the Master Kuthumi.

The Third Ray of Active Intelligence

This is the ray of the abstract thinker, the philosopher and metaphysician. The people on this ray would be highly imaginative and excellent at higher mathematics. They are idealistic dreamers and theorists. They are able to see every side of a question in a very clear manner.

One of their main characteristics is their perseverance. They have an ability to hold on to something and not let go until completion, even if it should take a whole lifetime. Members of the third department are the organizers of the Hierarchy. They are the souls both in and out of incarnations who "get things done."

Their method of approach to the spiritual path is through deep philosophic and metaphysical work until realization is reached. Thomas Edison was one outstanding example of a third ray type. Others were Eleanor Roosevelt Paramahansa Yogananda, and Ernest Holmes.

Third ray types are very often perfectionists. They may ignore everything but their pet projects, which they will do with great precision. They tend to be independent. On the negative side, they have the potential to try to make everyone partake of their own perceptions.

They are very focused, concrete, logical, clear-minded, and organized; however, they are not always aware of consequences. One of their great abilities is to be able to hold on to the thought of perfection and true divinity and not veer from this course until it is realized.

The special virtues of the third ray person are wide views on all abstract questions, sincerity of purpose, clear intellect, capacity for concentration on philosophic studies, patience, caution, and an absence of the tendency to worry over small matters. The vices of this ray are intellectual pride, coldness, isolation, inaccuracy in details, absent-mindedness, obstinacy, selfishness, and too much criticism of others. The virtues to be acquired are sympathy, tolerance., devotion, accuracy, energy, and common sense.

The Fourth Ray of Harmony through Conflict

This ray has been called the "ray of struggle."' As with all the rays, it has a lower and higher aspect. When this ray is governed by the lower-self, then conflict and havoc ensue. When governed by the Higher Self, harmony occurs.

The fourth ray is connected with the emotional body and the solar plexus chakra. It is also very connected with physical existence. The fourth ray has a very reflective quality, which, in a sense, forces one to look at what one hasn't finished or completed yet. In this sense it reacts rather like a mirror.

The color of this ray is emerald-green. This ray is also very connected with the arts. Some of the most beautiful art, music, and sculpture on this planet has been created by people of the higher aspect of this ray. Mozart, Leonardo da Vinci, Richard Strauss, and Rubens all had a great deal of fourth ray energy. Mozart, believe it or not, had a soul, personality, mind, and emotional body that were all of the fourth ray in that incarnation.

The danger of this ray is the possibility of getting too entangled in the emotional body, which most people have tended to do. This us why the fourth ray works well with the first ray of will or with the third or fifth ray, which are more mental in nature. The fourth ray type of person needs these for balance.

Djwhal Khul has also told us that this ray seems to have an equal balance of the qualities described in the East as rajas (activity) and tamas (inertia). The average person lives in mortal combat between these two energies until soul infusion and soul merger are achieved. Examples of this type are Vincent Van Gogh and Pablo Picasso. They had great artistic ability but weren't balanced with the mental, emotional, and soul aspects, which caused greatness on one level but great torment on another.

The fourth ray person often lives on an emotional roller coaster until evenness of mind and equality can be achieved. The study of the *Bhagavad-Gita* would provide a good teaching model for the fourth ray person.

Since the fourth ray people are so connected to the Earth and aesthetics, they often have a hard time meditating and getting up into the spiritual area. Fourth ray types are often very focused on a lot of physical activities such as hiking, mountain climbing, horseback riding, driving of vehicles, and relating to animals. This is fine as long as it is balanced with the proper heavenly and spiritual integration.

One of the dangers of fourth ray people is that they can tend to be manipulative. They often like everyone to experience the same focus in life that they have. It is essential for fourth ray types to dedicate their lives to their spiritual path. If not, they tend to be manic-depressive. The method of approach on the spiritual path will be through self-control which leads to evenness of mind and equilibrium of the warring forces of their nature.

The special virtues of the fourth ray type are strong affections, sympathy, physical courage, generosity, and quickness of intellect and perception. The vices of the fourth ray are self-centeredness, worrying, inaccuracy, lack of moral courage, strong passions, indolence, and extravagance. The virtues to be acquired are serenity, confidence, self-control, purity, unselfishness, accuracy, and mental and moral balance.

The Fifth Ray of the Concrete Mind

This is the ray of science and research. The person of this ray has a keen intellect and likes great accuracy of detail. This ray is connected with the mental body. Many people, at this time in our history, are stuck in the mental body and have not allowed themselves to open to their intuition and soul body. This is a danger of this ray type.

Being stuck in the mind prevents a person from being interested in esoteric studies. Once the fifth ray person opens to the spiritual path and begins to study in this area, he is able to understand it much better than some of the other ray types.

The fifth ray is very important on the Earth at this time. People who are more emotionally based tend to be cut off from fifth ray energy. They have not learned how to use this energy to balance their emotional bodies. On the other side of the coin, the fifth ray type must learn how to shut off the mind at times, also. For this reason meditation is extremely important for this type. The color of this ray is orange.

The fifth ray person is extremely truthful and full of knowledge and facts. The danger here is of becoming pedantic and too focused on the most trivial details. It is the ray of the great chemist, the practical electrician, the first-rate engineer, the great surgeon, or the head of some special technical department.

An artist on this ray is very rare, as the energy here is so scientific. The fifth ray approach to the spiritual path is through scientific research pushed to ultimate conclusions. This type of person can thrust to the very heart of a matter.

A fifth ray mind can probe any learning experience and dig out the very essence of it. The third ray person has a very excellent mind, but does not have the ability to pierce into the very essence and core of things as the fifth ray person can.

Wherever there is a lot of fifth ray energy there will be a lot of New Age churches. These churches are connected with the "new thought" movement which is a strength of the fifth ray. The hope of the Hierarchy is that the tremendous amount of fifth ray energy on the planet now will lead people into the core and essence of things, which is ultimately the soul and spirit. In this sense, the fifth ray is helping to focus the New Age. The fifth ray puts the focus of the mind there, and the seventh ray and higher rays ground it and cause the activity.

Another one of the qualities in the pattern of the fifth ray that many people are not aware of is unconditional love. This is because the fifth ray accesses the higher mental body, which is the realm of the soul. The fifth ray helps in the process of finding balance and integration within the psyche.

The special virtues of the fifth ray include the making of strictly accurate statements, justice, common sense, uprightness, independence, and keen intellect. The vices of the fifth ray are harsh criticism, narrowness, arrogance, unforgiving temper, lack of sympathy and reverence, and prejudice. The virtues to be acquired are reverence, devotion, sympathy, love, and wide-mindedness.

The Sixth Ray of Devotion

The sixth ray is the ray of devotion and idealism. The person on this ray is full of religious fervor. Everything is seen as either perfect or intolerable. It is an emotionally based ray that is also very connected with the subconscious mind. Its color is indigo. It has the ability to help individuals go beyond a mere Earth-oriented focus.

This type of person also needs to have a personal god or incarnation of a deity to adore and devote himself to. The higher type of person on this ray becomes a saint. The lower, personality-based type of person becomes the worst kind of bigot and fanatic. The fundamentalist

Christians are very connected to this ray. All religious wars and crusades have originated from the misuse of this ray.

The person on this ray is often very gentle but can move into intense anger and wrathfulness quite easily. He will give up his life for his chosen ideal of devotion. This type of person, as a soldier, would hate fighting except if roused to battle over some great cause he believed in; if this is the case he will fight like a man possessed. The sixth ray type makes a great preacher and orator but a poor statesperson and businessperson.

The sixth ray person is often a poet or a writer of religious books in either poetry or prose. He enjoys beauty and aesthetics but is not always great at producing. The method of healing for this type of person would be through faith and prayer. The way of approaching God would be prayer and meditation that aim at union with God.

The sixth ray is moving out of incarnation at this time. Its highest manifestation was the life of Jesus Christ and the Lord Maitreya. The sixth ray was made available two or three thousand years ago because humanity was only at a "ten-year-old stage" of evolution. Given this fact, the sixth ray was the perfect ray to take humanity to the next step.

Humanity has matured now and this ray is no longer useful. It is really being replaced now with the seventh ray energy on a large scale. The positive side of the sixth ray in our history focused humanity on devoting itself to God and to becoming obedient to Him and His laws. It facilitated humanity's coming out of a pattern that it was stuck in. At this present period of history, the sixth ray has a heavier energy because its purpose has really been completed. A lot of the work in the sixth department, which the Master Jesus heads, is about uniting the world's religions.

As the Earth moves fully into the New Age after the turn of the century, there will not be a focus of the sixth ray on Earth. It will have completed its service. Most churches in our world today are utilizing this sixth ray energy in their services.

The sixth ray was also connected to devoting oneself to a guru, teacher or Master. In the New Age and seventh ray cycle, the ideal will be more to own one's power and recognize one's inherent equality with the spiritual teachers, for all are the eternal self, in truth.

Some examples of sixth ray souls are John Calvin, Meister Eckhart, and Saint Francis (Kuthumi). Saint Francis had a sixth ray soul, a sixth ray mind, and a sixth ray personality.

The special virtues of the sixth ray person are devotion, single-mindedness, love, tenderness, intuition, loyalty, and reverence. The vices of this ray are selfishness and jealous love, over-dependence on others, partiality, self-deception, sectarianism, superstition, prejudice, over-rapid conclusions, and fiery anger. The virtues to be acquired are strength, self-sacrifice, purity, truth, tolerance, serenity, balance, and common sense.

The Seventh Ray of Ceremonial Order and Magic

The seventh ray energy is connected to the violet transmuting flame. The head of the seventh ray department is Saint Germain. This is the ray of the high priest or high priestess, the community organizer, or the court chamberlain. The motto of this type of person is "get all things done decently and in order."

It is Saint Germain who is in a sense turning the key that is unlocking the new Golden Age on this planet. He is using his violet transmuting flame to transform and transmute trouble spots around the planet.

The seventh ray helps to integrate Heaven and Earth and ground spirituality into the physical material world. It is the ray of form, and hence a person on this ray makes the perfect sculptor. The combination of the fourth ray and the seventh ray would make the highest type of artist. Leonardo da Vinci had a soul ray of four, a personality ray of seven, a mind ray of seven, an emotional body of four, a physical body of seven. Here we have the ultimate example of Djwhal's teaching.

The literary work of the seventh ray person would be remarkable. The seventh ray person delights in ceremony, observances, ritual, processions and shows, reviews of troops and warships, genealogical trees, and rules of precedence.

The unevolved seventh ray person is superstitious and will be too influenced by omens, dreams, and spiritualistic phenomena. The more evolved seventh ray type is determined always to do the right thing and say the right thing at the right moment. Hence, he has great social success.

The seventh ray type of person approaches the spiritual path through the observance of rules of practice and ritual and can easily evoke the help of the elemental forces. He also very much enjoys the practice of disciplining and ordering every aspect of his life in service to and in harmony with God.

The special virtues of the seventh ray person are strength, perseverance, courage, courtesy, extreme care in details, and self-reliance. The vices of this ray type are formalism, bigotry, pride, narrowness, superficial judgments, and over-indulgence. The virtues to be acquired are realization of unity, wide-mindedness, tolerance, humility, gentleness, and love.

Another example of the seventh ray person is Nicolas Roerich, the channel for the Ascended Master El Morya, who brought forth the books on Agni Yogi. He had a seventh ray soul, a seventh ray personality, a seventh ray mind, and a seventh ray body.

The Higher Rays

In the early 1970s a divine dispensation of five higher rays were granted to this planet because of its impending movement into the fourth dimension and into the New Age. These higher rays are combinations the first seven rays with a touch of Source Light, or white Light, which gives them a luminous quality.

Many newly incoming soul extensions now have these higher rays in their ray structures. Others are now beginning to access them in a very integrated manner. They are wonderful rays, and I highly recommend that you call them forth on a regular basis for personal and planetary healing.

All these rays come through our Planetary Logos, Sanat Kumara. There are actually rays beyond these twelve that exist in the universe; however, these are all that are planned for Earth at this time. Helios, our Solar Logos, directs them to Sanat Kumara who makes them available to us.

The Eighth Ray

Ray number eight is a cleansing ray. It helps clean out those characteristics and qualities within self that one no longer needs and wants to get rid of. This ray has a green-violet luminosity. It is composed of the fourth ray, the seventh ray, and the fifth ray with a touch of white Light, all mixed together.

Before bringing in the next ray which begins to attract on the body of Light, it is important that the four-body system be clean and pure. The eighth ray is good for cleansing the subconscious mind. It helps to raise one to a higher vibration level and frequency.

The Ninth Ray

The main quality of the ninth ray is joy. It is also the ray that attracts one's full potentials. It is the ray that begins to attract the body of Light. It also continues the cleansing process that the eighth ray started so effectively. It is composed of the first ray, the second ray, and white Light.

The color of this ray is greenish-blue luminosity. The body of Light is a beautiful, magnetic, transparent, white, luminous, electrical, life-force-filled, rainbow-like robe or body of energy that, ideally, one dons to begin each day. Over time it becomes integrated as a regular part of one's being.

It is the ninth ray that is used to attract the body of Light. It is the tenth ray that allows it to be fully anchored it into one's being. Fully integrating and anchoring the body of Light is integral to the ascension process.

The Tenth Ray

The tenth ray allows all the changes a person has been seeking to make to be locked in. Divinity is truly recognized when one meditates on this ray. It has a pearlescent-colored luminosity. It helps to facilitate the soul merge experience. It helps to code the pattern of divinity into the physical body.

The tenth ray is a combination of the first, second, and third rays mixed with white Light. It must be understood here that the Earth as a whole has a body of Light, also. As each person anchors his individual body of Light, this helps the Earth Mother to anchor hers. The tenth ray allows the oneness of self to be experienced and allows the integration of the yin and yang aspects within self. The opportunity of the tenth ray is to fully realize the body of Light while still living in a physical body.

In the past the body of Light has not been accepted on the Earth and has lived in a higher dimension. A person has to refine and purify his being or raise his vibration to allow this integration to take place. The body of Light is not the soul itself, but it is the soul level that contains this aspect of self.

The body of Light is also connected to the monadic level. One can begin to experience this before taking the third initiation. It will not be completely locked in until after this initiation. There is a meditation at the end of this chapter to facilitate the anchoring of the body of Light.

The Eleventh Ray

This ray continues the process and is a bridge to the New Age. Its color is an orange-pink luminosity. It helps one to get in touch with Divine love/wisdom. It is a combination of the first ray, the second ray, the fifth ray, and white Source Light.

This ray is used to get to the New Age, to move up to the next level. One can call this ray in and blanket oneself or a particular area of the Earth that needs this impulse to move into the New Age. This ray has one of the most penetrating yet balanced types of energy matrix. This ray cleans up anything that was missed by the cleansing eighth ray.

The Twelfth Ray

The twelfth ray is the golden ray of the New Age. This is the ray of anchoring the Christ consciousness on Earth. It is the summit of all the higher rays. Djwhal Khul and Vywamus have predicted that the New Age will officially begin in 1996. The twelfth ray is a combination of all the rays with a sprinkling of white Light and Christ consciousness.

Even though it contains all eleven of the rays, the proportions are not all exactly the same. For example, there is less first ray than there is second ray. There is also a little less sixth ray since this ray is now going out of manifestation.

The twelfth ray also facilitates inner realizations. If there is confusion about a situation one can call this ray into consciousness and into the entire situation and it will facilitate proper understanding of it.

The twelfth ray brings in the highest invocation of the New Age. In the New Age, the main focus will be the twelfth ray. It is the highest type of energy made available to the Earth except for the energy of the Mahatma, the Avatar of Synthesis, which is an even higher frequency. It is good to can on both of them on a regular basis.

How to Determine Personal Rays

The main way a person can find out what his rays are is by careful examination of this material and by using both the rational and intuitive minds. In conjunction with this a pendulum can be used to double-check left-brain conclusions. Thirdly, it is possible to have channelings from the Ascended Masters through a qualified channel or from a qualified psychic who can give you this information. I would recommend using all three methods.

How to Use the Rays

Each of the twelve rays embodies a certain quality of energy. The idea now is to study this material and become familiar with the functioning of each ray. Then one can call forth whatever type of energy is needed at any given moment. If one wants more will and power, he calls forth the first ray. If he wants more love, he calls forth the second ray. If he wants more devotion, he calls forth the sixth ray. If he wants the violet transmuting flame, he calls forth the seventh ray. If he wants cleansing, he calls forth the eighth ray. If he wants the body of Light, he calls forth the grand tenth ray. If he wants Christ consciousness and the New Age, he calls for the twelfth ray. All a person has to do is say, within the mind or out loud, "I now call forth the twelfth ray." A ray can be called by number, by color, or by quality of energy. For example, one could say, "I now call forth the golden ray." One could say, "I now call forth the ray of love/wisdom." One can use any one of these methods or a combination of them. A combination might be, "I now call forth the golden twelfth ray." The energy and ray will flow in instantly, no matter what a person's level of evolution. All she or he has to do is ask.

One can not only call forth the rays for oneself, one can call forth these rays for world service work. It is not spiritually permissible to send a ray to another person unless one has his permission and he has asked for it. One can send rays, however, to certain areas of the world for planetary healing. For example, one might consider sending the second ray of love/wisdom into Bosnia or the Middle East. An area of the world might need the violet transmuting flame or any of the higher rays. The only two rays that are not appropriate to send for planetary healing would be the first ray and the fourth ray. These should be used only under the direction of an Ascended Master. The first ray is very explosive and has a destructive quality that could be misused. The fourth ray of harmony through conflict is one most people are not currently dealing with very effectively. It is an emotionally-based ray that, when guided by the personality or negative ego, creates nothing but more conflict and havoc.

Aside from these restrictions one is really free to use his intuition and imagination in this regard. All the higher rays (rays eight through twelve) are excellent for personal and planetary service.

The next tabulation I would like to share from the Alice Bailey book on esoteric psychology deals with the higher and lower expressions of each ray. Just as each of the astrological signs under which a person is born has a higher and lower expression, so the same is true of each of the seven rays. Which one is being expressed is governed by whether a person, with his free choice, is serving his personality or his soul in terms of the ray's usage.

Ray Methods of Teaching Truth

Ray I
Higher expression: The science of statesmanship and of government
Lower expression: Modern diplomacy and politics

Ray II
Higher expression: The process of initiation as taught by the Hierarchy of Masters
Lower expression: Religion

Ray III
Higher expression: Means of communication or interaction; radio, telegraph, telephone, and means of transportation
Lower expression: The use and spread of money and gold

Ray IV
Higher expression: The Masonic work based on the formation of the Hierarchy and related to Ray II
Lower expression: Architectural construction; modern city planning

Ray V
Higher expression: The science of the soul, esoteric psychology
Lower expression: Modern educational systems

Ray VI
Higher expression: Christianity and diversified religions; note relation to Ray II
Lower expression: Churches and religious organizations

Ray VII
Higher expression: All forms of white magic
Lower expression: Spiritualism in its lower aspects

The Rays and the Corresponding Professions

The following information shows each of the rays and the corresponding professions. It must be understood here that the type of work one is involved in may change depending on whether one is polarized in the body ray, personality ray, soul ray, or monadic ray.

Ray I   Government and politics; international relations
Ray II   Education and teaching; writing, speaking, radio, TV
Ray III   Finance, trade, business and economics
Ray IV   Sociology; race and culture cooperation and conciliation; the arts
Ray V   Sciences; including medicine and psychology
Ray VI   Religion, ideology, philosophy
Ray VII   Structuring of society; ordering of power through ceremony, protocol and ritual

The Chakras Associated with each Ray

The Crown Center	Ray I	Ray of Will or Power
The Ajna Center	Ray V	Ray of Concrete Konwledge
The Throat Center	Ray III	Ray of Active Intelligence
The Heart Center	Ray II	Ray of Love/Wisdom
The Solar Plexus	Ray VI	Ray of Devotion
The Sacral Center	Ray VII	Ray of Ceremonial Magic
The Base of the Spine	Ray IV	Ray of Harmony

The Rays Affecting Humanity

To demonstrate the enormous influence of the rays on individual lives, the following list shows all the different rays that are influencing everyone.

1. The ray of the solar system
2. The ray of the Planetary Logos of Earth
3. The ray of the human kingdom itself
4. The particular racial ray, the ray that determines the Aryan race
5. The rays that govern any particular cycle
6. The national ray, or that ray influence which is peculiarly influencing a particular nation
7. The ray of the monad
8. The ray of the soul
9. The ray of the personality
10. The rays governing:
    a. The mental body
    b. The emotional or astral body
    c. The physical body

The Rays and the Solar System

In occult thought it is understood that there are seven progressive solar systems that incarnated personalities evolve through. Personalities on Earth are evolving through the second solar system. The first solar system operated under the third ray. The current solar system operates under the second ray. The next solar system will operate under the first ray.

In regard to this solar system, the seven rays emanate and are expressions of seven great lives embodied by the seven stars in the constellation of the Great Bear. Since this solar system, governed by Helios, is a second ray system, the other six rays are really subrays of the cosmic second ray.

The rays from the seven stars of the Great Bear reach the sun by way of the twelve constellations. Each ray transmits its energy through three of the constellations and reaches the Earth through one of the seven sacred planets. There are also seven solar systems in the galactic sector of which Earth and its solar system are a part.

The Rays and the Planets

The following list shows the eight sacred planets and the rays they are associated with. Sacred status as a planet occurs when the Planetary Logos takes his third cosmic initiation.

Sacred Planets and Their Rays

Earth*	Ray IV
Vulcan	Ray I
Mercury	Ray IV
Venus	Ray V
Jupiter	Ray II
Saturn	Ray III
Neptune	Ray VI
Uranus	Ray VII

The Non-Sacred Planets and Their Rays

Mars	Ray VI
Earth*	Ray III
Pluto	Ray I
The Moon	Ray IV
(veiling a hidden planet)	
The Sun	Ray II
(veiling a hidden planet)	

*There has now been a slight adjustment in this understanding that was brought forth in the Alice Bailey material, given the fact that Earth has now become a sacred planet.

The Rays and Dimensions of Reality

The next tabulation shows the seven rays and the plane or dimension of reality each is connected with. Djwhal Khul has delineated seven dimensions of reality that humankind is working through on what is called the cosmic physical plane. There are also seven cosmic dimensions. The seven dimensions listed here are the seven subplanes of the cosmic physical, as described in the Alice Bailey book, *Estoeric Psychology*.

Ray I	Will or Power	Plane of divinity
Ray II	Love/Wisdom	Plane of the monad
Ray III	Active Intelligence	Plane of spirit, atma
Ray IV	Harmony	Plane of the intuition
Ray V	Concrete Knowledge	Mental Plane
Ray VI	Devotion, Idealism	Astral Plane
Ray VII	Ceremonial Order	Physical Plane

The Rays that are In and Out of Manifestation

The next tabulation shows which rays are currently active in a planetary sense.

Ray I   Not in manifestation
Ray II   In manifestation since 1575 A.D.
Ray III   In manifestation since 1425 A.D.
Ray IV   To come slowly into manifestation after 2025 A.D.
Ray V   In manifestation since 1775 A.D.
Ray VI   Passing rapidly out of manifestation. It began to pass out in 1625 A.D.
Ray VII   In manifestation since 1675 A.D.

The Rays and Their Method of Development

The following chart from the Alice Bailey book on esoteric healing shows the seven rays and their methods of development. Also shown are the planets as described by Annie Besant, the former head of the Theosophical Society.

Characteristics	Methods of Development	Planet
Ray I Will or Power	Raja Yoga	Uranus
Ray II Wisdom, Balance, Intuition	Raja Yoga	Mercury
Ray III Higher Mind	Exactitude in Thought Higher Mathematics Philosophy	Venus
Ray IV Conflict	Intensity of Struggle	Saturn
Ray V Lower Mind	Exactitude in Action	The Moon
Ray VI Devotion	Bhakti Yoga Necessity for an Object	Mars
Ray VII Ceremonial Order	Ceremony Observances Control over Forces of Nature	Jupiter

The Seven Types of People and the Main Divisions of Humanity

What makes people so different from one another? Why does one person become an artist, another an accountant, another a businessperson, and another a priest? Djwhal Khul has elucidated five main categories that make people the way they are.

1. A person's "racial division"; in other words, is he a Lemurian type, an Atlantean type, an Aryan root race type, or a Meruvian type?
2. The twelve astrological groups which greatly affect a person's focus in life.
3. Whether one is unawakened, awakened to his individuality, awakened to the soul, and/or monadically awakened. This, of course, deals with the person's level of psychological and spiritual development and level of initiation.
4. Whether one is watched from a distance by the Hierarchy, among those awakened and attracted to the Spiritual Hierarchy, or among those being integrated into the Hierarchy, called "the New Group of World Servers."
5. The last category that determines what type of consciousness a person has is the seven main ray types. These are:
   ◇ The power type—full of will and governing capacity
   ◇ The love type—full of love and fusing power
   ◇ The active type—full of action and manipulating energy
   ◇ The artistic type—full of the sense of beauty and creative aspiration
   ◇ The scientific type—full of the idea of cause and results; mathematical
   ◇ The devotee type—full of idealism
   ◇ The business type—full of organizing power; given to ritualistic ceremony

The Five Groups of Souls

Djwhal Khul, in his writings through Alice Bailey, has delineated five groups of souls that humanity falls into. Some of the places the souls originated from may surprise you.

1. Lemurian egos, our true Earth humanity
2. Egos that came in with Atlantis
3. Moon chain egos from the moon
4. Egos from other planets
5. Rare and advanced egos awaiting incarnation.

Yes, some souls even developed first on the moon before coming to Earth. This is not unique to Djwahl Khul's writing. Theosophy speaks of this, as do the channelings of Earlyne Chaney. There are apparently seven races and what are termed "seven rounds." Djwhal Khul said individualization upon the moon chain took place in the third round of the fifth race.

We are now in the fourth round of the fifth root race which is the Aryan root race. Individualization in Lemuria occurred in the fourth round of the third root race. Individualization in Atlantis occurred in the fourth round of the fourth root race. The unfoldment on the moon chain occurred much earlier than our Earth's history and that is why we know very little about it.

An interesting esoteric fact is that Lord Maitreya was the first of Earth humanity to achieve ascension, whereas Buddha was the last of the moon chain humanity to do so.

On the moon chain the souls were 75% third ray and 25% first and second ray. The Lemurian souls were 75% second ray and 25% first and third ray. The Atlantean souls were 80% first ray and 20% second ray.

Short Synopsis of the Twelve Rays

Ray I	Red	Will, Dynamic Power, Singleness of Purpose, Detachment, Clear Vision
Ray II	Blue	Love/Wisdom, Radiance, Attraction, Expansion, Inclusiveness, Power to Save
Ray III	Yellow	Active Intelligence, Power to Manifest, Power to Evolve, Mental Illumination, Perseverance, Philosophical Bent, Organization, Clear-Mindedness, Perfectionism
Ray IV	Emerald Green	Harmony through Conflict, Purity, Beauty, Artistic Development
Ray V	Orange	Concrete Science, Research, Keen Intellect, Attention to Detail, Truthfulness
Ray VI	Indigo	Devotion, Idealism, Religiosity
Ray VII	Violet	Ceremonial Order, Ritual, Magic, Diplomacy, Tact, the Violet Flame, Physicalness and Ground Spirit, Order, Discipline
Ray VIII	Seafoam Green	The Higher Cleansing Ray
Ray IX	Blue-Green	Joy, Attraction of the Body of Light
Ray X	Pearlescent	The Anchoring of the Body of Light, Inviting of the Soul Merge
Ray XI	Pink-Orange	The Bridge to the New Age
Ray X	Gold	The Anchoring of the New Age and Christ Consciousness

Summation

For those who want to study this material in real depth, I would recommend reading the three Alice Bailey book on this subject: *Esoteric Psychology*—Volumes One and Two, and *The Rays and the Initiations*.

5

The Importance of Learning to Balance Your Three-Fold Flame

We on the Spiritual path recognize the importance of the proper balance of the Three-Fold Flame. The Masters have guided me, however, to look at this subject from a more in-depth perspective for it is an issue that a great many lightworkers are struggling with. All of us on the Spiritual path certainly recognize the importance of unconditional love. The ability to demonstrate this however is easier said than done. The only way a person can be unconditionally loving at all times is if they have completely transcended the negative ego and all negative ego thinking and emotions. They secondarily must at all times think and process their reality from the Melchizedek/Christ/Buddha attitude system. There is also, in truth, no way a person can be unconditionally loving at all times if they do not 100% own their personal power at all times. The owning of your personal power is what allows you to maintain self-mastery and vigilance over your thoughts, feelings, emotions and energy. Most lightworkers do not fully understand how intricately tied together these two Christ/Buddha qualities are. You will never ever learn to be unconditionally loving if you do not learn to own your personal power. Without your personal power you will be a victim of your subconscious mind, emotional body, inner child and negative ego. There is no way you can be a Master instead of a victim or a cause instead of an effect in life if you do not own your personal power. There is no way you can control the negative ego and remain in Melchizedek/Christ/Buddha consciousness if you do not own your personal power.

On the other side of the coin, without unconditional love personal power becomes a total agent of the negative ego and becomes a corruption of the highest order. This is the masculine and feminine and/or Yin and Yang aspects of life working together in perfect balance and harmony. The third aspect of this trinity is wisdom. Wisdom is an essential ingredient and quality in the process of Self-Realization and successful living. We have all heard the expression "A little knowledge is a dangerous thing." We have also seen many people exemplify this most true full proverb. To use your personal power always in an appropriate manner in every situation of life takes much wisdom. To remain unconditionally loving at all times and in all situations takes enormous wisdom. To constantly monitor one's every thought, feeling, word and deed and to keep your energies and Three-Fold Flame always appropriately balanced takes enormous Spiritual wisdom, psychological wisdom and physical/earthly wisdom. To be joyously vigilant over one's every thought and impulse to make sure that one's motivations are always of the highest order and not tinged by the selfish desires and personal agenda's of the negative ego and self-centeredness takes enormous wisdom.

It is only when these three Melchizedek/Christ/Buddha qualities are perfectly balanced within self and within the sacred chamber of your own heart that true Self-Realization and full-fledged integrated ascension can take place. My beloved readers, strive at all times to keep these qualities and your own sacred Three-Fold Flame in balance, for it is truly one of the sacred keys to the path of God Realization and successful living!

6

How to Clear the Negative Ego through the Science of the Rays

The study of the science of the rays, also known as esoteric psychology is one of the most fascinating spiritual sciences a lightworker can ever study. If you have not read my first book *The Complete Ascension Manual* and the chapter on "Esoteric Psychology and The Science of the Twelve Rays," I would highly recommend you do so. That chapter will provide an important foundation for the focus of this chapter of how to use the science of the rays to clear the negative ego. To begin with, the following chart lists the twelve rays and their functions.

Short Synopsis of the Twelve Rays

Ray I	Red	Will, Dynamic Power, Singleness of Purpose Purpose, Detachment Clear Vision
Ray II	Blue	Love/Wisdom, Radiance, Attraction, Expansion, Inclusiveness, Power to Save
Ray III	Yellow	Active Intelligence, Power to Manifest, Power to Evolve, Mental Illumination, Perseverance, Philosophical Bent, Organization, Clear-Mindedness, Perfectionism

Ray IV	Emerald-Green	Harmony through Conflict, Purity, Beauty, Artistic Development.
Ray V	Orange	Concrete Science, Research, Keen Intellect, Attention to Detail, Truth
Ray VI	Indigo	Devotion, Idealism, Religious Fervor
Ray VII	Violet	Ceremonial Order, Ritual, Magic, Diplomacy, Tact, the Violet Flame, Physicalness and Grounded Spirit, Order, Discipline
Ray VIII	Seafoam-Green	The Higher Cleansing Ray
Ray IX	Blue-Green	Joy, Attraction of the Body of Light
Ray X	Pearlescent	The Anchoring of the Body of Light, Inviting of the Soul Merge
Ray XI	Pink-Orange	The Bridge to the New Age
Ray XII	Gold	The Anchoring of the New Age and Christ Consciousness

What is important to understand here is that even though each person has one of these rays that is specific to their monad, soul, personality, mind, emotions, and body, it is essential to integrate and master all the rays. Each ray in a sense can be looked at like an archetype as was described in the last chapter. Just as there were twelve major archetypes, there are twelve major rays. The following chapter will deal with astrology and the twelve signs and houses in the Zodiac which all must be integrated and mastered even though our sun sign is in just one of them. This is why we are born under a different sign in different lifetimes to get a more complete perspective.

The same is true of the rays. In different lifetimes the physical, emotional, mental and personality rays change to allow the incarnating personality to develop a more holistic perspective. Each ray although characterized by a specific quality is, in truth, whole and complete within itself and carries within it the qualities of all of the other rays. This is a new concept that I, myself, have just recently come to understand.

Each ray is whole within itself, and its blending with the other rays, which is essential, creates an even greater whole. Many Lightworkers are under the belief that if their ray structure for their soul and monad is second ray, for example, then they don't have to deal with the other rays. This is not true. Whatever your monadic and soul rays are determine what inner plane ashram you are connected to of the Chohans of the seven rays.

First Ray: El Morya
Second Ray: Kuthumi and Djwhal Khul
Third Ray: Serapis Bey
Fourth Ray: Paul the Venetian
Fifth Ray: The Master Hilarion
Sixth Ray: The Master Jesus/Sananda
Seventh Ray: Saint Germain

Every disciple and initiate on planet Earth is connected to one of these inner plane ashrams whether they realize it or not. This doesn't mean that you can't work with the other Masters, but rather your main planetary home, so to speak, will be in the ashram of your soul up to the fourth initiation, and of your monad from fourth onward. After you move into the sixth and seventh initiation the Great White Lodge on Sirius and Melchizedek, the Universal Logos, come into play. Just because you are a disciple of Saint Germain, doesn't mean that you don't have to integrate and master the other rays, and for that matter the teachings of the other Masters. Disciples and initiates usually carry the ray pattern of being a 2,4,6 or of a 1,3,5. These ray influences mark that the different aspects of Self have an enormous effect. In my opinion they are even more influential then astrology, and astrology is very influential. It is amazing how accurately one can read a person's personality by just understanding their rays and astrological horoscope.

I, for example, am a second ray soul and a second ray monad. That is why I am so connected to Djwhal Khul, Kuthumi, and Lord Maitreya and why spiritual education of the masses is my all consuming desire in life. Even though I am a second ray, it is essential that I develop myself in all of the rays.

Let me give an example of what happens if you don't. Let's say a lightworker is a first ray monad and hence is very connected to El Morya and therefore also to enormous personal power. The ray pattern is probably I, 3, 5. This, one could say, is the line of least resistance. If this type of soul does not develop their second ray, they will be powerful but not with the proper amount of Love/Wisdom to balance this power.

What happens to the person with a fourth ray monad, who is often the artist type, if they are not developed in one of the more masculine rays such as 1, 3, 5, 7, is the classic artist stereotype who is incredibly creative but can't function effectively in life.

The following chart lists the seven types of people narrowed down to one-word descriptions.

The Seven Types of People
A. The power type	Full of will and governing capacity
B. The love type	Full of love and fusing power
C. The active type	Full of action and manipulating energy
D. The artistic type	Full of the sense of beauty and creative aspiration
E. The scientific type	Full of the idea of cause and results; mathematical
F. The devotee type	Full of idealism
G. The business type	Full of organizing power; given to ritualistic ceremony

Every person needs all seven types of quality. Every person needs personal power, love, activity or action, artistic development, scientific development, devotion, and business acumen. Your ray read out of your spiritual constitution does not mean that you should only be that focus. Your ray readout is just telling you how God created you and what you came in with this lifetime. The goal is to integrate and master all the rays.

The exact same thing is true of astrology. Your astrological horoscope is a reading of the heavenly spheres you came under at the moment of your birth. Lightworkers often study this like it is the only thing they need to understand. All twelve astrological signs or astrological archetypes must be understood, integrated and mastered, if not now then in a future incarnation. When all your a twelve archetypes, twelve rays, and twelve astrological signs are integrated, and balanced within Self then by definition the negative ego has been cleansed. This is because another definition of the negative ego is "imbalance." Negative ego takes the form of being too yin or too yang.

We all want to be balanced, whole, well-integrated people although we each will have an inclination for a certain type of profession and work because of the ray of our monad and soul. So even if you are a fifth ray monad and gravitate to being a scientist, you still need to balance your power, your love, your wisdom, your devotion to God, your business pursuits, and your artistic expression although your main service focus will be in the sciences.

Each person is ideally a Renaissance man or woman within each ray type. Remember what I said earlier about each ray being whole within itself if properly understood. The problem comes when Lightworkers become unfocused or put all their eggs in one basket and are then not well-balanced people. The imbalances can manifest in an infinite number of ways, including being extremely gifted in one area and dysfunctional in others.

My new proverb as to the ideal is "jack of all trades and master of one." This is why we change rays and astrological horoscopes each lifetime to create this balance. This development on all levels is already within us from our 200 to 250 lifetimes so all we have to do really is just allow it to come forward. All this knowledge, information and abilities are already in our subconscious mind. We have probably lived out each one of these types at least thirty or forty times. One is not better than another is. They are all of equal importance to the perfect fulfillment of God's Divine Plan.

The following charts from the Alice Bailey book *Discipleship in the New Age, Volume One and Two*, show the ray method of teaching truth and distinctive methods of service and professions.

The Rays and the Corresponding Professions

Ray I   Government and politics; international relations
Ray II   Education and teaching; writing, speaking, radio, TV
Ray III   Finance, trade, business and economics
Ray IV   Sociology; race and culture cooperation and conciliation; the arts
Ray V   Sciences; including medicine and psychology
Ray VI   Religion, ideology, philosophy
Ray VII   Structuring of society; ordering of power through ceremony, protocol and ritual.

In this first chart, we see the well-balanced distribution of professions the seven rays give us. Look at government and politics. Why do we have so many corrupt and egotistical politicians? Because they are highly developed in first ray but not in second ray and sixth ray. Second ray initiates are great spiritual teachers but they are often dysfunctional in business, which is third ray or have not learned how to fully own their personal power and move into leadership. Initiates on the third ray may be well developed in dealing with money, and business, however, if they are not developed in second ray they will not use love and wisdom and integrity in their dealings. If they don't have first ray they won't be powerful and decisive. If not developed in the sixth ray their devotion may be to man rather than God.

The fourth ray type may be an artist but without the fifth ray energy they are too yin. The fifth ray type may be a great scientist but without sixth ray may be focused on science and not God. They may not be able to deal with money effectively without third ray. They may not be loving in the way they work and may be cruel to animals without second ray. They may be pushed around by their boss because of lack of development in the first ray. Do you see how this process works?

All the rays are Christ qualities just as are all the astrological signs. The true Ascended Master and Self-realized being is developed in all of them. The sixth ray person may have devotion but without the first ray may manifest as giving one's power away to a guru. They may be a minister but without third ray do not know how to deal with money.

I think you get the point now of how all these rays need to work together. It is like the concept of the three-fold flame of "love, wisdom and power" being balanced in the heart. If you are deficient in any one of these, your whole personality will become imbalanced. We all know this.

Well, there is also a seven-or twelve-fold flame in your heart that also must balanced and this is the science of the rays, archetypes and astrology which all dovetail together. The problems that arise when these twelve aspects are not balanced are infinite. It can manifest as health problems, relationship problems, emotional problems, mental problems, money problems, spiritual problems, blocked creative expression, inability to concentrate, inability to deal with detail, feminine and masculine imbalance, not being well rounded, and on and on and on.

The next chart is interesting in that it begins to get into the understanding that there is a higher and lower expression for each of the rays just as there was a higher and lower expression of each of the archetypes. Each of the twelve rays can be used in service of the negative ego and/or in service of the soul and monad. This chart shows the methods of teaching truth as to its lower and higher expression. The chart needs no further explanation.

Ray Methods of Teaching Truth

RAY I
Higher expression: The science of statesmanship and of Government
Lower expression: Modern diplomacy and politics

RAY II
Higher expression: The process of initiation as taught by the Hierarchy of Masters
Lower expression: Religion

RAY III
Higher expression: Means of communication or interaction; radio, telegraph, telephone, and means of transportation
Lower expression: The use and spread of money and gold

RAY IV
Higher expression: The Masonic work based on the formation of the Hierarchy and related to Ray II
Lower expression: Architectural construction; modern city Planning

RAY V
Higher expression: The science of the soul, esoteric psychology
Lower expression: Modern educational systems

RAY VI
Higher expression: Christianity and diversified religions: note relation to Ray II
Lower expression: Churches and religious organizations

RAY VII
Higher expression: All forms of white magic
Lower expression: Spiritualism in its lower aspects

The Rays and Their Distinctive Methods of Service

Each ray type has a unique and distinctive method of service.

Ray One: Servers on ray one work through the imposition of the Will of God upon the minds of men. They do this through the powerful impact of ideas, and by emphasizing of the governing principles. This is a process of death of the old form and rebirth of the new idea. Servers on this ray are God's destroying angels in a positive sense. Servers who still operate on the personality ray often misuse this energy. Hitler would be the worst example of this.

Ray Two: Servers on the second Ray meditate and assimilate ideas associated with the Divine Plan and by the power of attractive love, teach people to respond to the Plan. This educates others to do the same work and carry these ideas even deeper into the masses of humanity.

Ray Three: The servers on this ray function to stimulate the intellect of humanity. They help the mass consciousness of humanity to achieve greater comprehension through the manipulation of ideas.

Ray Four: There are no fourth ray souls in incarnation at this time, however there are fourth ray personalities. Their major task is to harmonize the new ideas with the old ideas so there is no schism. They are involved in the bridging process for they are initiates and have the potential for the art of synthesis.

Ray Five: This ray is coming into more prominence at this time on a mass level. The servers on this ray investigate form in order to find its hidden idea, meaning, and power. Their job is to prove ideas as being either true or false, hence the focus on concrete science.

Ray Six: This ray has been very strong in our past history, however, is now waning in power as the seventh ray is starting to pour in. Servers on this ray are focused on the art of recognizing ideals, which are the blueprints of ideas. They train humanity to seek the good, the true and the beautiful.

Disciples on this ray work very much with the desire aspect within man, and seek to scientifically evoke its correct usage. People who are galvanized into action by an idea are usually first ray souls. Persons galvanized into action by an ideal to which they subordinate their lives, serve the sixth ray energy. This ray, when it is focused on the personality level, can be quite destructive because of the fanaticism of the personality rather than the soul focus.

Sixth ray servers have the danger of being too one-pointed and full of personal desire. The fundamentalist Christians come to my mind as a good example of this. The sixth ray server also evokes desire in a positive sense for the materializing of an ideal on the physical earthly plane. The sixth ray builds the emotional desire for this and the seventh ray using this desire energy actually physicalizes it.

Ray Seven: This is the ray that is coming into power now in a very strong way. The seventh ray server organizes the ideal and physically manifests it on the earthly plane. The Great Invocation prayer is the inaugurating mantrum of the new incoming seventh ray.

Summation

All the rays are essential to the completion of God's Plan, and no ray is better than another is. All the rays work for the carrying out of a specific group idea of the seven Chohans of the seven rays.

This next chart from the Alice Bailey material begins now to give a little deeper focus as to each ray type's distinctive methods of service. If you have never had a ray reading and you don't know the rays of your monad, soul, personality, mind, emotions and body, I highly recommend you call me and I will set you up with an appointment and you can then apply this information to your particular constitutional makeup as well as study the material from a holistic perspective. For an appointment call me at (818) 706-8458 and leave your phone and address if you want to be on the mailing list.

The Rays and Their Glamours

In the discussion of the science of the rays and how to clear the negative ego it is now time to take a deeper look at the glamours connected with each ray. I am purposely trying to move slowly here with little bits of information so you don't get overwhelmed. Esoteric psychology and the science of the rays is a vast science much like astrology, so I am trying to make this as simple, easy to understand and practical as possible.

The word "glamour" was used by Djwhal Khul in describing the phenomena of delusion which occurs on the astral plane. He called the delusion that occurs on the mental plane "illusion." The delusion on the etheric plane he called "maya." For a more in-depth understanding of this I recommend reading *The Complete Ascension Manual* and the chapter entitled "Glamour, Maya and Illusion."

The following chart depicts in a very simple way the glamours or astral delusion of each of the seven major rays. As you go through this list, do a personal inventory and check any ones that you feel need to be cleared. Glamour is caused by the negative ego, which misuses the seven great rays and distorts them towards a lower instead of a higher expression. This chart is from the Alice Bailey book, *Esoteric Psychology* and will be enhanced if you understand your personal ray configuration.

The Rays and Their Glamours

Ray 1 *Glamours:* Love of power and authority, pride, selfish ambition, impatience and irritation, self-centeredness, separateness, aloofness.

Ray 2 *Glamours:* Fear, negativity, a sense of inferiority and inadequacy, depression, constant anxiety, self pity, excessive self-effacement, inertia and ineffectiveness.

Second ray is the ray of the World Teachers. The student on this ray is never satisfied with his highest attainments. His mind is always fixed on the unknown heights to be scaled.

Normally has tact and foresight. Makes an excellent ambassador, teacher, or head of a college. The artist would produce work that is instructive.

Ray 3 *Glamours:* Glamour of always being busy, materialism, preoccupied with detail. Efficiency and self-importance through being the one who knows. Scheming and manipulation of others, deviousness self-interest.

Ray 4 *Glamours:* Diffusion of interest and energy, impracticality and glamour of imagination, changeableness, vagueness and lack of objectivity, constant inner and outer conflict.

Causing argument and acrimony, dissatisfaction because of sensitive response to beauty and that which is higher and better. The ray of struggle, Rajas (Activity) Tamas (Inertia) Balanced so man is torn in combat which leads to the "Birth of Horus" of the Christ born from the throes of constant suffering and pain.

Ray 5 *Glamours:* Constant analysis and splitting of hairs, criticism, overemphasis of form, cold mental assessment and disparagement of feeling, intellectual pride, reason, proof and intellectuality are sacrosanct.

The ray of science and research. Orderly, punctual. The ray of the great chemist. The first rate engineer. The surgeon.

Ray 6 *Glamours:* Fanaticism, possessiveness and over-devotion, narrow Mindedness, love of the past and existing forms, Reluctance to change, rigidity, too much intensity of feelings.

Man on this ray is full of religious instincts and impulses and intense personal feeling. Everything is either perfect or intolerable. He must always have a personal God. The best type is a saint. The worst, a bigot, fanatic or martyr. Religious wars and crusades all originated on the sixth ray energy. He is a poet of the emotions (Tennyson). Devoted to beauty and color.

Ray 7 *Glamours:* Rigid adherence to law and order. Over-emphasis of Organization and for love of the secret and the mysterious. Psychism, the glamour of ceremony and ritual superstitions, deep interest in omens.

This is the ray of the Court Chamberlain and High Priest, the born organizer, the perfect nurse for the sick, the perfect sculptor. Loves process-ions, ceremonies, military parades, naval reviews, and genealogical trees.

More on Glamours of the Rays

The next chart from the Alice Bailey book *Glamour: A World Problem,* is a very concise, easy to read list of what can be called the main archetypal negative ray archetypes or glamours. Again, I recommend going through this list and doing a personal inventory and checking the ones that need clearing. Once this is done, at the end of the chapter I will share the methods and techniques for removing these glamours and the negative ray archetypes.

Ray One:
The glamour of physical strength.
The glamour of personal magnetism.
The glamour of self-centeredness and personal potency.
The glamour of "the one at the center."
The glamour of selfish personal ambition.
The glamour of rulership, of dictatorship and of wide control.
The glamour messiah complex in the field of politics.
The glamour of destruction.
The glamour of isolation, of aloneness, of aloofness.
The glamour of super-imposed will, upon others and upon groups.

Ray Two:
The glamour of being loved.
The glamour of popularity.
The glamour of personal wisdom.

The glamour of selfish responsibility.
The glamour of too complete an understanding, which negates right action.
The glamour of self-pity, a basic glamour of this ray.
The glamour of the messiah complex, in the world of religion and world need.
The glamour of fear, based on undue sensitivity.
The glamour of self-sacrifice.
The glamour of self-satisfaction.
The glamour of selfish service.

Ray Three:
The glamour of being busy.
The glamour of cooperation with the plan in an individual not a group way.
The glamour of active scheming.
The glamour of creative work without true motive. The glamour of good intentions, which are basically selfish.
The glamour of "the spider at the center."
The glamour of "God in the machine."
The glamour of devious and continuous manipulation.
The glamour of self-importance, from the standpoint of knowing, of efficiency.

Ray Four:
The glamour of harmony, aiming at personal comfort and satisfaction.
The glamour of war.
The glamour of conflict. with the objective of imposing righteousness and peace.
The glamour of vague artistic perception.
The glamour of psychic perception instead of intuition.
The glamour of musical perception.
The glamour of the pairs of opposites, in the higher sense.

Ray Five:
The glamour of materiality, or over-emphasis of form
The glamour of the intellect.
The glamour of knowledge and of definition.
The glamour of assurance, based on a narrow point of view.
The glamour of the form which hides reality.
The glamour of organization.
The glamour of the outer, which hides the inner.

Ray Six:
The glamour of devotion.
The glamour of adherence to forms and persons.
The glamour of idealism.
The glamour of loyalties, of creeds.
The glamour of emotional response.
The glamour of sentimentality.
The glamour of interference.
The glamour of the lower pairs of opposites.
The glamour of World Saviors and Teachers.
The glamour of the narrow vision.
The glamour of fanaticism.

Ray VII:
The glamour of magical work.
The glamour of the relation of the opposites.
The glamour of the subterranean powers.
The glamour of that which brings together.
The glamour of the physical body.
The mysterious and the secret.
The glamour of sex magic.
The glamour of the emerging manifested forms.

The Seven Human Temperaments

Every disciple and initiate on this planet is made up of one main temperament or theme that has its effect much like one's sun sign in astrology. This temperament will be governed by your level of development. Prior to taking any initiations it will probably be governed by your physical and emotional ray. As development occurs and one begins the path of initiation, this may move to the mental ray. By the third initiation the personality ray and then soul ray will give your temperament. After the fourth initiation, the monadic ray will guide your temperament. An interesting exercise is to look at your self first and then look at friends who know their rays and see how accurate this is.

The Seven Rays and Seven Human Temperaments

The First Ray—The main qualities of first ray people are will, power, strength, courage, determination, leadership, dignity, independence, majesty, daring and, executive ability. This type of person is the natural ruler and leader, the statesman, empire-builder and colonizer, soldier, explorer and pioneer.

The Second Ray—The main qualities of this ray are wisdom, love, intuition, insight, philanthropy, unity, spiritual sympathy, compassion, loyalty, generosity. This type of person is the sage, the philanthropist, reformer, teacher, inspirer, humanitarian, healer, servant to mankind, imbued with a universal love which even flows into the lower kingdoms of nature.

The Third Ray—The main qualities of this ray are comprehension of fundamental principles, understanding, a deeply penetrating and interpretative mind, adaptability, tact, dignity, recognition of the power and value of silence, capacity for creative ideation. These type of people are philosophers, organizers, diplomats, strategists, tacticians, scholars, economists, bankers, chess players, judges, allegorists, the interpreters and cartoonists.

The Fourth Ray—The main qualities of this ray are creative ideation, harmony, balance, beauty, rhythm, the special faculty to perceive and portray through the arts and through life, the principle of beauty in all things. Strong sense of form, symmetry, equilibrium, artistry.

The Fifth Ray—The main qualities of this ray are analytical, deductive, formal mind, the acquirement and dissemination of factual knowledge, unwavering patience and extreme thoroughness and method, particularly in the repeated examination and classification of intricate and minute details. This type of person is a scientist, mathematician, lawyer, detective, physical scientist or occult and metaphysical scientist.

The Sixth Ray—The main qualities of the sixth ray are sacrificial love, burning enthusiasm for a cause, fiery ardor, one-pointedness, single-mindedness, selfless devotion, adoration, intense sympathy for the suffering of others, idealism expressed as practical service and loyalty. This type of person is the mystic, devotee, saint, philanthropist, martyr, evangelist, missionary, reformer.

The Seventh Ray—The main qualities of this ray are nobility, chivalry of character and conduct, splendor of estate and person, ordered activity, precision, skill, grace, dignity, great interest in politics, the arts, ceremonial pageantry, magic, discovery, control and release of the hidden forces of nature. This type of person is the politician, stage director, pageant master, ritualist, magician, occultist and priest in ceremonial orders. Order in conduct of life tidiness of appointments.

Advanced Information on the Rays

This next chart from the Alice Bailey book *Esoteric Psychology*, gives a little more advanced information about the rays that was not mentioned in my first book *The Complete Ascension Manual* on the science of the rays. This is very short, concise and easy-to-read, and again will help to expand your total sense of what these rays are about.

Advanced Information on the Science of the Rays

The First Ray

The six key qualities of the first ray are: clear vision, dynamic power, sense of time, solitariness, detachment, and singleness of purpose. The six qualities express how the first ray affects the human kingdom. It also must be understood that the rays affect the other kingdoms as well.

The purpose of the first ray is to bring forth the death of all forms in all kingdoms in nature, and on all planes. This could be the death of an insect, solar system, star, organization, religion, government, root race or planet. The cyclical nature of life is death and rebirth. The first ray performs this most important function. The first ray will bring forth the death of egotistical values and institutions so we can move into the golden age of soul inspired values and institutions.

The Second Ray

The key qualities are: Love Divine. Radiance. Attraction. The power to save, wisdom. Expansion or inclusiveness.

The Third Ray

The key qualities of the third ray are: The power to manifest. The power to evolve. Mental illumination. The power to produce. Synthesis on the physical plane. Scientific investigation. Balance.

The Fourth Ray

The key qualities of the fourth ray are: The dual aspects of desire. The power to reveal the path. The power to express Divinity and growth. The harmony of the spheres. The synthesis of true beauty.

The Fifth Ray

The key qualities are: Emergence into form and out of form. The power to make the voice of silence heard. The power to initiate activity, revelation of the way. Purification with fire. The manifestation of the Great White Light.

The Sixth Ray
The key qualities of the sixth ray are: The power to kill out desire. The spurning of that which is not desired. Endurance and fearlessness. The power to detach oneself. The overcoming of the waters of the emotional nature.

The Seventh Ray
The key qualities are: The power to create. The power to cooperate. The power to think. The revelation of the beauty of God. Mental power. The power to vivify.

Synthesis Chart of All That Has Been Discussed

This next chart is a little bit more in-depth and synthesizes for each ray the strength, the vice, and the virtue to be acquired. Again I recommend doing your personal inventory which will prepare you for the work to come. If you are overdosed at this point then just skim it quickly and you can come back to this at a later time when you are fresh. It is a wonderful synthesis of information. Unfortunately, I don't know where I got this from. I think it may have come from a radionics book written by Tansley who was into the Alice Bailey material but I am not sure. It was either from Tansley or Alice Bailey, and was given to me by a friend.

The First Ray of Will or Power

Special Virtues:
Strength. Courage. Steadfastness. Truthfulness arising from absolute fearlessness. Power of ruling. Capacity to grasp great questions in a large minded way and of handling men and measures.

Vices of Ray:
Pride. Ambition. Willfulness. Hardness. Arrogance. Desire to control others. Obstinacy. Anger

Virtues to be Acquired:
Tenderness. Humility. Sympathy. Tolerance. Patience.

Glamours:
Love of Power and Authority. Pride. Selfish Ambition. Impatience and Irritation. Self-Centeredness. Separateness. Aloofness.

The Second Ray of Love-Wisdom

Special Virtues:
Calm. Strength. Patience and Endurance Love of Truth. Faithfulness. Intuition. Clear Intelligence, and a Serene Temper.

Vices:
Over Absorption in Study. Coldness. Indifference to Others. Contempt of Mental. Limitations in Others.

Virtues to be Acquired:
Love. Compassion. Unselfishness. Energy.

Glamours:
Fear. Necessity. A Sense of Inferiority and Inadequacy. Depression. Constant Anxiety. Self-Pity. Excessive Self-Effacement. Inertia. and Ineffectiveness.

The second ray is the ray of world teachers. The student on this ray is never satisfied with his highest attainments. His mind is always fixed on the unknown, the heights to be scaled. Normally has tact and foresight. Makes an excellent ambassador, teacher, head of a college. The artist would produce work that is instructive.

Method of Healing:
To thoroughly know temperament of patient and nature of disease so as to use his will power to best advantage.

Approach to Path:
By close and earnest study making them more than mere intellectual knowledge.

The Third Ray of Active Intelligence-Higher Mind

Special Virtues:
Wide Views on all abstract questions. Sincerity of Purpose, Clear Intellect, Capacity for concentration on philosophic studies, Patience, Caution, Absence of Tendency to Worry Himself or Others over Trifles.

Vices:
Intellectual Pride. Coldness. Isolation. Inaccuracy in Details. Absent Mindedness. Obstinacy. Selfishness. Overly Critical of Others. Seeing too many details may paralyze action.

Virtues to be Acquired:
Sympathy, Tolerance, Devotion, Accuracy, Energy and Common Sense. Good at higher mathematics.

Healing Methods:
Use of drugs made of herbs and minerals belonging to the same ray of the patient under treatment.

Approach to Path:
Deep thinking and study on philosophic and metaphysical lines.

Glamours:
Glamour of always being busy. Materialism Preoccupation with detail. Efficiency and self-importance through being the one who knows. Scheming and manipulation of others. Deviousness. Self-interest.

The Fourth Ray of Harmony Through Conflict

Special Virtues:
Strong affections. Sympathy. Physical Courage. Generosity. Devotion. Quickness of Intellect and perception.

Vices:
Self-Centeredness. Worrying. Inaccuracy. Lack of Moral Courage. Strong Passions, Indolence. Extravagance.

Virtues to be Acquired:
Serenity. Confidence. Self Control. Purity. Unselfishness. Accuracy. Mental and Moral Balance.

Glamours:
Diffusion of Interest and Energy. Impracticality and Glamour of Imagination. Changeableness. Vagueness and Lack of Objectivity. Constant inner and outer conflict causing argument and acrimony. Dissatisfaction because of sensitive response to beauty and that which is higher and better.

The Ray of struggle of Rajas (activity), Tamas (inertia) balanced so man is torn in combat which leads to the birth of Horus of the Christ from the throes of constant suffering and pain. Varies from brilliant conversations to gloomy silences. Loves color.

Approach to Healing:
Massage and magnetism uses with Knowledge.

Approach to Path:
Self-control thus gaining equilibrium thus gaining balance amongst the warring forces of his nature. Hatha Yoga is said to be very dangerous for this ray type.

The Fifth Ray of Lower Concrete Mind

Special Virtues:
Strictly accurate statements. Justice without mercy. Perseverance. Common sense. Uprightness. Independence. Keen Intellect.

Vices:
Harsh criticism. Narrowness. Arrogance. Unforgiving temper. Lack of sympathy and reverence. Prejudice.

Virtues to be Acquired:
Reverence. Devotion. Sympathy. Love and Wide Mindedness.

Glamours:
Constant analysis and splitting of hairs. Criticism. Over-emphasis of form. Cold mental assessment and disparagement of feeling. Intellectual pride. Reason "proof" and intellectuality are sacrosanct.

The ray of science and research. Orderly punctual. The ray of the great chemist. The first rate engineer. The surgeon.

Approach to Healing:
Surgery and Electricity.

Approach to Path:
Research pushed to its ultimate conclusion and the acceptance of the inferences which follow.

The Sixth Ray of Devotion

Special Virtues:
Devotion. Single-mindedness. Love. Tenderness. Intuition Loyalty. Reverence.

Vices:
Selfish and jealous love. Over-leaning on others. Partiality. Self-deception. Sectarianism. Superstition. Prejudice. Over-rapid conclusions. Fiery anger.

Vices to be Acquired:
Strength. Self-sacrifice. Purity. Truth. Tolerance. Serenity. Balance and Common Sense.

Glamours:
Fanaticism. Possessiveness and over-devotion. Narrow mindedness. Love of the past and existing forms. Reluctance to change. Rigidity. Too much intensity of feeling.

Man on this ray is full of religious instincts and impulses and intense personal feeling. Everything is either perfect or intolerable. He must always have a personal God. The best type is a saint. The worst a bigot, fanatic or martyr religious wars and crusades all originated on the sixth ray energy. He is a poet of the emotions (Tennyson). Devoted to beauty and color.

Approach to Healing:
By faith and prayer.

Approach to Path:
Prayer and meditation aimed at union with God.

The Seventh Ray of Ceremonial Magic or Order

Special Virtues:
Strength. Perseverance. Courage. Courtesy. Extreme Care in Details. Self-Reliance.

Vices:
Formalism. Bigotry. Pride. Narrowness. Superficial judgments. Self-opinion. Over-indulged.

Virtues to be Acquired:
Realization of unity. Wide mindedness. Tolerance. Humility. Gentleness and love.

Glamours:
Rigid adherence to law and order over-emphasis of organization and for love of the secret and the mysterious. Psychism. The glamour of ceremonial and ritual superstitions. Deep interest in omens.

This the ray of the court chamberlain and high priest. The born organizer. The perfect nurse for the sick. The perfect sculptor. Love processions, ceremonials, military parades, naval reviews, genealogical trees.

Approach to Healing:
Extreme exactness in carrying out orthodox treatments.

Approach to the Path:
Observance of the rules of practice and of ritual can easily evoke and control the elemental forces.

Methods for Clearing the Negative Ray Glamours and Archetypes

Self-Inquiry

This method as mentioned in the previous chapter is always the most important method. It is just the process of monitoring your thoughts and feelings at all times, and when a negative ray quality tries to enter your consciousness or mind "push it out and deny it entrance." Immediately focus your attention and consciousness on the positive ray quality that is its opposite. This is the process of denial and affirmation or attitudinal healing. It requires constant vigilance and personal power, and the understanding that it takes 21 days to cement a new habit into the subconscious mind.

Keeping a Log

The next method for clearing the negative ego ray glamours is to make a list of all the ones you checked in your personal inventory. I recommend you create this list in a positive form by rewording the negative qualities into qualities you want to develop. In other words, if superiority was coming up then you might write the word "equality" as the quality you are trying to develop. The idea here is three times a day give yourself a percentage score or grade point average as to how you are doing manifesting this quality. Keeping a log such as this forces you to be conscious and is also a positive game you are playing with yourself to try and have as high a score or grade as possible. Do this for 21 days and these new qualities will start becoming positive habits.

Ray Symbols

The following seven symbols correspond to the Seven Great Rays, and can be used as a type of meditation tool to access or balance the ray energy you would like manifest at any given moment.

This method is a more right brain method. It is absorbing the positive archetype by meditating on all the symbols or one of them. These symbols trigger the positive aspect of the rays in an auto-suggestion and right brain fashion.

Ray Reading from Djwhal Khul

In this reading through a qualified channel Djwhal will tell you the rays of your monad, soul, personality, mind, emotions and body. In this reading you can ask how these rays area affecting you currently and where the areas of ray glamour are present. Sometimes the Masters are able to see things that we aren't always aware of. You can also ask how you are doing integrating all the rays and getting rid of all the negative aspects of all the rays. Again, call me if you are interested in such an appointment at (818) 706-8458.

Dialoguing

As mentioned in the previous chapter this can be a very valuable tool. In chairs or in your journal isolate a particular glamour you are trying to correct. In one chair put the glamour and in the other chair put the opposite Christ ray quality, which is the correction. Whether in a chair or journal let each side speak almost as if you are channeling these subpersonality parts. You want to give them expression first to see how they are operating within you. Sometimes it is helpful to do this with a friend who can ask questions to these parts to facilitate the gathering of information.

Once each part has fully expressed itself, move back into the conscious mind which is a chair in the center of the two polarities. As the president of the personality talk to each part and basically with your personal power tell the part how you, the Ascended Master are going to organize your personality. In essence you are telling the glamour goodbye. If you want you can go back to the glamour and see what it says. If you really own your power and mean business it will not have a choice. If you are weak in your first ray energy, it will give you back talk. If you want to realize God you are going to have to minus your negative ego.

The Matrix Removal Program

Request to be taken by your Mighty I Am Presence to Djwhal Khul's Synthesis Ashram on the inner plane. Immediately call forth Djwhal Khul and Vywamus. Request the installation of the core fear matrix removal program. This, again, is a lattice work of Light that will be anchored into your entire four-body system which will highlight all imbalances.

Go through your personal inventory list and request Djwhal Khul, Vywamus and your own Mighty I Am Presence to remove like a vacuum cleaner or a gardener pulling weeds the glamours you read forth. Give the Masters at least two or three minutes for each one, unless guided otherwise. If not clairvoyant you will feel them energetically being subtlety pulled right out of the crown. Just trust that this is being done for it works every time and this service is always there for the asking.

If you want to get fancy, you can do a comprehensive program of going through all the glamours I have listed, over a three-week period and have a complete clearing. You would be amazed how many weeds and dark energies they will pull out of your four-body system. It has been stored there not only from this lifetime but all your 250 past lives. Always end this process by calling in a downpouring of core love or golden white ascension light!!!

The Wisdom Seats in the Seven Ashrams of the Christ

There are seven great ashrams of the Christ Maitreya that are headed by the seven Chohans or Lords of the Rays. These Chohans and Ashram Heads are:

- El Morya: First Ray
- Djwhal Khul: Second Ray
- Serapis Bey: Third Ray
- Paul the Venetian: Fourth Ray
- Hilarion: Fifth Ray
- Sananda: Sixth Ray
- Saint Germain: Seventh Ray

Each of these ashrams has a wisdom seat within it. The wisdom seat is for viewing other people on this planet as to their positive and negative uses of the ray of any given ashram you have requested to visit. To do this call on your Mighty I Am Presence to take you to the ashram of your choice and ask to sit in the wisdom seat. If you are clairvoyant and clairaudient you will see a viewing screen as you sit in this large heavy chair. The Chohan of the ray or high level initiate in the inner plane ashram will be your guide as to positive and negative examples of the use of the ray of the ashram you are visiting. This process usually takes 30 minutes.

If you are not clairvoyant or clairaudient it doesn't matter for your spiritual self is absorbing the information and you can feel rather than see what is going on. All the techniques I give in my books work, and they work every time. If you are not clairvoyant and clairaudient sometimes a little faith is needed.

After you are finished there request to go to the holographic screen room. This is a room where you can sit or stand and view your own personal use of the ray of that ashram. If, for example, you are visiting Djwhal Khul's ashram you will be looking on the holographic screen at how you have used the second ray in all your past lives and this life. The way this works is first you will be shown a negative or misuse of this ray. Then this holographic screen presents the correction to the misuse and automatically shows you how to use it properly. This has the affect of reprogramming the glamour.

The holographic screen at first looks like going to a movie, however, as you look closer it is like a 3-D movie which you are inside of. It is like you are in the movie hovering and just above yourself watching yourself misuse the ray energy, and then using it properly.

So the first wisdom seat was for viewing others. The holographic seat and room is for viewing yourself and clearing all misuse of that ray. The second ray ashram is of special importance because it is the synthesis ashram whose job it is to synthesize all the other rays. The holographic screen in the synthesis ashram is connected by tubes of light to all the other holographic screens and Akashic records in all the other six ashrams.

The value of these wisdom seats and holographic room seats cannot be overstated. The Masters have recommended spending about 15 minutes in the holographic seat, so as to not be overwhelmed or get spiritual indigestion. For this reason you may want to return a number of times, until the total clearing and reprogramming is complete. You might also ask for the matrix removal program in conjunction with the holographic screen room but not with the wisdom seat. What I am recommending here is to systematically go through all seven wisdom seats and holographic screen room seats so as to clear all seven ray glamours and seventh ray negative ego archetypes.

Now there is one more part which I haven't mentioned yet which is essential to do to complete the process. First is the wisdom seat, then the holographic room and seat, and third to complete your experience each time you come to any one of the seven ashrams is to call forth the ray energy of the ashram you are working in. If it is El Morya's Ashram you will call forth the first ray or red energy. This will pour down through your head into your heart and through all your chakras. This will help to cleanse and cement in the work that was done this day. Always conclude your visit by doing this for five or ten minutes.

This process in conjunction with the matrix removal program and the other tools and study material I have given you should do the trick. These are revolutionary Ascended Master tools and techniques that have never been available to mankind before. Just reading about them won't help you. You must now manifest the self-discipline to follow the exercises I have given you. It is very enjoyable and can be done in the comfort of your home and it costs nothing, except your love, devotion, and commitment to service.

7

Integrating the Seven Rays and Ray Types

The Importance of the Rays

In regard to a discussion of the seven rays comprising our solar system, I remind you here that the five higher rays have only been recently activated in relationship to humanity's evolution. The three major rays are the first, second and third, the third being the major ray department which overlights rays four, five, six and seven. In my books—*The Complete Ascension Manual, Cosmic Ascension*, and *Your Ascension Mission: Embracing Your Puzzle Piece*—I have gone into great detail explaining these rays and therefore will not repeat myself here. Very specific charts have been drawn up which are easily accessible and easy to follow in these books. In fact, several other of my books make definite references to these various charts, exploring their various facets in great detail. I therefore refer you to these sources for any specific or detailed breakdown of the rays that you might be seeking. These charts are purposely omitted from this book and section in order to refrain from repeating what has already been explained.

I am therefore writing with the assumption that you, my beloved readers, are quite familiar with the basic ray structure and tendencies. If this subject is very new to you, then I highly recommend that you do make use of the extensive charts drawn up in the aforementioned books. For the beginner, *The Complete Ascension Manual* might be the best choice for this resource, as the rays are explained from the point of view of basic introduction and understanding. Any serious student of the occult should certainly familiarize themselves with the rays and the Ray Masters, as they form an intrinsic part of our development, growth, evolutionary process, process of initiation and ascension, and ultimately our Planetary and Cosmic destiny.

Looking at the Rays through the Lens of Integration

As you are aware, we cycle through the various rays in order to develop specific qualities, attributes, and aspects of the rays within ourselves. Our monad, or Mighty I Am Presence, stays constant upon one ray throughout our cycles and rounds of birth and death of the physical form. The ray of the oversoul or Higher Self is fairly consistent, but it too makes cyclical changes when it is deemed appropriate by the Hierarchy of Masters and our own Higher Selves. The ray of the personality is in constant flux and cycles through the various rays, much as it cycles through the various signs of the Zodiac.

Each successive birth that the personality takes upon a ray that it has cycled through before is designed so that the personality will manifest higher and higher attributes and facets of that particular ray. An astrological corollary to this would be a person being born under the Sun Sign of Leo at various cycles of their evolution. This would be very much like being born as a first ray personality. Both of these represent fiery will. The goal is that each successive time within that particular influence the individual demonstrates higher, clearer, purer, more spiritualized facets of that ray or that sign. The same is obviously true for all the various signs and all the various rays.

What simultaneously occurs is that various aspects of the personality likewise cycle through various rays. For example, the emotional and mental bodies are each found upon a very specific ray, as is the dense physical body itself. This is continuously changing, even as do the various governing planets change from life to life. All of this is for the purpose of learning the lessons of each particular ray, developing the higher frequencies and attunements to each particular ray, as well as raising our point of focus so that it ultimately expresses the highest qualities that any given ray carries within its core matrix light structure.

Due to the fact that this is an ongoing process, what we are essentially doing is integrating the seven major rays and later the five higher rays within our four-body system. Ultimately we ascend upon the ray of our monad, which forms part of the energy field of the Master of that ray, a fact not generally considered. When we do this, however, what is hoped for is that we have integrated the various other rays within our monadic essence as well. The fact that we ultimately ascend upon one of the rays does not discount the fact that one of our essential goals is to ascend with each of the various rays brought to a point of integration within each of us. This serves to round out our own individualized essence.

Nothing is Ever Lost

One of the most important concepts to grasp is that, in truth, nothing that exists is ever lost. This is a concept that is commonly bantered about, yet seldom contemplated or understood. Within the essence of this basic truth is the fact that all we have ever been, done, or experienced is incorporated within our monadic essence at the time of our full ascension. The specifics are obviously let go of, but the essence of all that has transpired within the rounds and cycles of our many births upon the many planes and various worlds that we have traveled upon is absorbed within the Mighty I Am Presence. It's colors, tones, qualities, and frequencies all contribute to the regeneration of our Beingness itself.

This is not to say that our negative ego, fragmented, divisive, manipulative, non-integrated acts go with us, for they do not. When dealing with any of the negative energies they will ultimately be transcended or transmuted before the time of our actual ascension. They certainly will not come with us "...unto the High Places." At some point they will be worked through and cleaned out. Their negative energy vortex will be transmuted and changed into a higher frequency. This is known as "alchemical transmutation." So, even in the case of the lower frequencies, nothing indeed is ever lost.

Basically, however, what we were in fact designed to do was to cultivate the highest aspects of each of the rays so that we may enrich the whole by carrying within our unique monadic essence the integrated best of all of the rays. This is quite a different lens than those used by various lightworkers who blatantly say things such as, "I am a 1st, 2nd, 3rd, etc., etc., etc., ray person and therefore do not really care about the other rays within my life." Beloved readers, you must care, for although you are indeed a specific ray type in regards to your monad, your soul, and the various personality aspects, you are also a compilation of all that you have cycled through before.

The intent should not be to disregard any of the rays. The only true intent should be to work on overcoming the lower aspects of all of the rays in order that you are free to manifest each ray's highest potential within your Being. I trust that you now have a pretty good sense regarding the facts about the integrated various ray expressions and their relationship to the "whole." What we do at the soul level we will ultimately do at the monadic level. This process of assimilating the essence of our many and varied ray experiences is then directly absorbed into the core matrix of He whom is the Lord of our particular Monadic Ray. This is then repeated on a Planetary level, a Galactic, Universal, Multiuniversal, and ultimately Cosmic level. Therefore, beloved readers, nothing of our basic experience is truly ever lost, but expands and expands enriching and adding various qualities to the Eternal Whole of which we are a part.

Integrating the Rays within a Given Lifetime

Let us now move our thoughts from the cosmic scope of things and bring them down into the particular life in which each of us presently finds ourselves. The practical question then arises as to exactly how to proceed with proper ray integration. We shall therefore consider certain specific possibilities, and how we can use the atmosphere, frequencies, tendencies, and motivations of a given lifetime to integrate the various rays.

To begin with, we must first realize that depending upon the ray structure of our monad, soul, and personality, we will definitely have certain very specific ray tendencies and inclinations. These are not meant to be denied in any way, but rather to be raised to the highest level possible. The main point to be aware of is that when we consider the integration of all the various rays we are not meant to do this by trying to escape the specific ray configuration with which we are born. We come into each incarnation stamped with a certain ray structure in order to explore and cultivate the potentiality within that particular ray patterning.

When I talk about integrating the various rays into each incarnation, I am specifically referring to the incorporation of the rays into who and what we each essentially are. The truth is, the more we get in touch with our particular ray configuration and the qualities and tendencies of that structure, the more we will be able to add the various other ray aspects into our Being and expression. I do not, therefore, suggest avoiding your "ray reality" by any means! Rather, I suggest exploring it to the fullest, which includes finding out what your specific ray patterning is, and then and only then, working at the integration of the other rays into your core ray structure!

If you are a person who is very much first ray, i.e. first ray overall personality and first ray monad, you will be very strong within the will. Personal power, which I emphasize so often, will most likely not be one of your major concerns, as that would come to a person dominated by first ray qualities quite naturally. You could easily find yourself within the arena of politics, a firm and powerful leader of nations. In essence, you may be doing quite well in the honoring, manifesting and expressing of the first ray. If this is done from a spiritual vantage point, and we will assume for the sake of discussion that you are acting from that vantage point, it can serve as a great transformative force of politics and of civilization itself!

Upon the Cosmic planes, and more directly in relationship to our planetary expression, the Head of the First Ray is the Manu Allah Gobi. His function, although shrouded in mystery, is clearly related to planetary government as a whole. Under His Divine auspices works beloved El Morya, Chohan of the ray itself. The individual whom I am using as an example would be holding a similar position within the ring-pass-not of the four lower worlds. In a sense they would be representative of both the Manu and El Morya's frequencies and purpose.

Having taken human birth, however, they would have some of their own personal refining that yet remains to be done. True to the title of this book, they would most likely be faced with the task of integrating their eight major quotients, as well as integrating the other rays that are not functioning as prominently in their life as is the first ray. This integration of the rays is what we shall confine our focus to in this section, as that is what we are presently exploring.

Our wonderfully first ray centered political leader may have some very definite issues with regard to the proper and required integration of the love aspect of the second ray, as well as integration of the sixth ray of devotion. He may have the ability to be devoted to an ideal, an abstract political concept, but when it comes to the appropriate devotion and loyalty to those with whom he lives and works, he is at a total loss. His heart center, through which love and devotion flow, is shut down. We then have a being who has fully actualized his monadic ray and expressed it through his personality ray, both of which are first ray, but who is completely unintegrated with two highly vital rays.

There is always the hovering danger that his staff will desert him, for they do not trust that he will remain in support of them. That is because they rightly sense that he is entirely cut off from his emotional nature. Although he can be devoted to an ideal, as was earlier stated, they know he cannot demonstrate personal devotion, or even personal love for that matter, to anyone. All who know him therefore "walk on eggshells" around his most powerful first ray. They are not wrong in assuming that love, tenderness, devotion, or caring in any sort of personal way will not stay the wrath of his first ray unintegrated personality if it is crossed.

The people with whom he shares his life mourn for his heart center. They see before them a being who is quite adept and capable but who drastically and dramatically needs to integrate the love of the second ray and the devotion of the sixth into his life and into his work. Without that, they see him heading for a fall, as he is too unbalanced a personality to deal with. He himself feels an uncomfortable hardness within himself, but does not know how to deal with it.

One simple solution, when looked at through the lens of ray integration, would be to invoke the second and sixth ray into his life. He could call upon Kuthumi the Lord of the Second Ray, and Sananda, Lord of the Sixth Ray, to help stimulate and activate the qualities of those rays within his very Being.

The Masters of each ray are extremely eager to help anyone who requests assistance in whatever way he or she needs it most. All of you, my friends, should be aware that any ray imbalance that you feel can be activated simply by either calling upon the Master, Lord or Chohan of that ray or upon the ray itself. If you are familiar with the colors of the rays you can help activate any particular ray simply by sounding the frequency of its color!

The person in our example might very well consult with a ray-reader or someone who does ray clearing. In this way he could find out exactly what his total ray structure is. The channel could tell him which ray his soul is on, as well as break down the personality ray into its component parts. More than likely, the ray of love/wisdom comprises either his soul body or a particular aspect of his personality, such as the mental body. This could equally be true with regards to the sixth ray, or perhaps the fourth ray of harmony and art. He would then be able to work directly with that aspect of himself that these rays are anchored upon and begin the process of integrating them fully into his life.

If he chooses a path such as those suggested, it would work wonders for him. It would also work wonders for those with whom he shares his life both personally and professionally, as well as to help add balance to his career. This type of healing is specifically called "healing through ray integration." It is even possible to do this by accessing rays that are dormant in your present life, but are nevertheless part of your essential make-up because they were active in a previous life. The possibilities for this type of healing integration are exponential. I do hope that you take this idea and run with it. Use it and apply it to your own life.

The fact is that most of us are unbalanced within our rays. We generally focus upon one ray to the exclusion of others. The successful artist, demonstrating a highly developed fourth ray personality and having a fourth ray monad may be in exactly the same position as our first ray politician. He would, however, be at the opposite spectrum of things. He would be immersed in love, beauty, poetry, and harmony with the likelihood of having no backbone, no "will" to speak of whatsoever. "Healing through ray integration" would work just as well on him as it would on the first ray individual. In fact, it does not matter what the particular scenario is; the cure is always within the proper integration of the rays. This is a most effective tool for healing, balancing, and integration work in general, and as I have stated, it is my sincere hope that you make as much use of it as possible.

Individual Points of Balance

Another important consideration is that based upon ray configuration, each person will hold his or her own unique balance within any given incarnation. Ray integration and ray balancing will therefore be a unique and individualized process.

Each of us has come into incarnation with a specific Divine blueprint. We each are encoded for the fulfillment of a specific ascension mission and we each have our own puzzle piece within that mission. Because of this, we will each be configured differently with regards to the rays. This is again a parallel situation to that of astrological configuration. Our specific patterns have been given us with Divine intent. We therefore must tend to the best cultivation of them, for this is literally what we were born to do.

In doing this, however, the ultimate goal is to do so with as much integration on all levels as possible. We therefore strive to reach the heights of our Divine blueprint and particular ray configuration while simultaneously calling forth for the full integration of all of the various rays to play their perfect part within our given puzzle piece and design. This must obviously take various shapes, as each person finds their own particular point of balance within their own unique destiny.

For example, an individual who is a strong second ray being, with perhaps both soul and monad upon the second ray of love/wisdom, would obviously be very dominant within those areas. If their overall personality ray is upon the fourth ray, they will probably teach the spiritual principles of love and wisdom through one of the arts. When this person seeks to integrate and balance the other rays within themselves, they may prove to be extraordinarily successful at it. If we were to compare that person with the earlier example of our first ray politician, and assume that both of these individuals were equally successful at healing through ray integration, we would find two distinct results, and rightfully so.

The point of maximum balance for the predominantly fourth ray person would necessarily be different from the point of maximum balance for the predominantly first ray person. This would not be the earmark of imbalance, but of balance and success! As each and every one of us does indeed have our own unique mission and calling, we were, in a sense, breathed forth from the Heart of GOD differently. In other words, we each have a different blueprint for each specific lifetime and even for the life of the monad itself. That higher blueprint is called the Monadic Blueprint, which replaces the Soul's Blueprint as we continue to evolve.

The basic point, however, is that no two of us were created or configured exactly alike. By Divine design, we were each designed to hold a specific energy matrix. This basic fact is the reason why no two of us will ever achieve the same exact point of balance. The mistake that many lightworkers make is in thinking that we should!

All too often, the vision of what is right for one person is foisted upon another person. While it is true that we all can be mirrors for one another, and that it is often easier to perceive a situation from outside of it rather than from the inside of it, it is also true that no one is better qualified to know what you "need" than your own GOD Self! That, my beloved readers, is fact pure and simple.

The wisest of us knows when to speak and knows when to keep silent. In this moment, I am speaking on the behalf of your own uniqueness and individuality. I am telling you that the balancing of the rays is a wondrous opportunity for healing and coming to center within yourself. I am *not*; however, presuming to tell you what your own point of balance is, for there is no way in which I could know that.

There are sometimes insights that can be revealed by consulting with a qualified channeler in regard to this. As previously mentioned, they are able to see into your basic ray configurations and can offer some guidance and assistance. What neither they nor anyone else can do is to tell you **how** to best manifest your point of balance, or exactly where your point of maximum balance lies. That is between you and GOD.

A complete understanding of this process would take into account not just this one life, but your many lifetimes. It would also take into account the specific point of balance that you are not only meant to hold within yourself, but to hold within the complex of the world. During the Victorian era, for instance, any soul in male embodiment who demonstrated a great tendency at dreaminess or fancifulness or even beauty in a certain sense was greatly criticized and thought weak, although these qualities in women were expected. The truth is that things were so "proper" then that any male who held a strong fourth ray energy would have appeared unbalanced to the casual onlooker. In actuality, they were holding a point of balance that was sorely needed for the planet as a whole. A woman who was assertive and demonstrating her free expression would also serve to hold a planetary balance.

This type of planetary balancing is still going on, beloved readers. In countries that are extremely first ray, a person apparently out of balance because they are overly emotional, overly sentimental, or artistic may, in fact, be holding their very civilization together! While it is true that for their own integration they would probably do well in seeking a point of greater balance, I would be very much surprised to find that their personal point of maximum balance would not still have them somewhat sentimental, dreamy, and artistic. GOD, the Karmic Board, and the Masters deliberately look for individuals that are predominately structured in just such a capacity in order that they provide the greater function of helping to balance a community, city, state, and even an entire nation!

We must, therefore, be extremely careful not to ever judge any situation, particularly one regarding the delicate balancing of anyone's ray configurations. Each individual has their Divine work to do; part of which is deliberately governed by the total structure of all the active rays with which they came into embodiment. While it is their ultimate destiny and for their greatest good to find balance and integration within that ray structure, it is also extremely vital that they properly honor the specific ray configuration with which they were born. There is then the greater work of helping to balance our community, nation, and planet as a whole. We can do this best by first being who we are and living our ray to its highest potentiality and possibility of expression and simultaneously having the courage to find our own unique optimum point of balance within that structural patterning.

As you can see, the subject of ray balancing is vast and extremely intricate. It is one that most assuredly involves each of us individually, but equally involves the part we have to play within the greater scheme of things. Our planet is itself a fourth ray planet, and so we must realize that all of us in incarnation upon Earth are balancing within a sphere that has its own particular hue, frequency and point of balance. The greater solar system of which we likewise form a part is upon the Ray of Love/Wisdom. All of us involved in the evolution of this particular solar system are therefore going to be balanced a bit in the "favor" of Love/Wisdom! When we tune into Melchizedek, our Universal Logos, we find that our entire universe is build upon courage. This influences all within our universal sphere and is so vast that we can only pretend to fathom the true significance of this. However, there is a corresponding point of balance within the Universal and Multiuniversal levels which affects all initiates at the appropriate time in their cosmic evolution.

It behooves us all to be humble within our approach towards balancing the rays, and to not presume we know what is best for any of our brother and sisters upon this planet anymore than we would dare presume to know what is best for a species evolving in another galaxy or universe all together. We, therefore, must simply work with what is revealed to us in the moment.

Beloved readers, we are all smart enough to know when we are out of balance in regard to the rays, as well as in regard to anything else. If we can summon the courage, which is the keynote of our universe, then we will be well on our way to balancing ourselves through the process of ray integration. In doing this we will *not* under any circumstances compare ourselves to anyone else! The point of balance for one person may very well be the point of imbalance of another, and that other person may be you. If you try to fit into someone else's conception of what balance looks like to them, you may indeed end up walking a path that is not yours!

Trust yourself and your own inner senses. Seek your own point of maximum balance, and do avail yourself of the Master's help in doing so. Do not, however, ever try to be who or what you are not. If you do, you are endangering the balance of the greater whole in which you live and move and have your Being, and in which you have a specific and deliberate part to play, as well as doing a great injustice to yourself. Ray integration and balance is the key, however, it must be your rays and your personal point of balance. Just as does the Kingdom of GOD, balance lies within! It is never to be measured against anyone else's, but to be aligned and integrated within your own individualized being, in the fulfillment of your own ascension mission!

Integrating the Rays within Various Bodies

Earlier in this chapter I have explained to you that each of the four lower bodies are upon their own individual ray. In brief review, there is the overall ray of the personality, and then there are the specific rays of the physical body, the feeling or astral body, and the mental body. There is, of course, the ray of the monad, which is the dominating source for the higher initiate, as well as the ray of the soul, which is highly active from the third initiation onwards. These various rays must all be brought into alignment and balance in order to function at your maximum capacity. In this regard, the proper integration of the rays of the four lower vehicles within themselves, as well as within soul and monad, is vital!

Getting a ray reading from a qualified and trusted professional can be helpful in this regard. This is a service we provide at the Melchizedek Synthesis Light Academy. For those of you who can directly access the Masters and Inner Plane Guides, I suggest that you ask them to enlighten as to which ray each of your various bodies is on. With this greater knowledge available, you will be able to work more clearly, directly, and specifically on the process of integration and balance.

This can be one of the most valuable tools towards working on your own integration process. For example, to know that one of the prime reasons that you are overly sensitive and prone to mood swings or outbursts of intense emotion is due to the fact that your emotional body is upon the sixth ray, and you are therefore extremely devotional and highly emotional, offers you a deep understanding of self. If your astral body is on the fourth ray while your overall personality ray is upon the second ray, the feelings within you will be quite intense, and the heart space, if not properly balanced, open to the point where it knows no boundaries and feels too much. I am not talking about the higher aspect of "heart" here, but specifically that which is focused upon the four lower planes and susceptible to the emotions of humanity en masse, as well as and especially to those who you associate with closely.

Now, if your ray reading reveals that you have a mental body that is upon the third ray and a soul that is upon the Scientific, or fifth ray, then you have conscious knowledge of your basic make-up, as well as a clear understanding of where you need to work. If further investigation reveals your monad to be upon the second ray of Love/Wisdom, you can likewise access the higher aspect of love and the greater scope of wisdom that comprises your Mighty I Am Presence itself. The adjustments that you can make with this type of information are enormous.

To begin with, you can immediately start to bring your mental body, which is well-endowed with intelligence, mental illumination, and clearmindedness, into the picture. Integrate the more feeling or emotional rays within the four lower bodies with that of the mental body. Ask to see with the clearmindedness and active intelligence that is the primary qualities of this ray. Before you go into emotional overload by allowing the two lower vehicles, as well as the overall personality vehicle and their attendant rays to completely dominate you, consciously bring in the energy and lens of the mind. This will be extremely transformative in and of itself.

Realize that your over emotional nature has most probably cut you off from the energetic frequencies of your soul and monad, and attune to these higher aspects of self at once! If the ray of your oversoul is that of the fifth, it is structured quite scientifically and rationally. Invoke it, meditate upon it, call beloved Master Hilarion who is the Chohan of that ray, even envision the color of that ray, which is a pure and clear orange, as a stream of light surrounding and penetrating all your four lower bodies. Each and every one of us who are lightworkers, and I am certain that if you are reading this book you fall into this category dear friends, certainly have access to the ray of our own soul. Call upon its great, potent overlighting power to help you integrate all of these facets of your Being within one whole. Also, call upon the Higher Self or soul to help you raise the frequency at which each of the four lower bodies is functioning.

If you recall, very early on in this book we addressed the varied vibratory rates of frequency that each of the four lower bodies can function at. If you have not done the work of fully integrating, balancing, and clearing these vehicles completely so that your true self, the Mighty I Am Presence is the one and only guiding force of your ship, then you can be certain that these bodies could use a bit of a raise in frequency. Both calling upon the Higher Self, regardless of what ray it is upon, and asking that the ray structure of all of your bodies be brought into balance and harmony will most definitely raise the frequency and vibrational tone of each and every one of these bodies.

In order to have full and complete personal integration, and to help raise the vibrational qualities of all of your many bodies, it is imperative that the ray of the monad, or Mighty I Am Presence, be fully anchored and integrated within the whole. Remember that the fifth initiation is that of monadic merger, wherein the monad begins to take an ever increasingly active role upon the life of the initiate, which is, in truth, an incarnated aspect of itself! Almost all, if not all of you who were drawn to this book, have taken at least the fifth initiation. For the very few of you who have not, the Masters tell me that it is right around the corner.

The monad and the monadic ray, therefore, have quite an influence upon each and every one of you who are reading about it in this moment. For most of you it is literally what you know yourself to be, as the majority of readers have already passed through the gateway of ascension. The remainder of you simply needs a bit of time to catch up with the full realization that you are yourself the monad. Therefore, for all of you, my beloved readers, the ray of the monad is of utmost importance.

The ray of the monad itself has, in truth, the greatest impact and influence upon each of our lives. It is that which can bring to balance and fully integrate each and every aspect of self. It holds the greatest power for it is upon the highest level of GOD-attunement, knowing itself to be a spark of the ever-burning flame of GOD!

What is needed in the example that is being used, as well in all possible ray configurations, is that you attune to the frequency and level of Beingness of the monad itself. In dealing with the rays, you would specifically invoke the ray energy of the monad, which in the above example would be the second ray of Love/Wisdom. Request that your monad, or Mighty I Am Presence, completely overlight and integrate all the rays of all your various bodies within the sphere of its own Divine radiance. Ask that all other ray frequencies present within you adjust, harmonize, and balance themselves within the total infusion of the monadic ray.

Until the lower bodies are totally and completely balanced and integrated on all possible levels, there will always be some degree of fragmentation within your system. One of the ways that this fragmentation often manifests is in the non-integration of the various rays that are active within you. By invoking the intervention of the monadic ray, you are immediately putting yourself in alignment with the highest resonance of your Divine configuration. As was previously stated, the monad truly holds the point of maximum influence within the initiate. When you specifically ask for the intervention of the monadic ray frequency, it is guaranteed to call all the rays comprising its lower vehicles into alignment with its radiant purpose.

If the ray of the monad is indeed that of Love/Wisdom, it will impart this quality into all other aspects of itself. Being the primary ray, it will help each of the bodies function in Divine attunement to itself. The over-emotional, over-devotional aspects that have gotten out of alignment will become infused with the light and love of the Heart of GOD, flowing from The Great Central Sun through the monad and into every cell of your multidimensional bodies. The lower aspects of each of the rays that have taken hold of the personality will vanish within the Divine fire, leaving in their place only the highest aspects of each of the rays that jointly govern each of the bodies. The soul or Higher Self will serve as a direct channel through which the Mighty I Am Presence radiates, and the process of ray integration will be brought to levels of unity and harmony that would not be possible without the direct intervention of the monad in this specific manner.

In truth, it does not matter at all what ray your monad is on. The ray of Love/Wisdom simply serves to complete the given example. If your monad is upon the first ray, that of Will, it would likewise provide the same function in the process of harmonization, upliftment, and Divinely transforming all of the other rays so that they become totally aligned with its Divine intent. The only difference is that the signature of the first ray is obviously different than that of the second, or any other ray. A first ray monad would overlight all the various bodies with a keen sense of personal power and will.

You must, however, bear in mind that the "will" I am speaking of here is the Will of GOD Itself! No matter what the particular ray anyone's monad is upon, it is focused within the light, love and power(Will) of that which is GOD, and therefore brings rays of all the lower bodies into the same attunement with the GOD-Self as does any other monadic ray. The fact that each monad has its own distinct frequencies is obviously by Divine design, and is one of the primary components of individuality. There is no distinction, however, in the fact that attunement to the monadic ray is attunement to the ray of one's own Mighty I Am Presence, and ultimately to GOD Itself.

When dealing with the rays, beloved readers, I cannot urge you strongly enough to seek to fully integrate the rays that you are composed of into one beautifully functioning, interdependent "whole." This "whole" will be established and maintained throughout any given incarnation when brought under the direction and guidance of the ray of the monad, Mighty I Am Presence, or GOD-Self! Within the many tools I am sharing with you in regard to becoming fully integrated Ascended Masters, the integration of one's personal ray structure is a little known gem.

Integrating Rays that are NOT Part of Your Basic Configuration

Sometimes we are configured in such a way that a particular ray or group of rays is not built into our basic ray structure. This again, is by Divine design, as our puzzle piece and ascension mission would obviously require a specific type of vehicle. This does not mean, however, that we cannot call upon those rays, or the Masters of those rays, in order to help us and perhaps add a bit of balance to our overall configuration.

We may be structured according to certain rays in a manner that would present us with a particular destiny in a particular line of work. As I have said, we are working at helping to balance the planet, even as we work to balance ourselves, and if there is a certain gap that needs filling and the Lords of Karma and our Mighty I Am Presence see that we can easily fill that gap, we will come under the ray structure that will most quickly and efficiently see that we proceed along our chosen path.

Chances are that this particular ray structure will leave us somewhat at a disadvantage in other areas. This may all be well and good, as this is not our purpose, and cultivating our own personal point of balance within that given incarnation requires very little in regard to these other rays and their properties. More often than not, however, at some point down the line we will find that in order to proceed upon our given path, and even to be at maximum harmony within our personal life, we do require the qualities of certain other rays than those upon which the monad itself has built its other vehicles upon. In fact, it is almost a 100% certainty that we will.

What I suggest in this case is to simply invoke the activation of that ray in the area or vehicle where you feel in most need of it. For example, if you are definitely serving the purpose of a visionary artist and channel, you may possibly be constructed without any first ray. At least for this example, suppose then that your work is flowing perfectly, all your personal ray configurations are aligned and in harmony with the Divine plan and purpose of the monad. Out of the seeming blue, a specific situation arises that requires you to hike up a very high mountain in order to participate in a global visionary art and channeling conclave. You look within, but find that the physical vehicle has little if anything to draw upon to make this arduous and seemingly physically dangerous trek.

This, my beloved readers, is the time to invoke the aid of El Morya and the power and Will energy of the first ray over which he presides. You would invoke it specifically into your physical vehicle, as the task you will be undertaking requires the use of "will" within the physical body. Most likely, you would also want to invoke it into your emotional body, as I imagine there would be some fear present. You could, however, be experiencing the lack of the first ray specifically in the physical vehicle, as you have never had to "will" it to exceed a certain limit. It therefore has grown a bit tender, lazy, weak, and mistrusting of its own abilities. Perhaps it is a most delicate second ray body, and cannot fathom even putting on hiking boots and knapsack, much less taking the journey!

The advantage that the study of the rays and the study and integration of the various ray structures that we each have provides us in this instance is with the understanding of what to ask for and where it needs to be directed or applied. In a situation such as this, I would definitely encourage you to call upon both El Morya and Archangel Michael. Lord Michael is, as you know, the Archangel of the first ray, and is focused upon protection of all kinds. His energy, in combination with that of El Morya's, would serve to both stimulate your own will power and to provide you with the needed protection.

As you know exactly what area, or what body you need strength of will and protection in, you would specifically put this request forward. This would engender a dramatically quick response, as your invocation would be direct and to the point. You would not be vaguely asking for willpower in general, but for the power of will to directly pierce into your physical vehicle!

You could also help hasten this process by invoking the color red into the etheric structure surrounding your physical vehicle. I would definitely suggest the actual wearing of the color red, as the color of the ray is itself a stimulant of the specific ray that you are calling upon. Since hiking would be your major challenge, I would definitely advise wearing red about the feet or leg area. Red socks would be perfect, or a red ankle band. Anything red upon the physical body would greatly aid in the facilitating of this process and send direct signals to the physical vehicle, which would serve to stimulate and infuse it with the power of Divine Will.

If there is more of an emotional need, then what I have said regarding the physical body would be applied, only directed toward the emotional body instead. For example, if a similar situation was occurring, except that in this instance you had to fly for 18 hours to get to the conclave, and you had a great deal of fear concerning flying, then it would be the emotional vehicle that would need to feel the strength of will to proceed upon the journey.

The same Masters would be called forth, but their help would be requested within the emotional vehicle. Wearing the color red could still prove quite helpful, as it is a visual and energetic reminder of what ray frequency you wish to stimulate. More importantly, however, would be to do a specific meditation wherein you clothe your emotional body itself within the frequency tone of red, or Will. Wearing a medallion or amulet, or a gemstone such as a ruby or garnet that touched the heart area, would be quite helpful. The red amulet or stone should be placed at stated intervals upon the solar plexus area, for in truth that is where the energies would be the most helpful.

This situation has countless permutations; however, the above examples provide enough basic information upon which to build. Whatever ray structure you may be in need of is available for the asking. It does not matter if you are configured in a certain way that allows you to fulfill 98% of your life's mission and purpose without the direct activation of a specific ray energy. If there ever comes a time when you find yourself in need of that energy, and you most likely will, simply apply all the techniques that I have given you in the previous examples to your particular circumstance. Remember to call upon the particular Ray Master whose assistance you desire, as well as to activate the color of that ray within the body where it is most needed. It is always beneficial to wear at least a little bit of that color, preferably around the area that needs the stimulation, as the color itself emits the tone and frequency of the ray you are invoking.

There is one other point that I would like to add here. It is also quite helpful to get help from another ray that works in harmony with the particular ray that you are invoking. Using the previous example, you might also benefit greatly by calling upon a ray that already exists within your personal ray structure which can help facilitate the needed results in its own way. If your physical body is lacking in the necessary trust of itself to take the required hike up the mountain, definitely do what I have suggested in regard to invoking the first ray of Will directly into the physical body. Concurrently, if your emotional body is upon the sixth ray of devotion, you can also access that ray from within your own ray configuration to help motivate the physical body to take the journey. Your devotion to service within the sphere of your ascension mission would engender this activation and response.

In truth, it does not matter whether the ray is active within your four-body system or not, as Devotion works complementary with Will to motivate and stimulate a particular vehicle to fulfill its calling. I do want you to know, however, that you can absolutely access a ray that is active in one of your bodies in order that it can help stimulate another of your bodies. I have already explained how this can be done with the Higher Self and monad, or Mighty I Am Presence, however, I want you to know that it is equally as valid in regard to the lower vehicles as well.

Conclusion

It is always a good idea to call upon the Master, Lord or Chohan of whatever ray it is that you seek stimulation from and also extremely beneficial to ask them for specific help in the body where you require it. In this case, suppose you want to bring in the devotional energies that exist within the emotional body in order to motivate the physical body to take the trek to the conclave in the high mountainous terrain. Call upon beloved Master Sananda to help you radiate the sixth ray frequencies from your emotional body directly into the physical body. Remember that the Lords of the Rays are here to assist us in any way they can and what better way is there than in dealing with the direct application of a particular ray frequency?

If you feel that the Devotional ray energies would benefit you, then by all means do not limit yourself to accessing it only from within your own personal ray configuration. This can and is most beneficial, however, why not ask Sananda to directly infuse you with the frequency and currents of the sixth ray? This will help to facilitate the work that you are already doing when you are accessing the ray from within your own field.

Beloved readers, do not place any limitations on this process whatsoever. The rays hold one of the great keys to Integrated Ascension. The Masters, Lords, or Chohans of each ray are eagerly waiting to assist you and to help facilitate your process of Integrated Ascension. Call upon them, even if you simply think that there is some possibility of a certain ray's frequency assisting you. Once they come within your auric field, if they do not deem it appropriate to help you in that way, they will certainly help you simply by virtue of their Divine radiance.

I personally invoke each one of them at the start of every day. I ask for what I feel I require and then I turn it over to them. If I am in need of a certain outpouring of a specific ray, then I know I shall get that. If I am in need of healing in any way, I am certain they will provide that. The Chohans of the Rays are benedictions in and of themselves. I cannot emphasize the benefits of calling upon them in any and every regard, and certainly when dealing with the energies of the rays and their influence in our lives!

The subject of the rays is so vast that it could comprise the length of a book in itself. I have chosen instead to write about this subject throughout my many books in order that they can be explored through many various lenses and looked at through various perspectives.

What I do encourage you to do is to continue to explore the subject of the rays through the many and varied lenses that I have presented them in. Learn how they can best be integrated within your personal life. Explore as well, my friends, how they can best serve you within your unique field of service.

As I have alluded to throughout this chapter, the integration of the rays plays a most vital part in the total process of Integrated Ascension. This chapter demonstrates through example how the rays can best be used to help facilitate the process of integration as a whole. It offers as well very definite tools and examples of how the rays can be integrated in and of themselves. It is my earnest prayer that you make use of these tools and find the place of maximum balance within your own personal ray configuration.

8

The Negative Ego's Effect on the Seven Chakras

The subject of this chapter is a most interesting study! In this book and my other books on psychology I have studied the effects of the negative ego/fear-based/separative mind on the mind, feelings, the physical body, the Seven Rays, archetypes, tree of life, feminine and masculine energies, lenses, the initiation process, the laws of manifestation, astrology, channeling, psychic work, Spiritual teaching, Spiritual scientists, healers, relationships, the inner child, real children and all aspects of Spiritual life. One area I have not done this in yet is how the negative ego/fear-based/separative thinking and feeling affects our seven main chakras.

I always love to find a new area of exploration to decipher and uncover. It is like a "Holy Manuscript" that needs to be deciphered, or a magnificent Spiritual puzzle to be put together in an easy to understand and practical form! I share this with you to share my personal excitement and enjoyment in writing this chapter!

Let us begin this discussion with the first chakra. I should say before I begin that this discussion and these dynamics apply to all lightworkers regardless of how many chakras they have anchored or what level of initiation they have taken! The negative ego mind can enter at any time and Spiritually test a Master or initiate!

The first chakra deals with survival and grounding issues. When the negative ego mind or the mind of imbalance enters in, this chakra becomes overly focused on issues of survival, not having enough money to pay your bills and eat, and possibly homeless issues. There is a possible focus on finding a job! Health crisis or chronic debilitating health lessons would be another example. Another example might be manifesting your business! Instead of being able to focus on one's Spiritual life and service, just making it through Earth life and surviving becomes the focus. This is not a judgement of course for just about all people on Earth at one time or another have been in this place. The ideal is to get this earthly aspect of life together so one can focus on higher Spiritual pursuits! This is why it is so important to take care of the physical body and develop mastery of prosperity consciousness. It is also why it is important to master Earth energies and earthly life.

This now brings up another issue, which is that the first chakra can become out of balance by negative ego thinking. This deals with the Heavenly/Earthly Balance. Many lightworkers become very ungrounded on the Spiritual path. They do not live in their physical bodies. They may focus too much on celestial things or esoteric things and not feel earthly things are important! They may not get involved in Earth life. They may not ground their Spiritual mission on Earth. They may not be connected enough to the Earth mother, nature, the nature kingdoms, animals, plants, minerals, nature spirits, or the Devic kingdom. I have dedicated a whole chapter in this book to help lightworkers ground their Spirituality more! To become God on Earth! Being too vertical and not horizontal enough in life! Too isolated and not involved with people enough. Not loving the Earth and earthly life! Not loving their physical bodies! Not mastering Earth energies to the same degree they master psychological energies or Spiritual energies! Not loving, honoring and sanctifying the Material Face of GOD! All of these issues can create a little imbalance in the first chakra. This would be termed underactivity in the first chakra.

On the other side of the coin is the issue of being too materialistic, which many lightworkers are, even though they are on a Spiritual path! Being too materialistic, too focused on money, too focused on business, having an improper diet! Becoming too focused on earthly life. Becoming too horizontal! Too caught up in the enjoyments and pleasures of Earth life! Too grounded to the point of being disconnected from Spirit, or the psychological focus of life! Too focused on food, vanity, gaining things, relationships, and putting people and material things before GOD. All of these issues can manifest as imbalances in the first chakra.

So we are seeing here that imbalances come in the form of causing over or underidentification in each of our chakras. This is important for Spiritual reasons of God Realization. People who are too materialistic in an extreme can even get disconnected from their Higher Self and Mighty I Am Presence within their own consciousness. It is important in terms of your psychological balance and inner peace. I mention the psychological level, for an imbalance in the first chakra could throw someone into fear or worry over earthly matters which of course is a psychological issue. In reverse, someone who is too materialistic or earthly focused is going to be, by definition, run by the negative ego mind, which will cause other negative ego feelings and emotions. It is also important in terms of your physical health, for each chakra is connected to one of the seven major glands. Over-or underactivity in the glands affects your hormones! This is often why people are over or underactive in the function of their gonads, lydig gland, adrenal glands, thymus gland (immune system), thyroid gland, pineal gland and pituitary (master) gland. So, as we see this study of the chakras and the effect that the negative ego mind has in causing imbalance in each chakra, is quite an interesting study and Spiritual science in and of itself!

Let us now move to the second chakra. The second chakra deals first off with sexuality. So the negative ego mind will have one either be overindulgent in sexuality or underindulgent. Overindulgence causes a weakening of the lydig gland, and will put a strain on the kidneys and other organs as well. It must be remembered that everything is connected in our physical body and psychological system and Spiritual system. When one area gets weakened it affects other areas as well! The other side of the coin is non-sexuality, and this can manifest as no energy being in this chakra! The same thing can happen in the first chakra as well. Many lightworkers have no energy in this chakra! This affects one's energy level, and the energetic feeding of those glands and organs connected there. Now, some people choose to be celibate and this of course is a valid life choice for some. Then other adjustments need to be made to bring energy into these chakras. To be God Realized all chakras need to be balanced! God Realization does not mean having energy in your higher chakras and none in your lower chakras. This is called lack of "Integrated Ascension"! Physical exercise, doing Hatha Yoga, stretching, certain Polarity exercises and most of all just being "Integrated" Spiritually, psychologically and in a physical/earthly sense will do this!

Having friendships and relationships will help fill the energy in this chakra. This chakra is also connected to creativity! It is also connected very much to "integrating your feelings and emotions"! Those who are too closed to their feelings and emotions will have less energy in this chakra! On the other side of the coin are those who are too run by their emotional body, too focused on friendships and relationships, and too horizontal to the neglect of the vertical will have too much energy in this chakra. Always remember that integration and balance are the key. Too much or too little is not good! We must live in the "Tao" in each chakra and within the balance and integration of all the chakras! Too much or too little will overactivate or underactivate the lydig gland and all the organs energetically connected with this chakra. Over-or under-activity in this chakra could affect intestines!

We now move to the third chakra in our Spiritual, psychological, and physical/earthly scientific study of the effect of negative ego/fear-based/separative thinking and feeling on the chakra system! The third chakra is our solar plexus and deals with the mind and emotions, as well and with the will, will power or personal power! This chakra is connected to the adrenal glands. So overactivity in this gland will cause what is commonly known as too much adrenaline in our system. This is not good, for adrenaline is meant to be used for emergency energy only. Too much in the system will have a weakening effect. Too much tapping of the adrenal gland an also cause what a great many lightworkers have, which is "adrenal exhaustion"! This is why they are tired so much of the time. This causes the body's energy systems to have to pull on other glands for energy, which over time can weaken them as well! Underactivity in this chakra can be caused by a person not owning their 100% personal power, not utilizing the full power of the mind, or not causing their reality with the use of their mind. Also not causing their emotional life by seeing and demonstrating that their feelings are caused by their thoughts! On the reverse side, some overuse their will, will power, personal power, Spiritual Warrior energy, and deplete themselves this way. They may rely too much on their personal power for example, and not pray enough and call on GOD and the Masters for help. They may also not rely enough on the incredible powers of the subconscious mind to help in manifestation or whatever else they need! They may be lacking in faith, hence use too much personal power or effort! Others in reverse don't use enough of it! In the ideal state, life is a balance between personal power, prayer, and the power of the subconscious mind! So you do not want to overuse the mind or underuse the mind. The mind must be in perfect integration with one's intuition and/or Spiritual senses, feelings and psychic senses, instincts and sensation/function or five outer senses! No aspect of self is more important or better than another. GOD gave us them all to use in perfect balance and integration. Often lightworkers think one is more important than another, which is the direct negative ego key to create imbalance on all levels, which will be reflected in your chakra system!

The third chakra is still also very connected with one's feelings and emotions. Feelings and emotions, in truth, cannot be separated or disconnected from the mind, for it is our mind, thinking, interpretations, perspectives, belief systems, perceptions, and lenses that cause us to feel the way we do! When we allow the negative ego/fear-based/separative mind to interpret our life instead of the Spiritual/Christ/Buddha mind, we create all kinds of negative thoughts and negative feelings and emotions. This will all be reflected in the third chakra. It will be more and more in chaos, the more we allow the negative ego mind to interpret our reality! This again can cause stomachaches, ulcers, intestinal problems, and digestive problems, although these are not the only reasons these can occur. Sometimes there are physical reasons, electrical reasons, etheric reasons or Spiritual reasons. This kind of negative ego activity will also weaken the adrenal glands. It will also affect all the organs—liver, pancreas, spleen, gall bladder, kidneys, and so on. Overuse of will or personal power will cause a weakening of the pancreas. Underuse of personal power will do the same! Too much anger and too much thinking and planning will weaken the liver! Too little thinking and planning will do the same! All our thoughts and feelings totally affect our aura, chakras, glands and organs. This again is why "Integrated Ascension" is so important! The third chakra is often one of the hardest chakras for lightworkers to balance! It is for this reason and many others that this book has been written!

So we see that overuse or underuse of personal power, the mind, feelings and emotions will all cause imbalance in the third chakra. Only living in the "Tao" and achieving "Integrated Ascension" will bring each chakra and your entire chakra system into balance! The most important thing is to keep the negative ego/fear-based/separative mind and thought system out of your consciousness and to only think with your Spiritual/Christ/Buddha mind and feelings, for this is what will perceive balance and integration in all things and only create positive and Spiritual thoughts and feelings!

The fourth chakra is of course our heart chakra! It remains in balance and focused on unconditional love when we think from our Spiritual/Christ/Buddha mind! When we think from our negative ego/fear-based/separative mind the heart chakra becomes imbalanced, for conditional love, addictive love, anger, lack of forgiveness, guilt, impatience, irritation, judgment, intolerance and separative feelings and emotions have been allowed to enter your consciousness and are hence reflected in your fourth chakra. The heart chakra is interestingly enough your immune system, for it is connected to the thymus gland. When you learn to see life only from the eyes of the Spiritual/Christ/Buddha mind, your physical immune system will function much more perfectly. Isn't that interesting! Unconditional love is the key to perfect health! Conditional love of the negative ego mind will have a weakening effect on the thymus gland and heart chakra!

The fifth chakra deals with communication! Virginia Satir, the well-known marriage counselor, said something to the effect that "Communication is to a relationship what breathing is to living"! I thought that was well stated. We are here to communicate, to talk to GOD and the Masters, to share, to have fellowship with our Brothers and Sisters, to have romantic relationships, to have personal relationships, friendships, and to serve and help others. We do this through various forms of communication. When this chakra is in balance we communicate from our Spiritual/Christ/Buddha consciousness, not our negative ego/fear-based/separative consciousness. We hence share that which GOD, our own Mighty I Am Presence, our Higher Self, our Soul, the Masters, and the Angels would have us share. We share things of Unconditional Love, Oneness, and Godly matters and issues! The fifth chakra becomes imbalanced when it is used by the negative ego mind! This chakra will also become imbalanced when overused or underused! Some people or lightworkers spend too much time communicating. They can overuse this chakra, which drains the thyroid gland and can create thyroid problems. This type of person may process too much, or be too overidentified with service. They may have fear so they look too much to try to overcome the fear they have not mastered. They may communicate too much to try to increase their business they are worried about. They may talk too much for they do not have enough faith, trust, and patience in GOD. They may communicate too much, for they do not know how to quiet their mind, feelings, and emotions. They may communicate too much because they have too many negative feelings and emotions that are too stirred up from negative ego thinking! They may talk too much because they are not whole within themselves and do not love themselves! They may communicate too much because they do not know how to meditate and appreciate just "Being and/or being in the Silence"! They may communicate or overuse this chakra because they are so busy doing and achieving they do not know how to just "be"! They also may communicate too much because they do not know how to set boundaries with self or others!

On the other side of the coin, there are many people and lightworkers who undercommunicate. As the Universal Mind said through Edgar Cayce, "There are sins of omission or commission"! There are many that undercommunicate. This is commonly seen, of course, in men in romantic relationships. We don't want to stereotype, for of course this can happen to anyone. Women on the whole, however, as a fair generalization, tend to communicate more freely, especially about their feelings! There can be a danger here if there is too much of a preoccupation with the emotional body, which hence then will create an imbalance as well in the fifth chakra. Balance, once again, is the key! The lesson here is to know when to talk and when to be silent. Don't talk when it is time to be silent and don't be silent when it is time to talk. Part of coming into one's Spiritual service work is the proper opening of this fifth chakra! In relationships, when a person is afraid to express their thoughts, feelings and emotions, this can create an imbalance in the heart chakra and throat chakra. The inability to express love or even to say the words "I love you!" would be an imbalance of the heart chakra and throat chakra. Any place in a person's life where they need to be communicating and are not as GOD would have it be shows an imbalance in this chakra. All imbalances in the chakras, and all imbalances and problems in life, are caused by only one thing, which is negative ego/fear-based/separative thinking! It is the negative ego that causes us to make imbalanced choices. This book is dedicated to showing you all the different ways the negative ego does this, so we can be more conscious, aware and joyously vigilant to always think only with our Spiritual/Christ/Buddha mind!

Other examples of imbalance and the negative ego mind creating problems in the fifth chakra are: gossip, speaking judgmentally about others, bad-mouthing others behind their back, breaking confidentiality, backstabbing and speaking negatively about others! As the saying goes, if you don't have anything nice to say, don't say anything at all!

The sixth chakra is our Third Eye and Spiritual vision center. The Third Eye is properly opened by the study of many of the things you are studying in this book! Spiritual vision occurs really on four levels. There is awareness of Spiritual things and esoteric knowledge and wisdom, which opens the third eye in a positive balanced manner! There is psychological wisdom, the likes of which you are also studying in this book, which greatly opens the Third Eye. For this is the Spiritual science of how to think with your Spiritual/Christ/Buddha mind and not your negative ego/fear-based/separative mind! The thinking with your negative ego mind is what closes the Third Eye and causes blocks and imbalances in it. It is what creates blind spots and limited lens seeing! Every person either has negative ego vision or Spiritual vision. We don't just see with our physical eyes, we see through our mind and belief systems! Our thoughts create our reality! Our thoughts create our feelings and emotions. Our thoughts create our behavior! Our thoughts create what we attract and magnetize into our lives! You have been learning in this book the Spiritual science of proper psychospiritual vision, which is hardly discussed in Religion and the New Age Movement, and is, in truth the foundation of your Spiritual life!

Then there is your physical/earthly vision, which is connected to how you integrate and ground your Spiritual life into your physical body and into Earth life! Are you a fully integrated Ascended Master living in your physical body? Have you fully manifested your Spiritual mission on Earth? Are you fully integrating your Spiritual life into your earthly life? Have you found a way of being of service on Earth? Are you mastering and fully integrating Earth energies? Are you balancing and integrating the God/Goddess within? These are all issues of Spiritual sight on an earthly level.

Many do not realize that your Spiritual/Psychological/Earthly mastery and integration will affect your physical sight. "As within, so without! As above, so below"!

A great many lightworkers think that Spiritual sight is being clairvoyant and being able to see into the Spiritual world! This is a type of opening of the Third Eye. However, you do not need this to achieve God Realization or Integrated Ascension! A great, great, great many of those who have clairvoyance of this kind do not have the type of Spiritual vision and Third Eye opening of esoteric knowledge and wisdom, psychological wisdom and clarity, physical/earthly psychospiritual vision! They have what I call "Mystic vision" but not occult, psychological, and physical/earthly psychospiritual vision! So, we see that this type of vision is only one quarter of what the true opening of the Third Eye is about. A person can have mystic clairvoyance, they can be a Spiritual, psychological, and physical/earthly mess, and often are! This lack of clear third eye vision on these other levels also greatly contaminates and distorts their mystic vision. It is impossible to separate a person's consciousness from their mystic vision or channeling abilities. This is why it is to your best interest to be much more Spiritually discerning before you give your power to an external channel or clairvoyant!

The opening of the third eye is also connected to the opening of all your Spiritual senses such as: intuition, knowingness, comprehension, knowledge, wisdom, Spiritual idealism, all knowledge, beautitude, active service, divine vision, revelation, healing, Spiritual telepathy, response to group vibration, Spiritual discernment, discrimination, emotional idealism, and imagination, to just name a few! A person could have their mystic clairvoyance opened and not be very developed in the rest of these inner senses that open the Third Eye! This is not even counting all the Spiritual and esoteric knowledge and wisdom, psychological vision, and physical/earthly psychospiritual vision, and for that matter just plain physical/earthly vision, which is a type of Spiritual vision in truth! Some people have better physical third dimensional vision than others. The ideal is to have good Spiritual vision in all these levels, and it is all of them that open the Third Eye and sixth chakra. Mystic vision is less than ten percent of what fully opening the Third Eye is about! Let this be a lesson to all of those lightworkers that think mystic clairvoyance or channeling is the be-all or end-all and will give them all they want. I know channels, who are clairaudient channels, but very weak in all these other senses and in the three basic levels of Spiritual knowledge, psychological vision and physical/earthly psychospiritual vision. My Beloved Readers, this is more often the norm and that is why you must be extremely careful about not giving away your personal power, Spiritual discernment, and not giving too much credence to what comes through external channels and psychics!

Not only is it very likely they are not developed in a lot of these other areas, they also do not know you from Adam! Their channeling and psychic work is not only based on all that I have stated so far, but is also based on the knowledge and attunement they have of you. Their channelings are coming through all their filters, subconscious mind, belief systems, personality, psychological clarity and development, Spiritual knowledge or lack thereof, earthly mastery or lack thereof, Ray structure, archetypes, astrological configuration, perceptions, negative ego agendas, chakra balance or lack thereof, information banks from this life or past lives, fatigue level, personal opinions, overall integration and balance, philosophy, psychology, Spiritual path they are on, lenses they are stuck in, blind spots, and on and on. All of these things are acting as filters to what an external channel is telling you or what their mystic vision is telling you. I am not saying that it is not of value. I am just saying, "Be discerning!" If any channel says they are not affected by any of these considerations "run for the hills!" It is when a mystic clairvoyant or channel can admit to themselves and to you that all these things can affect clairvoyance and channeling that they might be able to be trusted a little more! Any channel or mystic who thinks that these things do not affect their channeling or clairvoyance, with no judgment intended, is living in faulty thinking! Every channel on planet Earth, including myself, is affected by these aspects of consciousness! When channeling comes through it has to be interpreted by the subconscious and conscious mind of the person doing the work. It is not like some open telephone call, and if anyone thinks so, they are deluding themselves. Even Edgar Cayce had filters. Why did the channelings come through in a "stilted" English? This was Cayce's past life programming. The Universal Mind through Cayce said that Cayce's abilities were stemming from a past life and lives in Egypt. Sai Baba in India is a Universal Avatar and his channelings are totally affected and colored by his Indian upbringing and background! He does not speak of the Ascended Masters or Ascended Master teachings as we do in the West. His work is colored by the lens of Indian teachings. This is not a judgement, for Sai Baba is incredible! Lightworkers must understand how channeling, clairvoyance and psychic abilities really work. There is this incredibly naïve and undiscerning belief that these abilities are separate and not influenced by a person's consciousness, mind, emotions, psychology, subconscious, negative ego, philosophy, Spiritual development, psychological development, physical/earthly development, and so on. This is ludicrous, my friends! Lightworkers are way too naïve and impressionable. They give away their personal power too easily. They believe anything they read! They think if it is channeled it is true. Nothing could be farther from the truth!

The reason all this takes place is that their Third Eye and sixth chakra is not fully open on all these levels I am speaking about here! They are so enamored with channeling, clairvoyance, or psychic abilities they are blinded to the truth. The are not seeing from a "Full Spectrum Prism Vision"! They are overidentitified with the Spiritual level and do not see the astronomical effect that the consciousness, psychology, and physical/earthly psychospiritual aspect, as well as all these other filters I have mentioned, are affecting the process. They are not recognizing the 90% of other inner senses they have forgotten about! My Beloved Readers, please take these other factors into consideration. I am attempting to more fully open your Third Eye in reading this chapter! I am attempting to help you develop your Full Spectrum Prism Vision from all levels, not just one fragmented lens or type of vision! The third eye will never ever be fully open until all these factors are taken into consideration!

Now, it is possible to open the Third Eye too much or too little. I have been talking about what causes the Third Eye or sixth chakra too open to little! There is also a need for protection in life, which a lot of lightworkers say is unimportant. This of course is not true. The Third Eye is like the physical eye in some ways. The pupil of the eye opens and closes in terms of how much light is coming into the room. There are times to close the Third Eye a little. If you go to the movies and there are some violent scenes you might want to close it a little. Too many stimuli can be coming in at times. This needs to be monitored.

There is also the aspect as well of overusing the third eye. Lightworkers may spend too much time working with this chakra to the neglect of others! This may cause headaches, eyestrain, or depletion of the pituitary gland! This is very important to not let happen, for this is the Master Gland of our body and affects all the other glands and organs. It is interesting that the Third Eye or sixth chakra is connected to the Master Gland or pituitary, is it not! In this discussion we see the incredible importance of having a clear Spiritual, psychological and physical/earthly vision in our lives. We see from this discussion the enormous effect our Spiritual/Psychological/Physical/Earthly vision has on our lives! It is our thoughts and images in our mind that creates our reality! Would it not make sense, given that the Third Eye and sixth chakra are connected with the vision for our whole life, that it would be connected to the Master Gland of the body, the pituitary? Is not GOD ingenious!

So the key here is to not underuse or overuse your Third Eye and sixth chakra, but to fully open it and keep it in balance with all the rest of the chakras! For we don't want to overactivate or underactivate the pituitary gland, among other things!

The seventh chakra is, of course our crown chakra and connection to GOD, Christ, the Holy Spirit, our Mighty I Am Presence, our Higher Self, our Soul, the Oversoul, the inner plane Ascended Masters, the Archangels and Angels, Elohim Councils, Christed Extraterrestrials, the Universal Mind, Universal Knowledge, Spiritual knowledge and wisdom, anchoring of Higher Light Bodies, anchoring of Higher Chakras, Divine Plan, Monadic Conscious-ness, Ascension, The Godhead, Esoteric knowledge, Revelation, Inspiration, Intuition, Meditation, Prayer, Chanting the Names of GOD, reciting Mantras of GOD, using the Power Names of GOD, Highest form of Spiritual Healing, All Knowledge, Higher God Senses, the Highest form of Channeling, Perfection, Realization, Active Service, Beatitude, Highest form of Egolessness, Spiritual idealism, Divine vision, Highest Form of Spiritual telepathy, and overlighting by Masters!

It is, of course, the ideal to open one's crown chakra! However, one does not want to be overidentified with it to the point of overactivating and stimulating it to the improper integration and balance of the other chakras. If one does this, for example, improper grounding can take place. All the energy in the etheric body will be in the upper chakras and not in the lower chakras. This could cause headaches! Not being in the physical body! Not embodying the physical body! Not grounding your Spiritual mission on Earth! Being too preoccupied with esoteric knowledge and not doing service work. As Sai Baba says, "Hands that help are Holier than lips that pray"! Living in the Heavenly world, but not properly integrating the psychological level, or physical/earthly level! Having Spiritual wisdom but not psychological or physical earthly wisdom! Being overidentified with the guru or Spiritual teacher role! Being too vertical and not integrating the horizontal aspect of life! Not living in the marketplace! Not being involved enough in relationships and with people! Spending too much time channeling and not living! Spending too much time meditating and not fulfilling your Spiritual mission on Earth. Thinking the Spiritual worlds are more Spiritual than the psychological world and physical/earthly world. Being Spiritual but not mentally and emotionally balanced. Having an open crown but a closed heart! Not dealing well with relationships or people, but being a Spiritual teacher. Being so Spiritual you don't communicate with others effectively. Being highly developed Spiritually, but totally fragmented and not integrated on other levels. Being so Spiritual you can't take care of yourself in a physical/earthly sense! I have seen many of these types in the Spiritual movement! This is not the ideal and not what we are meant to embody!

All these things I have mentioned are examples of how someone can become overidentified with the crown or seventh chakra and hence overactivate it and create massive imbalance in other areas of your life which are equally important! If the crown chakra is not opened enough, the pineal gland will be understimulated or nourished. If the crown chakra is overactivated, the pineal gland will become overstimulated and eventually exhausted! It is integration and balance we seek my friends! Any chakra that is over or under identified will create "blind spots" Spiritually, psychologically and in a physical/earthly sense, which is, in truth, antithetical to God Realization! God Realization in terms of our chakra system is the proper integration and balance in our daily lives of all seven chakras, so that no chakra is overactivated or underactivated in a long-term sense. There are times, of course, where it is quite appropriate to focus on one chakra more than another for a certain Spiritual purpose or project. However, in the greater scope of one's life and in the big picture of one's life the seven major chakras need to be basically balanced! This, my Beloved Readers, is another one of the real golden keys to achieving God Realization! It is my sincere hope and prayer that this Spiritual study of this most important subject has been enlightening and helpful in helping you to make some subtle Spiritual, attitudinal, emotional, energetic, and physical/earthly adjustments to make this Spiritual ideal of "Integrated Ascension" even more of a reality in your life!

9

The Seven Rays and Chakras and the Importance of Making Decisions from an Integrated Perspective

One of the most important aspects of becoming a Self-Realized Being and being successful in all areas of one's life deals with the process of making decisions. The ideal is to make all your decisions from a full spectrum prism perspective integrating all seven rays. A great many lightworkers have not been trained in this work, and often tend to emphasize one ray over another, which can skew or cause an imbalance in their decision making process. Let me explain here what I mean.

Although every person has one specific ray that characterizes their Monad, Soul, personality, mind, emotions and physical body; the true ideal is to become a master of all the rays. A person may have a different ray structure for each of their bodies, but one should not strive to only embody one's ray structure. One should strive to be a master of all seven rays.

If a person overemphasizes the First Ray then the decisions they make will be based on achieving power and political gain. There is nothing wrong with this as long as this serves Spiritual power and political concerns, not negative ego power and political gain. We see the corruption of this in our Government, with many political leaders making decisions for power and politics to serve the negative ego and not the Spirit.

If someone is overly identified with the Second Ray, which is love/wisdom, they may make all their decisions to serve love and harmony but be unable to integrate the proper balance of personal power, and consider the political implications of the decisions they are making. The word "political" here is not a negative word. In our government and society it has become a negative word because of how much political corruption and negative ego usage of the First Ray there is. A positive Spiritual use of a political decision might be, for example, having a party and inviting a certain family member to keep the peace in the family, for if you did not a big emotional explosion would take place. Intuiting this in advance, you make a political decision to take this action, which in the bigger picture is a much better move even though your personal feeling in the moment might be that you do not have a preference for this. Second Ray overidentification may bring someone to making decisions only out of how they feel, rather than out of their intuition or mind. The ideal is to integrate all three. All decisions should, in truth, integrate all seven rays to come to a balanced perspective.

The first person might make their decision out of power and political rightness but may not make it out of unconditional love and/or achieving oneness and harmony. The person who is overidentified with the Third Ray will make their decisions out of "Active Intelligence" which is out of a mental place that considers the physical action. For example, they make a decision not just out of the feeling of being Spiritual, but out of how this Spiritual feeling translates into actually physically helping self and others. The Second Ray person might only consider the feeling of love and not how this love translates to physical service. I am again reminded of Sai Baba's famous quote, "Hands that help are Holier than lips that pray"! The Third Ray is also concerned with business. So the decision making process would consider, how does this decision affect my business? The Second Ray person would be more concerned about how this affects their Spiritual education and the Spiritual education of others. The First Ray person only sees the political implications.

Are you beginning to see that each of these are like "lenses" we see through?

The Fourth Ray person is interested in beauty and harmony. All decisions will be made out of more artistic and aesthetic concerns. Here we have the artist and musician. They are not concerned with power or politics. They may not even be concerned with love/wisdom and active intelligence. They see through the lens of artistry and aesthetics. You can see why many artists have a difficult time making it in the world. They are not integrated in their decision making with the other rays.

The Fifth Ray focuses on Spiritual science. So this type of person will look at the decision making process through the lens of a scientist. Hopefully, a Spiritual scientist and not just a materialistic one. The danger here is also that if the other odd-numbered rays are integrated, the decision may be too rational and not include the Second Ray heart, the Fourth Ray artistic concerns or the Sixth Ray devotion.

The sixth ray is devotion and idealism. All the rays have Spiritual and negative ego usage or application. Devotion and idealism is a beautiful thing if applied Spiritually and in a balanced way. However, if someone is too devotional and idealistic this can be a limiting lens as can all the rays. Their decisions become focused on devotion to a Spiritual teacher, guru, or ideal. If this ideal is not integrated and balanced, you can see the problems it can cause.

The Seventh Ray Person is focused on ceremonial order and magic, freedom, transmutation, alchemy and economics. For example, the Seventh Ray person may make their decisions out of a desire for freedom, but may miss the power, love, active intelligence, artistic, scientific and devotional concerns.

So you see, my friends, from this very simple discussion, how all decision making must consider all seven lenses in an integrated and balanced fashion to make sure you are making the right decisions. This is how GOD and the Masters make decisions! This is called decision making from a full spectrum prism perspective. Karma and/or wrong decisions are often made because the person is unconsciously seeing through one or two Ray lenses and doesn't realize it. This occurs extremely often in life among most people, including lightworkers and is not a judgement of any kind. It is just a good lesson to examine right now to not make decisions too impulsively and to make sure you are embodying a "Seven Ray Decision Making Process"!

Now, to add to this a little more, people make decisions out of overidentification with their chakras. A person overidentified with their First Chakra will make their decisions out of survival and/or fear. If they are underidentified, they make decisions because of a lack of groundedness, or lack of connection to Mother Earth. The Second Chakra person may make decisions out of sexual or overemotional reactions or responses. Or they may make decision out of a lack of emotional response if underidentified with this chakra.

The Third Chakra-identified person may make their decision out of, again, personal power or a mental response, or lack thereof. The Fourth Chakra-identified person may make their decision out of love, but, we all know there are different types of love. Is it a Spiritual and integrated love? If not, we have all heard of the book, *Women Who Love Too Much*. Perhaps they are too Fourth Chakra-identified and too Second Ray, which causes imbalanced decision making. If the person is too Fifth Chakra-identified, the decision process might be based on a desire for communication. Have you ever heard of people who process and communicate too much in an almost obsessive manner? Under-identification can cause one to make decisions based on avoidance of proper communication.

The person overidentified with the Sixth Ray may, again, make decisions too much out of a mental focus not considering the Earth, emotional concerns, power concerns, heart concerns, communication concerns, or Transcendent concerns. Underidentification will cause the reverse to take place.

The Seventh chakra is the center of truly transcendent and religious concerns. This is beautiful, but again, so are Earth, survival, emotions, mind, heart, communication, and integration. All must being considered.

So, my Beloved Readers, I think you can see that decision making is a tricky business. In truth one must trust one's intuition, one's heart, one's mind, one's feelings, one's instincts and one's physical body to come up with the proper decision. One must do this in an integrated and balanced manner.

If your Spiritual practice is astrology, then all the houses of the horoscope must be considered, for each is a lens and can be over-or underidentified! The same can be said of the Tree of Life! Are you over-or underidentified with one Sephiroth over another? Or are you integrated and balanced and seeing life from the full Cosmic Tree of Life? Are you making decisions from just a Planetary lens, or a Solar, Galactic, Universal, Multiuniversal and Cosmic Perspective?

Are you making decisions out of all the 12 major Archetypes, or just seeing life through one or two? Are you seeing life through all the cards of the Tarot Deck, or from a limited and fragmented perspective?

My Beloved Readers, are you getting a sense now of the Full Spectrum Perspective that GOD and the Masters make decisions out of? This is really not that complicated, once you develop Spiritual mastery in an integrated manner. Then the decision making process can occur automatically and very quickly. This chapter has been written to make sure you have done your Spiritual and psychological homework to develop yourself in these different areas, so that every time you make a decision, automatically the full integration of your entire being is being brought into the process. It is also to ensure that you do not have any blind spots, or over or underidentification in your Spiritual philosophy and psychology! Once you become an Integrated Spiritual Master you will be able to trust your intuition, heart, mind, feelings, instincts and physical body, for they will all be working in an integrated and balanced fashion, and they will give you instantaneous and accurate guidance. This will be true as long as you also have done your Spiritual and psychological homework to release all negative ego/fear-based thinking and feeling and to only think and feel from your Spiritual/Christ/Buddha mind and perspective. As Sai Baba says, the definition of GOD is, "GOD equals man minus ego"!

10

Chakra Development and the Issue of Channeling

There has been such an incredible misunderstanding on how the process of channeling works in the New Age Movement that the Masters have asked me to explain this process as they would have it understood. A person's psychological consciousness plays an unbelievable part in filtering what comes through any given person's channelings and telepathic guidance and information.

This chapter is dedicated to explaining the channeling process from the lens of the chakra system. As we all know, every person has seven main chakras. These seven chakras are focused upon the following qualities and principles:

1st Chakra: survival and earth issues
2nd Chakra: sexuality and feelings
3rd Chakra: personal power
4th Chakra: unconditional love
5th Chakra: communication and GOD's Will
6th Chakra: spiritual vision
7th Chakra: connection to GOD and the Masters

Now we all know that we create our own reality by how we think. This manifests within the chakras as the chakras being too open, too closed or balanced. The overstimulation or understimulation of the chakras is, of course, connected to our seven major glands, which are listed as follows:

1st Chakra: Gonads
2nd Chakra: Lyden Gland
3rd Chakra: Adrenal Glands
4th Chakra: Thymus Gland
5th Chakra: Thyroid Gland
6th Chakra: Pituitary Gland
7th Chakra: Pineal Gland

This is why so many people have overactive or underactive glands. Their improper thinking causes the chakras to be overactive or underactive, which causes the glands to be overactive or underactive.

The only reason I bring this all up is that the same thing takes place in channeling! The only way I can explain myself here is to give you examples of how the overactivity or underactivity of any given chakra skews the channeling process as well as telepathic abilities and clairvoyance. To explain this, I will now go through each of the chakras and I will share with you what happens to a person's channeling if the chakra is too open or too closed.

Let's start with the first chakra, which deals with survival issues and the Earth. If a person is very grounded, has a lot of Earth in their astrological chart, and is very Lemurian in nature, then their channelings will be very attuned to the Earth Mother and nature. They will probably be able to bring through a great deal of physical health type of information. They might be a good channel for Pan and the nature spirits. This type of channel will do well with survival issues in the channelings.

If a person is undeveloped in their first chakra and/or has very little energy in this chakra, the channeling will be exactly the opposite. The channelings will be very heavenly orientated or mentally based. Very little practical Earth information will come through this channel. My Beloved Readers, you cannot separate a person's consciousness from their channel ability. Many lightworkers do not want to believe this, however, I assure you that this is true. I could write an entire book on the corruption of the channeling process from lack of understanding. I am not saying here, that you should never receive an external channeling. Just be aware of how the process works and the limitations within this.

If a person is overactive in their second chakra, the channelings will be highly emotional in nature and usually very creative and poetic, often very flowery, sometimes lacking in specific information. On the other side of the coin, if a person is undeveloped in this chakra and there is little energy in this chakra, a person's channelings from the other realms will be very dry and intellectual. We have all heard channels like this.

Now we will move to the third chakra. If the person is overactive in this chakra, the channelings will be very powerful and commanding, even militaristic. They will push the importance of self-discipline and self-mastery, but will be lacking the Goddess energy and the beauty of the feminine nature.

If a person is underactive in their third chakra, the channeling will be more timid, shy, and soft. They will usually be of a more emotional nature. They will focus more on sensitivity and feelings.

If a person is overactive in their fourth chakra, then their channelings will be extremely loving and flowery. I call this the language of the beloved and this is very nice as long as it is in balance. If the chakra is overstimulated, however, you will have enormous love and flowery language but no "beef" or real information. For vegetarians there will be no "tofu." We have all heard channels like that, so loving and flowery, but they don't say very much. We have all read channeled books like this as well. This is why I have tried to make my books filled with valuable information, but also filled with enthusiasm and Unconditional Divine Love.

If a person is underdeveloped in their heart chakra, then the channelings will be very scientific and dry. There may be information that comes through, but no heart connection is made and a certain disconnection from spirit takes place as well.

If a person is overactive in the fifth chakra, then the channelings will be highly communicative and will go on for hours. They will also be very attuned to GOD's Will and very verbal in nature.

On the other side of the coin, someone underdeveloped in their fifth chakra, will channel but using very few words. The channelings will focus more on attuning to the silence meditation. There is also the danger that the negative ego's will will be contaminating the channel, for a balanced understanding of GOD's Will has not yet taken place.

My beloved readers, it must be understood that every thought you think is reflected in the chakras. Every negative ego thought you allow in your mind will reflect itself in the chakras as being overactive or under active. It is only when you practice and realize the goal of becoming an Integrated Melchizedek/Christ and Buddha that your chakras can truly be balanced. Perfectly balanced chakras are a byproduct of becoming an Integrated Melchizedek/Christ/Buddha.

If the sixth chakra is overdeveloped and overstimulated in a person, then the channelings will reflect this. They will be highly mental and/or highly filled with visions and psychic experiences. This type of channel is often very clairvoyant. If the chakra is too open however, then the channel will be overwhelmed with too much thought and psychic information. There may be a certain disconnection from the heart and even from spirit, but packed with information and psychic and/or spiritual experiences.

The other side of the coin is: if this chakra is underdeveloped, then the channel will bring through very technical information and there will be no visuals to speak of. There will also be a lack of coherent spiritual vision to the totality of information coming through.

If a crown chakra is overactive, then there will be a tremendous downpouring of information and light, but it will be very ungrounded and not integrated. It will be extremely spiritually uplifting, but the person receiving the channeling will not know how to integrate it. This is also why in my books I have focused upon the Cosmic and Planetary Ascension material, but also focus upon spiritual psychology, physical healing, and even Earthly civilization. This is the problem with so many channels that they specialize in one area, which is good, but they are not what I call an "Integrated Melchizedek/Christ/Buddha channel. The ideal channel can bring through information, love, and wisdom, on a spiritual, psychological, and physical/earthly level, in an integrated and balanced manner that demonstrates not only the balance of the chakras, but the balance of the Three-Fold Flame of GOD, of Love/Wisdom/Power.

If a person is underactive in their crown chakra, then the Cosmic flow of information, light and love gets cutoff. The channelings will be more mental or more earthly in nature and will not be as exhilarating as when this chakra is properly balanced.

Summation

My Beloved Readers, this short synopsis of the relationship between the channeling process and your seven major chakras has been given by the Masters, and I to emphasize how incredibly important it is for you to develop your consciousness. A channel for GOD and/or the Ascended Masters is only as good as the development of their consciousness in a holistic perspective. If a person's consciousness is not developed and balanced the channelings that come through that person will reflect that imbalance and ultimately be in danger of negative ego corruption, personal agendas and contamination by the channel's belief systems. If you learn only one thing from this book, learn and fully understand this lesson. It will serve you well in your own channeling development, which I highly recommend you pursue, and it will serve you well in understanding other people's channelings, psychic readings, clairvoyance, and channeled book literature. The purpose of this chapter, and part of the purpose of this book, is to bring this point home so utterly and clearly that whenever you deal with channeling in any form; be it through others in a lecture or reading a book, or through yourself, you will approach this process with a little more spiritual discernment, and you will never give your power or your spiritual discrimination and sword of discernment away ever again!

11

The 22 Chakras

The most common understanding of our chakra system is that we have seven chakras. This is a valid understanding if we are only considering the third dimensions of reality. The fact is that we have eight fourth dimensional chakras and seven more fifth dimensional chakras.

There may possibly be more even beyond this on into the sixth and seventh dimensions of reality, however, this is far beyond my ability to explain or access information on.

This information concerning the 22 chakras was brought through by Vywamus through the Tibetan Foundation. The following diagram delineates these 22 essential aspects of our being.

The Chakras		
Third Dimension	*Fourth Dimension*	*Fifth Dimension*
0 Earth	8 Seat of the Soul	16 Ascension, Universal Being
1 Base	9 Body of Light	17 Universal Light
2 Polarity	10 Integration of Polarities	18 6th Dimensional Divine Intent
3 Solar Plexus	11 New Age Energies	No Correspondence
4 Heart	12 Christ Consciousness	19 Universal Energy
5 Throat	13 Manifesting Vibratory Communication	20 Beingness
6 Third Eye	14 Divine Plan	21 Divine Structure
7 Crown	15 Monadic Connection	22 Source Connection

The seven main chakras are the ones that connect the etheric body, or energy body, to the physical body; they are within the etheric body, not within the dense physical body. Each chakra has a specific pattern of energy for a specific purpose. Since the Harmonic Convergence, in August of 1987, an energy structure has been developed that will allow the fourth dimension to come into physical existence.

The Third-Dimensional Chakras
The Root Chakra

The first chakra is the seat of the physical body. It focuses your Earthly life, connecting you very specifically to the Earth. It deals with issues such as grounding and survival. In the early Lemurian period it was the base chakra that was most open. The first chakra deals with consideration about being here on Earth. Its color is red; it is connected with the gonads.

The Second Chakra

The second chakra is the polarity chakra. It has to do with creativity, masculine and feminine balance, and our sexual energies. The back side of the second chakra relates to the seat of the subconscious. The gland that it is connected to is the ludig, or lyden gland which relates to the lymphatic system. The color of this chakra is usually designated as orange. This chakra was focused on in the latter Lemurian development.

The Solar Plexus Chakra

The third chakra is the seat of the emotional body. The gland that relates to this chakra is the adrenal gland. The color usually associated with this gland is yellow. The Atlantis period of earth's history focused on the development of this chakra.

The Heart Chakra

The fourth chakra deals with unconditional love. The gland that is associated with it is the thymus gland. The color most usually associated with it is green. This has been the focus in the Christian era.

The Throat Chakra

The throat chakra deals with communication, expression, and the use of will. The gland associated with this gland is the thyroid gland. The color most associated with this chakra is blue. This chakra is the one that is being developed in the Aquarian Age.

The Third Eye Chakra

The third eye chakra has to do with inner seeingness or spiritual sight and vision. The gland associated with this chakra is the pituitary gland. The color most often associated with this chakra is violet. The third eye chakra also relates to the conscious mind.

The Crown Chakra

The crown chakra has to do with the superconscious mind, the soul, the Higher Self, the Monad and/or God. It is truly our gate to bring through the higher energies. The color most often associated with this chakra is white light, or a rainbow speckled white light. The gland associated with this chakra is the pineal.

Chakra Toning

Besides using light and color to work with and open your chakras, it is also possible to use sound. Djwhal Khul has channeled the sounds that correspond to the seven three dimensional chakras. In parenthesis in the second column of the following diagram are words that will help you to enunciate the sounds properly.

Chakras	*Tones from Djwhal Khul*	*Hindu Tones*
Root chakra	O (oh)	Lam
Second chakra	SHU (shuck)	Yam
Solar Plexus chakra	YA (yawn)	Ram
Heart chakra	WA (way)	Yam
Throat chakra	HE (he)	Ham
Third eye chakra	HU (hue)	Om
Crown chakra	I (eye)	Aum

Chakra Colors

The standard, or most common colors that most schools of thought have used for the visualizing of the chakras are listed below. I have also included the updated colors that Djwhal Khul has most recently channeled to my wife and me to use in our work.

Chakra	Standard Color	Colors from Djwhal Khul
Root	Red	Violet
Second	Orange	Indigo
Solar plexus	Yellow	Yellow
Heart	Green	Pink (with a bit of violet)
Throat	Blue	Blue (with orange triangle in center of it)
Third eye	Indigo	Gold
Crown	Violet	Rainbow white

The Fourth Dimensional Chakras

My personal experience of becoming aware that we had more than seven chakras occurred a couple years ago when Djwhal Khul told me we had twelve chakras. I think we were working with my chakras at the time and he told me that as a person evolves, the higher chakras begin to move downward and descend into the former third dimensional chakras. In that conversation I asked if my higher chakras had descended. He told me during this initial conversation that my 10th chakra was in my crown, and my ninth chakra was in the third eye chakra. My eighth chakra was in my throat chakra, and so on all the way down my body and chakra system.

I found this piece of information fascinating. Since the time I knew that there were twelve chakras I began calling my twelfth chakra down into my crown. I also began working with focusing the energy and quality of this chakra more clearly in my life, which is the "Christ consciousness."

In a later conversation with Djwhal, he said I had stabilized the 12th chakra in the crown chakra and the eleventh in the third eye, and the tenth in the throat chakra and so on all the way down my chakra system. It was only in the last three months that I became aware from Vywamus that there are in actuality 22 chakras. My current focus in my own spiritual path has been to now anchor the 15th chakra into the crown. The 15th chakra having to do with our Monadic connection.

The 16th chakra, as I mentioned in a previous chapter, is the chakra that is anchored in the crown when an initiate ascends. Djwhal Khul has definitely recommended that prior to ascension that people **not** call down any chakra higher than the fifteenth chakra, for there is a danger of burning out the physical body with too high a frequency of energy. It is permissible to call forth the colors of energy that are associated with the fifth dimensional chakras.

These colors associated with each chakra will be explained as I go through the meaning and purpose of each of these chakras as explained by Vywamus through the Tibetan Foundation. I will begin with the fourth dimensional chakras.

The Eighth Chakra

The eighth chakra is the first chakra of the fourth dimension, and is the seat of the soul. In the third dimensional chakras the earth designated number zero represents physical existence. It is solid and concrete. The seat of the soul now becomes the seat of our existence, just as the earth was the baseline for our existence in the third dimension.

The colors of the chakras eight through twelve are exactly the same as the colors of the higher fourth dimensional rays. The color of the eighth chakra is emerald green and purple.

The Ninth Chakra

The ninth chakra corresponds to the base chakra in the third-dimensional chakra grid. The ninth chakra corresponds to the body of light. It has to do with joy. When this chakra is activated the body of light is now in your cellular and sub-cellular structure. The color of this chakra is blue-green.

The Tenth Chakra

The tenth chakra is associated with the polarity chakra in the third dimension. It has to do with the integration of polarities—the proper integration of male and female within self. This chakra actually starts functioning when the male and female energies are in total balance. This is experienced as a state of effortlessness, and alignment with one's soul. The color of this chakra is a pearlized color.

The Eleventh Chakra

This is the chakra of the New Age energies. It corresponds with the solar plexus chakra in the third dimensional chakras, connecting the third chakra to the eleventh chakra allows us to diminish the present and past life trauma stored in the third chakra. The eleventh chakra energy feeling will be like a wave, and it will move through your body and out again without staying in the body or without attaching itself to an area of misperception.

Before the fourth dimension was available, when someone responded in an emotional way, it would attach itself to some misperceptions already in the body. The color of this chakra is pink-orange.

The Twelfth Chakra

The twelfth chakra is the Christ consciousness, which is a transformational energy that connects all energy forms. It is associated with the heart chakra in the third-dimensional chakra grid. It is a shimmering gold color.

The Thirteenth Chakra

This thirteenth chakra has to do with the manifesting of vibratory communication. This is the chakra that is used in materializing and dematerializing things. It is also the chakra used in teleportation. This chakra is also used for healing. It is pale violet-pink in color.

The Fourteenth Chakra

The fourteenth chakra has to do with the Divine Plan. It allows the mental mind to surrender. The fourteenth chakra is saying that you are allowing the Divine Plan to show you the way without reviewing or evaluating from your mental thought beliefs.

This chakra corresponds to the third eye in the third-dimensional chakra system. It is bringing clairvoyance into the fourth dimension. It is beginning to activate your unlimitedness. The color of this chakra is deep blue-violet.

The Fifteenth Chakra

The fifteenth chakra has to do with your Monadic connection. It corresponds to the crown chakra in the third-dimensional chakras. The seventh chakra is your spiritual connection. With the fifteenth chakra your new spiritual connection is to the Monadic level as discussed in the chapter on initiation, when one passes the fourth initiation.

At the fifth initiation we become merged with the Monad. This brings us to the doorway of ascension. When this chakra is operating it is saying that the structure of your soul is stable enough to handle the energy and the scope of the information coming from the monadic level. It is a light golden-white.

The Fifth Dimensional Chakras
The Sixteenth Chakra

The sixteenth chakra, as mentioned earlier, has to do with ascension and becoming a universal being. Again it is the sixteenth chakra that descends into the crown chakra at the time of ascension. When this chakra has been activated, the Master needs to decide whether he or she is going to stay in physical existence. The universal being moves from any time frame, any dimension into different bodies and can adapt to the energy form needed.

This chakra is the first chakra of the fifth dimensional chakra grid system. The chakra of ascension into the Monad and I Am Presence and becoming a universal being becomes one's new base line, just as the eighth chakra, the seat of the soul, was the base line in the fourth dimensional chakras. The color of this chakra is light violet white.

The Seventeenth Chakra

The seventeenth chakra has to do with universal light, which corresponds to the ninth chakra, or the body of light in the fourth-dimensional chakra grid. We are going from the third dimension, which is solid, to the fourth dimension, which is solid and light, to the fifth dimension, which is total light. It is multi-white in color.

The Eighteenth Chakra

The eighteenth chakra has to do with sixth-dimensional divine intent. This chakra when activated will bring in the ability to bring in the sixth dimension of reality. In looking at your charts of the chakras you will see that there is a gap between the eighteenth and nineteenth chakra that says, "*no correspondence.*" The reason for this is that at the fifth-dimensional level there is no correspondence to the solar plexus because it has united with the heart chakra. It is pink-gold in color.

The Nineteenth Chakra

The nineteenth chakra has to do with universal energy. The heart energy was the focus in the third dimension. The Christ consciousness is the expanding energy in the fourth dimension. In the fifth dimension the correspondence is the universal energy. This universal energy is being felt by those that are allowing the new source energy to come through this source, through their Monadic level, through their soul level to their physical body. It is magenta in color.

The Twentieth Chakra

The twentieth chakra has to do with Beingness. In the third dimension you needed to communicate. In the fourth dimension you were able to communicate in a more expanded way through communication by vibration through light. In the fifth dimension there is no need for an exchange, it's a beingness where exchange is not necessary for communication. It is violet-gold in color.

The Twenty-First Chakra

The twenty-first chakra has to do with divine structure. It is creating from a point of evolution, which is really from a point of resolution. So as you have the third eye which allows you to be clairvoyant in the third dimension, now then you way in the fourth dimension, the Divine Plan. You are now beyond the structure of the fifth into the learning that took place during the Divine structure. Vywamus said in respect to this chakra, "Now I must tell you that none of you have to worry about this in the next two or three years." It is blue-gold in color.

The Twenty-Second Chakra

The twenty-second chakra has to do with Source or Godhead connection. It is platinum in color.

A Final Note

I would like to acknowledge The Tibetan Foundation and Dorothy Bodenburg for a transcript of the material she channeled from Vywamus, which I used as the basis for the information in this chapter. Some of the best channeled material I have ever seen has come out of The Tibetan Foundation, which was founded by Djwhal Khul through Janet McClure.

12

How to Open, Anchor and Activate the 50 Chakras

There exists a completely new understanding of the chakras that has never been written about. Most spiritual schools teach that there are seven major chakras and many minor chakras. Some New Age mystery schools teach that there are twelve chakras. Well, I am here to tell you that, in truth, there are thirty-six major chakras that must be dealt with if you plan to complete the seven levels of initiation. There are also some beyond that.

The best way to understand the chakras is to see that they basically come in sets of seven, according to the dimensional grid with which they are associated:

Third-dimensional chakra grid	Chakras 1 through 7
Fourth-dimensional chakra grid	Chakras 8 through 15
Fifth-dimensional chakra grid	Chakras 16 through 22
Sixth-dimensional chakra grid	Chakras 23 through 29
Seventh-dimensional chakra grid	Chakras 30 through 36
Eighth-dimensional chakra grid	Chakras 37 through 43
Ninth-dimensional chakra grid	Chakras 44 through 50

As you evolve spiritually, these chakras naturally descend, just as the soul and monad naturally descend in the process of initiation and ascension. The world has not known of these higher chakras because few humans have, until now, evolved beyond the third and fourth dimensions of reality. After Wesak of 1995, with its first wave of mass ascension, the situation changed dramatically.

Vywamus, through Janet McClure, was the first to come out with some detailed information on the twenty-two chakras. Since I have written about the third-, fourth-and fifth-dimensional chakra grids in other books, I am not going to repeat myself here. What I do want to say is that when you ascend and take your sixth initiation, your sixteenth chakra becomes anchored in the crown. What ascension really is, from the frame of reference of the chakras, is the complete anchoring into the four-body system of the third and fourth chakra grids—that is, chakras one through fifteen. When the sixteenth chakra (the first chakra of the fifth-dimensional chakra grid) anchors, you have ascended and are in the first stage of the fifth dimension. To complete your ascension you must then anchor and actualize the entire fifth-dimensional and sixth-dimensional chakra grids.

Now, you would think that to take the seventh initiation all you would have to do would be to complete the fifth-dimensional chakra grid and anchor the first of the sixth-dimensional chakras. However, that was not my experience. When I took the seventh initiation, I had already installed and actualized the thirty-third chakra. The seventh initiation is the entrance into the sixth dimension; the thirty-third chakra is actually in the seventh-dimensional chakra grid. I don't know if I was a little precocious or if this is the level all must attain in order to take the seventh. I tend to think this is a standard level, just as a certain Light quotient needs to be achieved.

To complete the seventh initiation it is required that all initiates fully install, anchor, and actualize all thirty-six chakras. In other words, at the completion of your seventh initiation, your thirty-sixth chakra will be in your crown, and so on. Following is a list showing the chakras and their corresponding areas:

Chakra thirty-six	Crown
Chakra thirty-five	Third Eye
Chakra thirty-four	Throat
Chakra thirty-three	Heart

The chakras from the previous sixth-dimensional grid will move down through your thighs, knees, ankles, and feet and into the Earth.

The most important thing to understand here is that the process anchoring your chakras can be speeded up. This is one of the main reasons I was able to move through the fifth, sixth, and seventh initiations so quickly. I began working with the ability to collapse time. Melchizedek told me that the evolutionary process has never before moved so quickly in the history of this planet. In that sense we are prototypes and guinea pigs. The Masters are watching this process of speeded-up evolution with great interest.

It is important to know that there are three levels of understanding in the process of anchoring the higher chakras: the first is installation; the second is actualization; the third is accessing the chakras' abilities, or utilization.

The first step in speeding up your evolutionary process is to request, in every meditation you do, the full anchoring and installation of your twenty-two chakras and your fourth-and fifth-dimensional chakra grids. Upon your invocation and request, these chakras will descend like bodies of Light. You can even channel the individual chakras and talk to them. Each has a consciousness. As they descend they will overlay the previous chakra grid.

I recommend that you request the anchoring and installation of the chakras through the completion of the fifth-dimensional chakra grid which is chakra twenty-two. You are allowed to work a little ahead of yourself. Always ask for this (and this is important) under the guidance and direction of your own Mighty I Am Presence and monad. These are, in truth, very powerful electrical energies and you don't want to "spontaneously combust" from too much spiritual current.

If you are just beginning your spiritual path, then begin anchoring chakras one through twelve. If you are more advanced, begin anchoring up to chakra fifteen. If you are very advanced and extremely devoted, then do all twenty-two chakras. No matter where you are, ask your Mighty I Am Presence to monitor and calibrate the whole process so you stay in the Tao.

Never forget that faster is not better; slower is not better. Staying in the Tao is the most efficient way to God-realization and, in truth, the only way to God-realization. People who have tried to force the evolution of their kundalini unwisely have sometimes set themselves back entire lifetimes because of the damage they have caused to their etheric bodies. I am not trying to scare you here, for this process is totally safe as long as you follow these instructions, but do not attempt, under any circumstances, to anchor chakras twenty-two through thirty-six until after you have taken your sixth initiation. You can always activate one grid above where you are, but no more than that.

I recommend asking the Ascended Masters, especially Djwhal Khul and the Arcturians, for help in this process, for the installation of the chakra grids is much like spiritual surgery. The Masters will not install the entire chakra grid, or all seven chakras of that grid, all at once. They will usually do two chakras at a time. This is the reason for the second phase of this process, which is actualization. The chakras might be installed but that does not mean that you have actualized them in the slightest. For example, as I mentioned previously, I have had all thirty-six chakras installed, but I was actualizing, at the time I wrote this, only up to the very beginning of the thirty-fifth.

The key question here is, "How do you actualize the chakras that have been installed?" It is done by living a God-inspired lifestyle. Meditation, I would say, is the key. You can pray to the Ascended

Masters and the Arcturians for help in actualizing your chakras as well as to have them installed.

The third step is being able to access the chakra's abilities. For example, I have now actualized almost all thirty-six chakras; however, I have not yet learned to utilize all of their abilities. Someone like Sai Baba is an example of one who has. his ability to materialize things, to be physically in two places at once, to teleport, and so on, are examples of utilization, the next step after installation and actualization.

You cannot go higher than the top of the sixth dimension while still retaining a physical vehicle. When you take the seventh initiation you are in the sixth dimension. The completion of the seventh initiation means you are accessing the top level of the sixth dimension without yet having switched over to the seventh dimension. You can, however, still access dimensions seven through nine in meditation and in the dream state. I am currently doing that. After the ninth dimension you are no longer dealing with physical existence. The most important point here is that you can continually ask in meditation for this anchoring to occur.

If you feel a need to know about the progress of the work, and if you can channel or if you have a friend who can channel, talk with the Masters. if not, it does not matter. You are God, and if you ask for this, it will be done.

There is so much that goes on in the spiritual world about which humans have not the slightest idea. A lot of what I am sharing with you here I ask you to take on faith, judging with your intuitive knowingness that what I am sharing with you is true and effective. To a third-dimensional scientist, this whole book might seem like hogwash; to a disciple and initiate, the information makes perfect sense and is as real as anything perceivable with the physical senses.

After taking your sixth initiation and ascension you can begin calling in the sixth-dimensional grid of chakras twenty-three through twenty-nine. The act of calling them in and anchoring them is no different from calling in one of the Ascended Masters. The process is not dangerous.

Having them installed is the next step; again, I suggest you have Djwhal Khul, the Arcturians, or Vywamus help you. Your good lifestyle, meditations, and Light quotient building work will help you to actualize the installation.

I have hesitated to share my experiences here because I do not want to give you unrealistic expectations; I share with you what is potentially possible so that it can motivate you to discipline yourself and get down to business so you can achieve full God-realization and hence be of greater service to humanity, as well as sharing in the extraordinary joy of it all.

We have just recently been given permission to anchor all fifty chakras. The process begins with a request for installation. Then follows the slow anchoring and activation of the eighth-and ninth-dimensional chakra grids.

The Chakra Chambers and Facets

The next major understanding about the chakra system came as a result of an advanced ascension workshop. During the workshop Djwhal Khul, for the first time, spoke of the seven chambers in each of the chakras, including the ascension chakra, that needed to be opened. The ascension chakra is a chakra located toward the back of the head where a ponytail might begin. It is the key chakra in the ascension process. As you know, each of the seven major chakras is connected to a gland: the crown to the pineal; the third eye to the pituitary; the throat to the thyroid, and so on down the line. The ascension chakra, Djwhal told us, is connected to the hypothalamus.

For full God-realization, each of the seven chambers in each chakra must be open and active. Djwhal told us that just completing the seven levels of initiation does not automatically ensure their opening and activation.

When the chambers are opened by your spiritual work, your Mighty I Am Presence, or the Ascended Masters, they are not opened all at once.

They are opened, in a sense, one facet at a time. The opening of one facet leads to the opening of another. The facets could be likened to the facets of a diamond or the triangles that make up a merkabah or geodesic dome. During the workshop Djwhal activated certain facets of these chambers. It is all done very mathematically and scientifically. For example, he might say something like, "Activate and open crown chakra, level one, facet thirty-five." This is not exactly the way he does it, but it does make the point. The whole process gets more complicated because although Melchizedek told us that a model of forty-eight facets was the best model to use, all the chakras do not necessarily have forty-eight facets. Nonetheless, it is enough to know that each chakra has seven chambers and they need to be opened for full God-realization.

Earlier I spoke of the stages of anchoring the thirty-six chakras—installation, actualization, and utilization of the abilities. The opening of the chambers is connected to the actualization and utilization of the abilities of the chakras. For example, teleporting will use certain chambers and facets that I have not as yet developed. This is the next step, and that is why the information is now being brought forward. The opening of all these chambers is the next step in my personal evolution. Now that I have installed and actualized nearly all thirty-six chakras (the fifth-, sixth-and seventh-dimensional chakra grids) it is time to move to the third stage of utilizing the abilities of all these chakras.

Here is some more information about this whole process. First, when you complete your ascension and take your seventh initiation, the chakras become one column of Light rather than seven individual chakras. In addition, this chakra column combines with the antakarana, or rainbow bridge, when the kundalini rises within the ascension column.

Of the three facets in each pie piece, the smallest one closest to the center represents the future, the middle one, the present, and the one closest to the outside of the circle, the past. Ideally. all three are open, activated, and working together. What often happens, however, is that just the past is open; people then end up projecting their past misconceptions onto the present and future because the facets are not integrated properly. When all thirty-six chakras are anchored and all chambers and facets are open, twelve strands of DNA move from the etheric vehicle into the physical vehicle.

Now, some of the facets and chambers open automatically in the process of evolution on the spiritual path. Melchizedek told us that the invocation of all the fire letters, key codes, and sacred geometries aids in the opening of these facets and chambers. I believe that sitting in the ascension seats also helps in this regard., as do other forms of Light quotient building and meditation techniques.

In essence, all the varied spiritual practices, from journal writing to affirmations to prayer, have their effects on the chakra system. Melchizedek said that all knowledge is stored somewhere within the chakra system.

It is also possible to ask your own Mighty I Am Presence and the Ascended Masters to, in a sense, collapse time and accelerate the process by opening them for you. This cannot and will not be done all at once, for that would be too dangerous. It can be done effectively by using the Huna prayer method of which I am so fond. However, before sharing that with you there is one more piece of the chakra puzzle I must discuss.

Vywamus on the Chakra Chambers

As I continued to research this subject from as many points of view as possible, Vywamus had some interesting things to add. He said that the chakras are means of focusing Light; in other words, they are vibrational focusing tools. The totality of the chakras and their chambers helps to create a tonal quality and tonal frequency for each person. He said that the ultimate goal is indeed to open all the chambers and all the petals, or facets, including those of the-minor chakras, to achieve your optimum octave and frequency. He said, however, that it was essential to understand, in the process of doing this, that there is a step-by-step process of chamber recalibration that must go on. If the chamber and petals are opened all at once the initiate would lose the physical vehicle. The recalibration process makes sure that a balance is kept among all energies to ensure the maintenance of a healthy and integrated Light frequency. The calibrating of Light should always be done in conjunction with your soul or monad. The relationship of the petals and chambers in the chakras is that a certain number of petals (for example one thousand in the crown chakra) are connected to certain chambers. The exact mathematics, he said, are too complicated to be more specific about.

At major initiations, recalibrations of Light frequency and chakra adjustment and opening take place. During minor initiations a similar process occurs but in a less intense manner. You can request a Light recalibration adjustment of the chambers and petals in the chakras to take you to the next step in your evolution. The Huna prayer at the end of this chapter offers just such a request.

The Chakras and the Petals

If you study Eastern spiritual literature and the Djwhal Khul/Alice Bailey books, you will find studies of the working of the chakra system. Among other things, Djwhal Khul says that each chakra has a specified number of individual petals which need to be opened.

Crown chakra	one thousand petals
Third Eye	two petals
Throat chakra	sixteen petals
Heart chakra	twelve petals
Solar plexus chakra	ten petals
Polarity chakra	six petals
Root chakra	four petals

As you can see, there is a relationship here between the Eastern system of opening all the petals of each lotus, or chakra, and the opening of the chakra chambers. What the exact relationship is, I am not sure. The study of the chakra system is such a vast undertaking, I believe you could spend a lifetime focusing on nothing else and you would just begin to scratch the surface. As Melchizedek said, "All knowledge is stored within the chakra system." In any case, I am choosing to use both systems in terms of the invocation and prayer work. I believe in covering all the bases.

One thing I do know is that the petals, chambers, and facets are connected to the etheric nervous system. They are also connected to the right and left hemispheres of the brain. The chakras themselves are connected to the glands, which affect the organs and the functions of the entire physical body.

The astral, mental, and spiritual bodies also have their effects on the etheric nervous system, the nadis, or spiritual filaments that connect with the facets, or petals. As you can see, this is one very synergistic, holistic, integrated process. The key is to get the entire seven-body system, the thirty-six chakras, the personality, soul and monad, all chambers, facets, and petals, the ascension column, kundalini, antakarana, heart and cosmic heart, upper spiritual triad, and lower spiritual triad, all working in perfect unison, harmony, integration, and balance as one unified system with no separate parts.

The metaphysical science of breaking all that down into its component parts, showing cause and effect relationships, can be quite complex and even, in some cases, incomprehensible, given the complexity of all the different functions that are taking place simultaneously. For current purposes, the most important thing is to open the chambers, facets, petals, and chakras so you can more fully realize God and be of greater service. This is the bottom line.

Huna Prayer for Opening

The prayer below is the prayer I used to open and activate the chambers and petals of my chakras. My recommendation is to ask to go to the ascension seat in Shamballa first. Then read the prayer three times out loud. If you do it with an ascension friend it is even more powerful, but that is not necessary. After repeating the prayer three times aloud, then say the second paragraph, which is addressed to the subconscious mind, one time. Wait thirty seconds to allow the subconscious mind to take the prayer where it needs to go. Then say the last paragraph and be silent for another thirty seconds to receive the initial blessing.

The exact wording of the prayer can be changed if you like. The timetable I used was what was right for me, given the coming of the 12:12 celebration and Wesak in May 1995; you must use your own intuition to determine what is right for you. What is nice about this prayer is that it applies not just to one meditation but invokes help on an ongoing, everyday basis for a substantial period of time. The use of Huna prayers has been absolutely invaluable and is one of the main reasons I have moved forward so quickly. I write one for whatever dispensation I need or am looking for. This action really locks the prayer in and makes it official. The prayers work every time.

Beloved Presence of God, Sanat Kumara, Vywamus, and Djwhal Khul:

We hereby call forth a divine dispensation on our behalf. We call forth, over the next (months to months), a full opening and activation of the seven levels of chambers in each of our chakras, including the ascension chakras. We ask that this work go on every night while we sleep and during our meditations and receptive periods during the day. We also ask that this work continue until fully completed. We also ask at this time for a full opening and activation of all the individual petals that make up each of the individual chakras. [For example, the one thousand petals in the crown, two in the third eye chakra, sixteen in the throat, twelve in the heart, and so on down the line.] We thank you and accept this as done in the name of the fully realized Christ so we may be of greater service. Amen.

(Repeat three times)

Our beloved subconscious minds, we hereby ask and command that you take this thoughtform prayer, with all the mana and vital force that are needed and necessary to manifest and demonstrate this prayer, to the Source of our being. Amen.

(Repeat only once. Then wait for twenty or thirty seconds while visualizing a fountain or some other suitable imagery shooting upward from within you and going straight to God, or Source)
Sanat Kumara, Vywamus, and Djwhal Khul, let the Rain of Blessings fall! Amen.

(Visualize the Rain of Blessings as it falls upon you)

13

Integration of the Seven Rays and Spiritual Leadership

My Beloved Readers, this is a chapter I've been really looking forward to writing, for I have had a great many insights on this subject in the process of demonstrating my own spiritual leadership and observing others, that I think you will find very interesting.

What I have come to realize in my spiritual observations and spiritual discernments of this subject is that for a person to be an effective spiritual leader, they really must be well integrated within themselves in all Seven Rays. I have observed a great many people who, when they move into spiritual leader-ship, have an enormous number of problems. In conjunction with the inner plane Ascended Masters, I have developed a model and/or paradigm that I think you will find quite fascinating, which deals with Integrating the Seven Rays and the subject of Spiritual Leadership.

To begin this discussion, I have presented a chart of the Seven Rays and their corresponding qualities and job functions.

Ray Methods of Teaching Truth

Ray I
Higher expression: The science of statesmanship, and of government.
Lower expression: Modern diplomacy and politics.

Ray II
Higher expression: The process of initiation as taught by the Hierarchy of Masters.
Lower expression: Religion.

Ray III
Higher expression: Means of communication or interaction. Radio, telegraph, telephone, and means of transportation.
Lower expression: The use and spread of money and gold.

Ray IV
Higher expression: The Masonic work based on the formation of the Hierarchy and related to Ray II.
Lower expression: Architectural construction. Modern city planning.

Ray V
Higher expression: The science of the Soul, Esoteric Psychology.
Lower expression: Modern educational systems.

Ray VI
Higher expression: Christianity and diversified religions. Note the relation to Ray II.
Lower expression: Churches and religious organizations.

Ray VII
Higher expression: All forms of White Magic.
Lower expression: Spiritualism in its lower aspects.

Short Synopsis of the Seven Rays and Their Colors

First Ray
Will, Dynamic Power, Singleness of Purpose, Detachment, Clear Vision–*(Red)*

Second Ray
Love-Wisdom, Radiance, Attraction, Expansion, Inclusiveness, Power to Save–*(Blue)*

Third Ray
Active Intelligence, Power to Manifest, Power to Evolve, Mental Illumination, Perseverance, Philosophical, Organization, Clearminded, Perfectionist–*(Yellow)*

Fourth Ray
Harmony through Conflict, Purity, Beauty, Artistic Development–*(Emerald-Green)*

Fifth Ray
Concrete Science, Research, Keen Intellect, Detailed, Truthful–*(Orange)*

Sixth Ray
Devotional, Idealistic, Religious–*(Indigo)*

Seventh Ray
Ceremonial Order, Ritual, Magic, Diplomacy, Tact, Violet Flame, Physicalness and Grounded Spirit, Ordered, Disciplined–*(Violet)*

As you all know, each of our Monads come from one of these Rays, which is also true of our soul, personality, mind, emotions and physical body. For those who have awakened spiritually, the strongest Ray influence is your Monadic Ray and/or Soul Ray. It is very helpful to know the configuration of your structure, for this causes a great influence over your spiritual and psychological self. The Ray influences are even stronger than astrology. By understanding your Ray configuration, this also gives you a clue as to which inner plane ashram you are most connected with and hence what inner plane Ascended Master you are most connected with. For those interested in receiving a Ray Reading, Initiation and Light Quotient Reading all in one, call the Academy and I will set you up with an appointment to receive a channeled reading from the Inner Plane Ascended Masters, to get this information. I also recommend that you read my book *The Complete Ascension Manual* and the chapter called "Esoteric Psychology and the 12 Major Rays."

Even though each person's Monad, Soul, personality, mind, emotions and body are all governed by an individual Ray, and in all cases a different combination of Rays, it is essential that every lightworker become a Master of all Seven Rays. This is essential in the understanding of becoming an Integrated Christ. If you do not do this, a great many problems will ensue when you enter the realm of Spiritual Leadership! Let me explain what I mean here. For example, if a person is a First Ray Monad, they will be highly developed in the power aspect of GOD and in political consciousness. These are excellent qualities for a spiritual leader. The problem is I have met many spiritual leaders with First Ray Monads or Souls who have great power and charisma, however, are undeveloped in their Second Ray of Love/Wisdom. Because of this, those leaders are not especially psychologically clear and are prone to self-aggrandizement and disintegration in their teachings. They also have problems being loving in their relationships with people in the areas of pleasure or work.

Now let's look at a Second Ray Monad or Soul and the issue of Spiritual Leadership. The Second Ray Monad or Soul, in demonstrating their Spiritual Leadership, has enormous love and words of wisdom flow from them like a fountain. People are attracted to them because of the radiance and effervescence of their poetic words and aura. The problem with the Second Ray spiritual leader is they often do not have First Ray energy properly integrated. They have tons of love and wisdom but they may not have the personal power, self-mastery, self-discipline, focused concentration, and political savvy to deal with the intense lessons that come from spiritual leadership and responsibility for others. This may come in the realm of dealing with many numbers of students or having lots of employees, or dealing with the politics of other spiritual leaders or the barrage of responsibility that comes from putting on large workshops. This might be a person who is an incredible channel for the Masters, but cannot deal with the fame, responsibility, and even attacks that come from people once you enter the limelight. To be an effective spiritual leader in any realm of life including business, you must have a good balance of First Ray and Second Ray energy, regardless of the Rays that are governing your Monad, Soul and other bodies. Now let's move to the Third Ray and spiritual leader-ship. The Third Ray person is developed in active intelligence and economic issues. This is excellent for spiritual leadership in the realm of business. This type of person is usually very active in the world. The question again comes, do they have enough Second Ray energy of love/wisdom to be effective in dealing with employees. Do they have enough First Ray energy to deal with the same concerns the Second Ray spiritual leader was deficient in?

This brings us to the Fourth Ray and spiritual leadership. This type of person is very attuned to the issue or aspect of GOD that focuses on harmony and beauty. This is the Ray of the artist, musician, and poet. To be honest, this type of person usually has enormous problems in the realm of spiritual leadership if they are not interested in all seven Rays. The are usually extremely creative people. Usually more feminine or yin in psychological makeup. Usually deficient in Rays 1,3 and 5, which have a more mental focus. Someone like Van Gogh, or the archetypal artist, is usually very lacking in the First Ray of power, self-discipline, and politics, and deficient in the Third Ray of business acumen. They also lack the scientific focus of the Fifth Ray. Their extremely emotional nature creates an opening for the negative ego, psychological unclairity, many highs and lows and fighting with people unless really mastered.

They are brilliant in their artistic work, but do not make good spiritual leaders unless they have really worked on themselves. I have met some that have done this, but most have not. This is not a judgment, it is just an insight, and key for those with a Fourth Ray Monad or Soul, on the Ray aspects they need to develop within self. This can provide a type of map for the integrating of the conscious-ness, to become a more effective spiritual leader.

This brings us to the Fifth Ray person and spiritual leadership. The Fifth Ray person has a very scientific mind, and is brilliant in giving forth New Age science. The danger for the Fifth Ray person in regard to spiritual leadership is that they do not have enough Second Ray energy of love/wisdom, enough Fourth Ray of artisticness and beauty in the demonstration of their spiritual leadership. They also may be lacking in Sixth Ray of enough spiritual devotion. This can lead to a scientist who is devoid of GOD in their focus. Without this proper integration, their spiritual leadership would be brilliant in a mental sense but extremely lacking on love and heart energy, which would not make an effective spiritual leader.

This brings us to the Sixth Ray person and spiritual leadership. The Sixth Ray person has enormous spiritual devotion and feeling, however, they are usually extremely lacking in personal power and political savvy. They usually have the Second Ray love/wisdom, but tend often to be too childlike, which does not make an efficient spiritual leader. They have wonderful love and radiance and are tuned to the Fourth Ray beauty, but are usually lacking in the Fifth Ray scientific focus.

This brings us to the Seventh Ray person and spiritual leadership. This type of person is very attuned to ceremonial order and magic. They have a good sense of order and structure, and are excellent at business. The dangers here in the realm of spiritual leadership are the same with all the others. Does this person have enough First Ray power and political savvy? Do they have enough Second Ray love/wisdom and spiritual education? Do they have active intelligence of the Third Ray?

Do they have the harmony, beauty, and aesthetics of the Fourth Ray? Do they have the scientific mind of the Fifth Ray and the proper spiritual devotion of the Sixth Ray to be an "Integrated Christ Spiritual Leader?"

So, my Beloved Readers, I think you can see the strengths and pitfalls, so to speak, of each Ray type, and how they will get in trouble in trying to be spiritual leaders if they are not integrated in all Seven Rays.

People tend to often fall into two lines, although this is not always the case. Often, however, people either fall into a 2,4,6 Ray focus or a 1,3,5,7 focus. These beings are on one side a little more emotional, and on the other side a little more mental; on one side a little more mystic, on the other side a little more the occultist. To be perfectly honest, neither of them makes effective spiritual leaders. The ideal of an "Integrated Christ Spiritual Leader" is when the person can integrate all Seven Rays in a balanced manner. If you are too much leaning in either direction, this is going to create problems in dealing with people and with all the situations that arise when you take on greater spiritual responsibility.

My Beloved Readers, developing one self in all Seven Rays is not the easiest thing to do. It may take some very focused work on your part to develop those areas that are a little deficient or underdeveloped. The question is what do you do in the meantime when you're already involved with spiritual leadership? I have come up with a very interesting insight to resolve this issue. What you do is ask your friends, family and/or hire people to work for you who are developed on those Ray functions that you are less developed in, to make your spiritual business mission and service more complete.

For example, if you are more of a 2, 4, 6, Ray type, you may not be good at computers. So hire someone, or make a trade with someone and you can do channelings for them, which they probably can't do for themselves.

If you are a little deficient in First Ray and political savvy, have a friend who is good at that deal with the sticky situations that come up in life. In your spiritual business, if you are more of a 1, 3, 5, 7, hire a 2,

4, 6, to answer your phone calls if you want more of a loving devotional vibration. If you are more of a 2, 4, 6, and business acumen is not your strong point, again make a trade or hire someone who is skilled in that, to bring balance to your business or organization.

For example, at the Wesak Celebration, I am not a professional musician or artist, although I love music and art and consider myself well developed in that Ray. Because I do not perform, however, I invite some of the finest musicians, artists, and singers from around the world to be a part of the Wesak Celebration. I have other artists decorate the entire auditorium, which holds 1500 people. I have spiritual vendors come and sell their spiritual wares. At the Wesak, I create with the Masters a synthesis event of all Seven Rays and this is part of the reason why it is so successful and has such a spiritual power.

One of the key principles of the New Age is group consciousness. Work with people who balance and compliment your energy. The same is true in romantic relationships. Sometimes some of the most effective and long lasting relationships are not necessarily those where you are the same, but those where there is a balance and complementation of Ray functions.

In conclusion, my Beloved Readers, if you find yourself deficient in any Ray function, work on developing yourself in that area to become a full, "Integrated Christ." However, as this process proceeds, align yourself in your personal and professional relationships with those that complement and balance your Ray structure and nature. One of the best ways to develop those rays and ray functions is to form personal relationships, friendships, and professional relationships with those of an opposite nature. You will integrate their vibration and qualities and they will integrate yours. In truth, this must be the quickest and most effective way to becoming an "Integrated Christ" in the realm of integrating the Seven Rays in the focus of Spiritual Leadership!"

14

The Development of Consciousness through the Rays and the Issue of Channeling

In this chapter I would like to look at channeling and telepathy through the lens of integrating the seven rays in the process of developing one's consciousness, and the effect it has on the channeling process. As has been stated many times in this book, the development of one's consciousness enormously affects the channeling process, even within the finest channels on this planet. This is not a judgment upon channelers; it is just the nature of the process of channeling itself. So let's continue this scientific study and exploration of this subject by looking individually at each of the seven rays in a given person, and see how the development of that ray affects how channeled information comes through that instrument.

Let us begin with the First Ray, which deals with the issue of power. If a lightworker is highly developed in that ray, the channelings will, by definition, be very powerful, commanding, charismatic, forceful, and again, if not balanced, even militaristic in nature. If a person is undeveloped in the first ray, then the channelings will come through that channel in a more timid, soft, sensitive, more shy kind of manner. The channel often blocks information coming through so as not to create waves or any kind of confrontation.

The Second Ray deals with love and wisdom. If the person is highly developed in the second ray, the channelings that come through that channeler will be filled with love and all kinds of spiritual wisdom. But if not balanced with the first ray, will again lack the power, or if not integrating rays three and five, will be more flowery but lack scientific and specific types of information. If undeveloped in the second ray, the channelings will not be very loving and will lack the spiritual information that is needed to make them useful. They will be probably more dry and intellectual, and will not connect with people's hearts, but be more concrete in nature.

The Third Ray deals with active intelligence. If a person is highly developed in this ray, the channelings will reflect keen intellectual knowledge and very practical information that is useful in dealing with Earth life. If the channeler is lacking in the Second Ray, it will not be as loving, however, and if lacking in the first ray, it will not be as powerful, charismatic and commanding. If undeveloped in the third ray, the channelings will lack a certain keen intellectual quality and not be as practical and applicable to Earthly life, without development of this Ray.

The Fourth Ray deals with harmony and beauty. If highly developed in this ray, the channelings will be very poetic and beautiful. The words will flow from the channeler's mouth like the words of a beautiful song with the most polished lyrics. If the channeler is not developed in the first ray, the channelings will lack a certain power and spiritual forcefulness, and if undeveloped in the second ray, lack a certain unconditional love and spiritual wisdom. If undeveloped in the third, fifth, and seventh rays the channelings will be beautiful and poetic, but lack any kind of specific scientific information or specific spiritual wisdom that the person receiving the channeling might need. If undeveloped in this ray, the channelings will lack a certain harmony, beauty, and aesthetic quality. They may have some important information, however, if undeveloped in this ray, it will not be as enjoyable and pleasing to listen to, to the emotional body and the higher senses.

The Fifth Ray deals with New Age science. If the person is highly developed in this ray, then the channelings will be filled with incredible New Age science information. If, however, the channeler is undeveloped in the first ray, the channeling will lack power. If undeveloped in the second ray, the channelings may be filled with incredible scientific knowledge, but will lack unconditional love and spiritual wisdom. If undeveloped in the third ray, the channelings may lack a certain grounded practicality; and if undeveloped in the fourth ray, the channelings will lack a beautiful, poetic quality. If overdeveloped in this ray there is a danger that the channelings will be filled with New Age information, but will be too dry and scientific. If undeveloped in the fifth ray, the channelings and telepathic information that come through the channeler will lack any type of spiritual, scientific information. The information may appeal to the concrete mind or be intellectual, but not New Age spiritual science.

The Sixth Ray deals with spiritual devotion. If highly developed in this ray, the channelings will be filled with information and feeling that lend itself to total devotion to GOD or a guru. This type of channeler usually brings through very loving information. If not balanced with the first ray, the channelings will lack a certain power. If not balanced with the second ray, may lack a certain amount of spiritual wisdom. If not balanced with the third ray, it will lack the keen intellectual knowledge and practical Earthly knowledge. If not balanced with the fourth ray, the channelings will lack the poetic beauty and harmony. If not balanced with the fifth ray the channelings may lack any type of scientific or specific spiritual information. In other words, the channelings may be very flowery and beautiful, but not as informative. If undeveloped in the sixth ray, the channelings will be a little bit too dry and intellectual. The channelings will lack love; and a certain enthusiasm and love for GOD and one's brothers and sisters.

The Seventh Ray deals with ceremonial order and magic and the Violet Flame. If the channeler is highly developed in this ray, then the channelings will come through in a very Divine order, spiritual ceremony, and with a certain pomp and circumstance. Every channeling will be like a very special ceremony and will have a very specified spiritual structure and order to the sequence of information given. The channelings may focus a great deal on alchemy and transmutation on all levels. If undeveloped in this ray, the channelings will lack a certain spiritual grandeur and majesty. The channelings may also be a little chaotic and lacking in spiritual order. If undeveloped in the first ray, they will lack the power. If undeveloped in the second ray, they will lack the love and spiritual wisdom. If undeveloped in the third ray, the active intelligence. If undeveloped in the fourth ray, the channelings will not be as poetically beautiful. If undeveloped in the fifth ray, not as spiritually scientific. In addition, if undeveloped in the sixth ray, will not carry enough spiritual devotion.

Channelers often fall into the category of being of the 2/4/6 ray types, or the 1/3/5/7 ray types. The 2/4/6 type of channeler is a little more emotionally focused. They bring through enormous love and spiritual wisdom, poetry, beauty, harmony, and spiritual devotion in the channelings. The channelings come through usually in a very flowery, beautiful way that is very pleasing to the emotional body and the soul. The only problem with this type of channeling is that it lacks the power of the first ray, the keen intellect and Earthly practicality of the third ray, and the specific New Age scientific information of the fifth ray. It also does not carry the ceremonial and ritualistic divine order of the seventh ray.

Channelers of the 1/3/5/7 type are exactly the opposite. Their channelings are very powerful and charismatic, carrying keen intellect and Earthly practicality. They are very spiritually scientific and bring through very technical and specific information. They are also very spiritually ordered and have great majesty and spiritual grandeur in what is brought forth. The only problem with the channelings of the 1/3/5/7 type is that it lacks a little bit of the unconditional love and spiritual wisdom quality of the second ray, as well as the poetry and beauty of the fourth ray. It also lacks the wonderful spiritual devotion of the Sixth Ray.

The Integrated Melchizedek/Christ/Buddha Channel

The ideal channel of information for the Aquarian Age, this New Millennium, and for the Seventh Golden Age, is to become as integrated and balanced as possible within self, so the Love, Wisdom, and Power that comes through your channel in whatever type of channeling you do is integrated and balanced in nature. This means carrying a balance of the seven rays. This means carrying a balance of the Three-Fold Flame of GOD—Love, Wisdom, and Power. This means reflecting a balance of the seven chakras, as well as the twelve major archetypes and twelve signs of the Zodiac. It is perfectly fine and in divine order for everyone to reflect a certain ray or theme of GOD for that is how GOD created us. Each of our monads and souls lies upon one individual ray and this is how it should be. So I am not suggesting here that everyone should be exactly the same, or do channelings exactly the same. What I am suggesting is that every person strive to become an "integrated Melchizedek/Christ/Buddha" in their practice of the presence of GOD on Earth, and in doing so, even though your channelings may have a tinge or theme of your own monadic and soul ray, your channelings will also be reflective of being an "integrated Melchizedek/Christ/Buddha"!

It is my deepest hope and prayer that this discussion of the Seven Rays as it relates to the process of channeling has given you, my Beloved Readers, a more refined perspective on the importance of "developing your consciousness," so as to become a more balanced and integrated expression and instrument of GOD and the Masters on Earth!

15

The Cosmic Rays

One of the most profound areas of research that has come through in recent times is in the area which I am calling the Cosmic Rays. This information along with the cosmology of the ascension seats is so exciting it is hard to contain myself. Let me begin by laying the foundation for this discussion. Prior to 1960 this planet for the last 3.1 billion years basically dealt with seven major rays. These seven rays are:

> First ray of Power, Will, and Purpose (Red)
> Second ray of Love/Wisdom (Blue)
> Third ray of Active, or Creative Intelligence (Yellow)
> Fourth ray of Harmony (Emerald-Green)
> Fifth ray of Concrete Science (Orange)
> Sixth ray of Abstract Idealism and Devotion (Indigo)
> Seventh ray of Ceremonial Order and Magic (Violet)

Then in approximately 1960, a most extraordinary event occurred on this planet. There was a special dispensation given to this planet of the introduction of five new rays. These five new rays are:

> Eighth ray: The Higher Cleansing Ray (Seafoam-Green)
> Ninth ray: Joy, attracting the Body of Light (Blue-green)
> Tenth ray: The anchoring of the Body of Light, inviting soul merge
> (Pearlescent)

Eleventh ray: The Bridge to the New Age (Pink-orange)
Twelfth ray: The anchoring of the New Age and the Christ
Consciousness (Gold)

The anchoring of these five higher rays was an extraordinary occurrence. The whole science of esoteric psychology and the twelve rays I have written about extensively in my first book *The Complete Ascension Manual.* It is probably one of the most important spiritual sciences known to man. It predates and is the causative factor of even the science of astrology. It is absolutely mind-boggling to me to see how totally unknown this science is and how much inaccurate information is floating around in regards to it.

If you have not spent time calling in these twelve rays and experimenting with them, I recommend that you do so. It is essential you do so for your spiritual training. The instructions for how to do this are in *The Compete Ascension Manual,* so I am not going to repeat myself here. These planetary rays function a lot like the ascension seats. It is just a matter of calling them forth and then bathing in their energy. They are there for the asking.

This is another one of these cases where God has given us everything, however most people, even lightworkers, don't know these rays are available or how to use them. It is really so simple. If you want personal power, call on the red ray. If you want cleansing, call on the eighth ray. If you are doing scientific work, call on the fifth ray. If you want devotion, call on the sixth ray. If you want transmutation, call on the seventh ray. If you want the pure Christ Consciousness, call on the twelfth ray. If you want to attract your body of Light, call on the ninth ray.

You can call the ray by number, color, or quality. Each of these methods works equally well. The five higher rays, which are combinations of the first seven rays with the added ingredient of White Light, are especially powerful.

Since completing my own planetary ascension and having worked with these twelve rays for a very long time I was ready for the next step. One day I had the idea that maybe it would be possible to map out the Cosmic Rays beyond these most extraordinary Planetary Rays. I don't know why I just hadn't thought of this before. Probably because the timing wasn't right.

Our core group and I sat down over a couple of months and were able to actually come up with this information. This, along with the ascension seats and the process of cosmic ascension, is some of the most profound information I have ever come across.

What is exciting to me is the process of bringing forth new information on the cosmic levels of creation that has never been brought forth before to humanity. What is also exciting is that these Cosmic Rays can be called forth in the exact same way that the ascension seats can for accelerating planetary and cosmic ascension. It is another method for tapping in. The following chart, which I have called the *Cosmic Rays Cosmology*, is my first unveiling of this new information.

COSMIC RAYS COSMOLOGY

Godhead Level
Clear Light; Translucent and Invisible

The Twelve Cosmic Rays
All 12 Clear Light; Translucent and Invisible

Multi-Universal Level
Platinum Ray

The Ten Lost Cosmic Rays of the Yod Spectrum
All Hues of Platinum

Universal Level Golden Chamber of Melchizedek
Purest and Most Refined Gold

Great White Lodge on Sirius
Gold; Second Level Purity

Melchior—Galactic Core
Silver-Gold

Helios—Solar Core
Copper-Gold

Shamballa—Sanat Kumara
White Light

Twelve Planetary Rays		
1: Red	5: Orange	9: Blue-green
2: Blue	6: Indigo	10: Pearlescent
3: Yellow	7: Violet	11: Pink-orange
4: Emerald Green	8: Seafoam-Green	12: Gold (third-level purity)

At the very top of the chart we have the Source or Godhead Level. This is the level of God from which all creation fans out. This might be called the place from where the first ray emanation stems from. Melchizedek told me that the color of the first emanation is "Clear Light." It is so pure and so refined it has no color. It is translucent and invisible.

The second level of the diagram leads one to the second step of Creation, which is the creation of the twelve cosmic rays. Just so there is no misunderstanding, I am talking about the twelve cosmic rays here, not the twelve planetary rays which I spoke of earlier. These twelve rays are connected with the Cosmic Council of Twelve at the 352nd level of the Godhead.

The twelve Cosmic Beings literally run God's infinite universe. This is God's leadership group, and God's core ashram members. These twelve Beings are so infinite and so vast "they are almost unfathomable." Each of these twelve Cosmic Council of Twelve members is connected to a cosmic monad (not planetary monad), which all of us come from. All the beings in God's infinite universe emanate form one of these twelve cosmic monads.

Cosmic ascension is the merger with this cosmic monad. Each member of the Cosmic Council of Twelve is in charge of one of the Cosmic Rays. The Planetary Rays that we deal with at our level are stepped down hundreds of times so the voltage doesn't burn us up.

I asked Melchizedek what color these twelve cosmic rays are. The twelve cosmic rays are so refined and rarefied that they also have no color, Melchizedek said. At this stage they are translucent and invisible. This reminds me of the Tree of Life and the very top Sephiroth called Kether, which is the Crown of the Cosmic Tree. At this stage we have not moved down the Tree to the next two Sephiroth, Binah and Chokmah, where creation as we know it begins to exist. In other words, we are still in the unmanifest, rather than the manifest state. The prism of God has not begun to refract color yet.

This then brings us down the Tree of Life to the multi-universal level, which is the source of the 43 Christed Universes for our Cosmic Day. Manifested reality begins. The first refracted color in the prism of divinity at the multi-universal level is "platinum."

Here begins another way to access this level rather than going to the actual ascension seat there. It is to call on the platinum ray from Melchizedek or Metatron. This is also a little less dangerous in the sense that in working with the ascension seat you are actually going to the source of that ray rather than just calling forth the ray and experiencing it. It is kind of like calling on the energies of the 43 Christed Universes. Here, however, we are specifically dealing with the Cosmic Rays.

That brings us now to the next level, which is a most extraordinary insight. This is what Melchizedek referred to as the Ten Lost Cosmic Rays of the Yod Spectrum. These are ten rays that have been lost by humanity until now. These Ten Lost Cosmic Rays are emanating out of the multi-universal level. They can be called forth by calling forth from Melchizedek, Metatron, or Lord Michael, the downflow of the Yod Spectrum and the Ten Lost Cosmic Rays.

Melchizedek has said that this work should not be done until you complete your seventh initiation. You can begin if you like as soon as you take your seventh. The "Yod Spectrum" is a term I first became acquainted with through the Keys of Enoch, and refers to the *cosmic* Yod Spectrum, not the planetary Yod Spectrum. The Yod Spectrum is the Light Spectrum. The planetary Yod Spectrum would be the full scope of the twelve planetary rays.

This brings us down to the next level, which is the Golden Chamber of Melchizedek. It is so funny to use the words "come down to the Golden Chamber of Melchizedek" because this chamber is such an extraordinarily high level of consciousness. Melchizedek told us that this universal core emanates a most refined and purified God energy.

Each color that one can work with has three graduations of purity, refinement, and clarity. This gold color from the universal core and Melchizedek is the most refined gold color and ray in existence. It is the cosmic ray at the core essence of our universe. You experience this energy when you sit in the Golden Chamber of Melchizedek. Melchizedek said you can begin calling in this cosmic ray at the beginning of the sixth initiation. The cosmic gold ray is different from the twelfth ray gold of the Planetary Rays. That is the highest gold of our planetary system, but not of the solar, galactic, and universal system.

The next level on the chart is the Great White Lodge on Sirius, which is governed by the Lord of Sirius on the inner plane. This is not the Extraterrestrial Sirius, but the inner plane Sirius. It is the true home of the Spiritual Hierarchy of which Shamballa is an outpost. It is where most of humanity will go in terms of the seven paths to higher evolution, which I speak of in my book *Beyond Ascension*.

The Cosmic Ray emanating from the Great White Lodge is again the color gold, but it is a second level purity, just beneath that of the Golden Chamber of Melchizedek, still extremely high in vibration.

This brings us to the galactic core, which is the home and charge of Melchior, the Galactic Logos. Melchizedek told us that the cosmic ray emanating from here is silver-gold. This is the energy that emanates when you sit in Melchior's ascension seat. It can be called forth once you attain the fourth or fifth initiation.

Continuing to move down the chart we come to Helios, the Solar Logos of the solar core. This is the cosmic ray of copper-gold. This is the energy that you experience when sitting in Helios' Central Sun ascension seat.

Moving down the chart we come to Shamballa, currently the home of Sanat Kumara and Lord Buddha. The cosmic ray emanating from here is the pure White Light. This is the energy you experience when you sit in the Shamballa ascension seat of Sanat Kumara and Lord Buddha, which is another very important and most excellent ascension seat.

We then have the twelve planetary rays. In going down this list it makes it sound like these twelve planetary rays are lowly unimportant rays that are not very powerful. Nothing could be further from the truth. These twelve rays are awesome, even the first seven, let alone the last five.

You must realize and put into perspective that I am mapping out God's infinite universe and we are all planetary Masters. We are all just little infants and babies in terms of cosmic evolution. I have spoken of our potential to activate 10% of our cosmic evolution while still on Earth. This is a great potentiality, however, no one has ever done it, and I am not sure anyone ever will. In actuality, if we could achieve one or two percent of our cosmic evolution while still on Earth, that would be enormous.

Please remember we are talking about God's infinite universe now, not just one planet. There are ten billion planets just in our universe, and there are infinite numbers of universes. The Source of our Cosmic Day, or the Source of our 43 Christed Universes, is just one source of infinite numbers of Sources that make up God's infinite universe. Do you have this in perspective? Even just 1% of God's full cosmic energy would be enormous. We are talking about the difference of being a fifty-watt light bulb versus being a million-watt light bulb. So please keep this in perspective as I give you these minimal restrictions I have outlined from Melchizedek.

The full installment, activation, and actualization of your solar, galactic, and universal bodies and/or 30% light quotient scale would be only an increase of 3% on the scale Sai Baba is working in. There are three light quotient scales. One for the planetary level, one for the cosmic level for seventh level completed initiates and a third light quotient scale for Masters who have gone beyond the seven levels of initiations who are Avatars on Earth. The true meaning of an Avatar is one who is totally God-realized at birth. This would also be the light quotient of those Ascended Masters who are out of incarnation.

So, my personal goal at this time is to get to this 30% level and to not only install and activate this level, but to also actualize it. It is in the actualization or third stage that all the advanced Ascended Master abilities that we have associated with the ascension process come. We are actually going much farther than Ascended Masters in the past went in terms of installation and activation of cosmic energies. However, we are going slower in terms of the development of the advanced Ascended Master abilities. This has a lot to do with the speed at which we are all going through this process and the fact that we are living in a period of "mass ascension," which is a different dispensation and program than that which Masters went through in the past.

Summation and a Few Shortcuts

Call on the rays that are appropriate to the level of initiation you are working with. The use of these planetary and cosmic rays is another awesome tool in conjunction with the ascension seats, light quotient building, chakra anchoring, and all the other ascension techniques and tools I have mentioned in my books. It also provides a variety, which is nice since I am recommending that you work with this 24 hours a day, seven days a week.

Even request before going to bed what process you want to work with. Now, I should mention here that you can overdo it, not so much with light quotient building as with the more intensive meditations in some of my other books. Use your intuition and cut back if you start not feeling well. In the beginning you will be releasing a lot of toxins. Drink plenty of water and eat as pure a diet as you possibly can. Once you clean your physical, astral, mental, etheric, and spiritual bodies out you will be able to bring in more and more Light.

If you ever have any physical health problems call on the Ascended Masters and the Angels of Healing. Also call on the Arcturians. I myself have had some chronic health lessons and I call on the Lord of Arcturus and Arcturians for light quotient building and for healing whatever is ailing me. They work on both simultaneously.

I find when I go for my ascension walks I prefer using the galactic level ascension seats and energies more because they are a little less refined then the universal level. That is just my preference. I like to call on the Arcturians early in the morning to get my energies flowing, and to building my light quotient which has a strengthening effect on my overall physical body and digestive system. I seem to be able to type and write for much longer periods of time by asking for their help in this manner. I like to call on the cosmic rays while meditating or if I need a particular quality of energy, of if I am watching television.

I actually have some of my best meditations while watching television. Sounds crazy, but it's true. I can soak in the energies for three hours and not get ants in my pants, as I do sometimes when I meditate. Once the spiritual current is activated you can do other things and it continues to flow quite nicely. If the current is too strong or too weak, you can always ask the Masters to make the appropriate adjustment.

Day by day, by doing this, your light quotient will slowly but surely build. Just make it part of your daily routine and soon it will become a positive habit. It will also help you to feel like you are making progress and accomplishing something. More and more as time has gone on, I do less actual meditating and more and more making my life my meditation. It is amazing how much spiritual work you can get done standing in line at the bank or market. You can do it inwardly in your mind and it takes all of five seconds to invoke. I have worked out systems with the Masters where all I have to say is five words and the whole process is activated. I will share a few of these with you:

◇ "Melchizedek, Golden Chamber, ascension seat." (This is all I say and it is immediately activated. The first time you may need to use more words to make sure you are connected, however, after a while it just takes a few words.)

◇ "Metatron, Call forth twelfth ray."

◇ "Mighty I Am Presence, I call forth transmuting flame."

◇ "Helios, copper-gold ray."

◇ "Lord of Sirius, Great White Lodge ascension seat."

◇ "Sanat Kumara, Shamballa, ascension seat."

◇ "Call forth Serapis Bey, Luxor, ascension seat."

◇ "Metatron, 100% light quotient increase."

◇ "Lord of Arcturus, Arcturians, 100% light quotient increase, heal and strengthen digestive system."

◇ "Metatron. 100% light quotient increase, revitalize."

I think you can get the idea from these examples how the process works. By having these short invocations I can do them in my mind. If I want to do them out loud, I can just whisper them and put my hand to my face while standing in line at the post office and do light quotient building while waiting.

16

The Rays and the Five Initiations Confronting Humanity

The First Initiation and Ray Seven

The first initiation, esoterically called "the birth at Bethlehem," is connected to the seventh ray of ceremonial order and magic. The effect of this ray will be as follows:

1. To bring about the birth of the Christ consciousness among the masses of aspiring human beings on this planet.
2. To set in motion certain relatively new evolutionary processes which will transform humanity into the "world disciple and initiate."
3. To bring about Good Will which is a reflection of the first ray energy of will-to-good.
4. To re-balance and readjust romantic relationships.
5. To intensify human creativity and hence bring in the new art forms which will serve as a conditioning factor for humanity as a whole.
6. To reorganize world affairs so as to instigate the new world order of the Christ.

In relationship to the individual the seventh ray will:

1. Bring upon the mental plane a widespread recognition of the relationship between the soul and the mind.
2. It will produce greater order in the emotional body of the disciple thus preparing him or her for the second initiation.
3. To enable the disciple on the physical plane to establish service relationships, to learn beginning white magic, and to demonstrate the first stage of truly creative life.

The Second Initiation and Ray Six

The second initiation is connected to ray six and has been esoterically called "the baptism in Jordan." The effects of this ray on humanity are as follows:

1. An embryonic realization of the will nature.
2. A magnified conflict between the lower and Higher Self. This, Djwhal has called, the conflict between the emotional nature and true realization.
3. The development on the part of humanity to clarify the world atmosphere, and the releasing of the energy of "goodwill."
4. The setting of the stage for humanity as a whole to take the first and/or second initiation.
5. The sudden and powerful emergence of the world ideologies.
6. A transformation of the astral plane.

In relationship to the individual initiate the sixth ray produces the following effects:

1. A vortex is created where all emotional and ideological reactions of the aspirant are intensified.
2. When this above-mentioned effect subsides, the initiate's alignment raises to an astral/mental/soul attunement.
3. Within the initiate's mental vehicle a crystallization of all thought occurs and a fanatical adherence to mass idealism.

The Third Initiation and the Fifth Ray

The third initiation is connected to the fifth ray and is esoterically called "the Initiation of Transfiguration," or "soul merge." The effects of the fifth ray on humanity are as follows:

1. It is the most potent energy of the planet at this time because in a previous solar system (we are in the third solar system) it was brought to full maturity.

2. It is the energy that admits humanity into the mysteries of the mind of God. It is the key to the universal mind.

3. This energy is esoterically related to the three Buddhas of Activity.

4. Its energy corresponds to the mental energy of a human being.

5. The quality of this ray is extremely responsive to impressions from the soul, and the upper spiritual triad via the antakarana.

6. This energy serves as a light bearer. It responds in time and space to the "Light of the Logos."

7. This energy transforms divine ideas into human ideals, relating the knowledge and sciences of humanity to these ideals, thus making them workable factors in human evolution.

8. The energy of the fifth ray can be regarded as "common sense." It receives various energies and synthesis and produces order out of them.

9. This energy is the thoughtform-making energy of mankind.

10. This ray of concrete science, along with the fact that humanity is in the fifth root race (Aryan age), which is a mental focus, also has greatly accelerated human evolution.

11. There is a close relationship between the second ray of love and the knowledge energy of the fifth ray.

12. The fifth ray energy produces three major areas of thought, or three prime conditions wherein the thoughtform-making energy expresses itself:
    A. Science..........Education.......Medicine
    B. Philosophy......Ideas............Ideals
    C. Psychology......In process of modern development
13. The fifth ray energy is also responsible for the rapid formation of the great conditioning ideologies of the planet.
14. It is the important factor in making possible the third or soul merge initiation.
15. In respect to the personality it works in three ways:
    A. As the transmuting agent of the physical body
    B. As the transforming agent of the astral body
    C. As the transfiguring agent of the mental body

The Fourth Initiation and the Fourth Ray

The fourth initiation is connected to the fourth ray of Harmony through Conflict, and is esoterically called "the Initiation of Renunciation." The fourth ray is out of incarnation at this time in terms of fourth ray souls coming into this planet.

From another angle, however, this ray is always active and present because it is the ray that governs the fourth kingdom (third kingdom is animals, fourth is humanity, fifth is the spiritual kingdom). Because of this relationship it is the dominant energy always exerting pressure on the kingdom of humanity.

This pressure began to exert itself primarily towards the end of the fourth root race which was the Atlantean race. Because of this influence, man began to give evidence of a growing sense of responsibility, and the power to demonstrate discriminative choice. The effect of this ray on humanity is more of a group effect since no fourth ray souls are incarnated at this time except in the ranks of the Great White Lodge, which is not a physical incarnation.

The key principle of the fourth ray is that of conflict. It is the conflict between the major pairs of opposites, which manifests most succinctly in the conflict between "spirit/matter," and "good versus evil." In Atlantean times the leaders with their power of free choice chose *matter*. In the present Aryan age it was this materialism that led to the world wars, which Djwhal says was really a sign of a shifting orientation.

The balance now is swinging most definitely over to the side of spirit. This principle of conflict clarifies for the individual and humanity as a whole, the choice we all have to make, to "renounce" glamour, maya, illusion and negative ego which is the result of attachment to the form side of life. It is only by doing this that a disciple can pass the fourth initiation.

Conflict is always present prior to renunciation. The fourth ray forces us to use our "discriminative power of choice." The fourth ray, in a sense, forces us to learn right discrimination which leads to the higher aspect of the fourth ray which is "harmony."

The fourth ray makes humanity aware of the dualism of the manifested world. This creates a battleground and field of experience which eventually leads to right choice, right perception, and right decision. It is the choice of the Christ consciousness over negative ego consciousness.

The conflict in the world today has increased because of the following factors as discussed by Djwhal Khul in the Alice Bailey book *The Rays and The Initiations*:

1. The crisis of ideologies.
2. The awakening of humanity to a better understanding.
3. The growth of goodwill which leads to the presentation of certain fundamental cleavages which must be bridged by human effort.
4. The partial "sealing of the door where evil dwells."
5. The use of the great invocation with its extraordinary and rapid effects, at present unrealized by you.
6. The gradual approach of the Hierarchy to a closer and more intimate relation to humanity.
7. The return of the Christ, the Lord Maitreya.

The effect of the fourth ray in conjunction with the second ray, which is also now coming in, is to create right human relationships and the growth of the universal spirit of goodwill among all people. It is this influence that is implementing the return and full coming declaration of the Christ. Each disciple and all groups of disciples should strive always towards a right orientation and a broad point of view, always preserving a calm, dispassionate and loving understanding.

The energy of the fourth ray produces conflict, which leads to inner or outer war, which leads to renunciation, which leads to "liberation," which is the result of passing the fourth initiation. The principle of conflict is active in the world today in all nations, religions, and organizations, which is leading to the emergence of the New Age. The conflict produces a point of crisis, then a point of tension, then a point of emergence. This principle of conflict is, in reality, paving the way for the return and full declaration of the Christ. As the individual disciple learns to harmonize himself through conflict, he sets an example for humanity as a whole.

The Fifth Initiation and Ray One

The fifth initiation is connected to the first ray and is esoterically called "the Initiation of Revelation." It signifies the power to wield light in the three worlds and to have a revelation to the next step to be taken upon the way of higher evolution.

The first ray manifests in three progressive stages. The first is, "God is Love." The second is "Good Will." The third is the "Will-to-Good." These are the three aspects of the first ray. When a master takes the fifth initiation, he already knows the first two aspects. It is the third, or will-to-good, that is now realized at the fifth initiation.

The first ray or Shamballa energy is not in incarnation at this time in terms of first ray souls incarnating. The influence of this ray on human-ity has been allowed to come in and throw off the effects of the First World War, and the fission of the atom, which resulted in the creation of the atomic bomb.

The first ray is the will energy and the energy of destruction. Ideally it is the destruction of the old forms, which allows the new forms to manifest. Another effect of the first ray energy from Shamballa is that the reasoning faculty within humanity will be stimulated so as to allow humanity as a whole to reach new heights.

In the beginning stages of this development can be found instability of the human mental mechanism, and in the human thinking process. At the fourth initiation, it was the energy of destruction of the first ray that allowed the disciple to destroy all which held him in the three worlds of human endeavor.

At the fifth initiation the first ray helps the initiate to attain a spiritual orientation that will remain permanent. At the fifth initiation all the initiate's spiritual and material realizations are renounced and hence he stands free from every aspect of desire.

This being the case, "spiritual will" has been substituted for "desire." The first ray from Shamballa, which embodies this will energy, reinforces this. This state of consciousness of the initiate/master allows him to receive this influx of energy that will enable him to see that which is to be revealed and to accept revelation.

The process is one of first the will to self-betterment, which leads to the will to human service, goodwill, and then finally to the will-to-good. The newfound master is able to look into the heart of all things. He becomes aware of the great central spiritual sun and the way of the higher evolution, which leads inevitably to the center of the "Most High God."

17

An Esoteric Understanding of the Seven Main Chakras

In this chapter I will be discussing the seven main chakras and their functioning as described by Djwhal Khul in his book by Alice Bailey called *Esoteric Healing.*

Before building the second and third floors we must first have the foundation built properly. This chapter will provide an in-depth understanding of seven major chakras and also how they affect the health and disease of the physical body.

In this chapter I will also be showing you a number of small charts and diagrams from Alice Bailey's book, *Esoteric Healing,* that give a fascinating glimpse into how the chakras work and function from an esoteric perspective of Djwhal Khul and the Great White Brotherhood. We will begin with the seven main chakras and their corresponding glands and number of petals.

Chakra	Gland	Petals
Crown chakra	Pineal gland	1000
Third Eye chakra	Pituitary gland	2
Throat chakra	Thyroid gland	16
Heart chakra	Thymus gland	12
Solar Plexus chakra	Pancreas	10
Second chakra	The Gonads	6
First chakra	Adrenal glands	4

In this second diagram we see: The chakra, the ray it is associated with, the quality of energy associated with each chakra and the dimension of origin or connection of each chakra.

Center	Ray	Quality	Origin
1. Head Center	1st	The Divine Will	Monadic
2. Ajna Center	7th	Organization	Atmic
3. Heart Center	2nd	Love/Wisdom	Buddhic
4. Throat Center	5th	Creativity	Mental
5. Solar Plexus	6th	Emotion/Desire	Astral
6. Sacral Center	3rd	Reproduction	Etheric
7. Base of Spine	4th	Harmony/Union	Physical through conflict.

This next diagram is a fascinating one that shows the negative aspect of the chakra, the disease that is produced when the chakra isn't working effectively. It also shows the good aspect of each chakra and the ray and astral force quality connected with each ray.

Center	Bad Aspect	Disease	Good Aspect	Astral Force
Head	Self-pity The dramatic I	Cancer	Sacrifice Dedication of the I	First ray Will or Power
Heart	Self-love Personality	Heart trouble Stomach trouble	Soul love Group love	Second ray Love/Wisdom
Sacral	Sexuality Over-activity	Social diseases	Parental love Group life	Third ray Activity
Ajna	Selfishness Dogmatism	Insanities	Mysticism	Fourth ray Harmony
Throat	Lower psychism	Wrong metabolism Certain cancers	Creativity Sensitivity Inspiration.	Fifth ray Knowledge
Solar Plexus	Emotionalism	Nervous diseases Gastritis Liver trouble	Aspiration Right direction.	Sixth ray Devotion
Base of the Spine	Self-interest Pure selfish Black Magic	Heart diseases Tumors	White Magic	Seventh ray Organization

The Crown Chakra

The crown chakra is, of course, located at the very top of the head. It is often called the "thousand petaled lotus" or the "Brahmarandra." It corresponds, esoterically, to the central spiritual sun (not the physical sun). It begins to function effectively after the third initiation and is the organ for the distribution of Monadic energy, or the Will aspect of God.

It is related to the personality through the antakarana which, of course, the disciple must build. It reaches its full usefulness only after the fourth initiation, which has to do with the burning up of the causal or soul body.

The crown chakra is the Shamballa center in the physical body. It functions to register divine purpose and corresponds to what Djwhal Khul has called the "electric fire" of the solar system.

The dense physicalization of the crown chakra corresponds to the pineal gland. This gland remains active during infancy until the Will-to-be is sufficiently established. This allows the personality or soul extension in incarnation to be fully and firmly anchored into physical expression.

The crown chakra is the only one of the seven chakras that, at the time of liberation from the wheel of rebirth, retains the position of the inverted lotus. All the other lotuses are turned upwards. Only the stem of the crown chakra, which is really the antakarana, is reaching upwards. All the other chakras start by being inverted, however in the process of evolution, turn upwards.

The Ajna or Third Eye Chakra

This chakra is between the eyebrows and is found in the region of the head above the two eyes. Djwhal Khul, in the Alice Bailey book *Esoteric Healing*, says that it "acts as a screen for the radiant beauty and glory of the spiritual man."

The third eye chakra corresponds to the "physical" sun, and is the expression of the integrated personality, first as the disciple and then as the initiate. It achieves this full functioning activity by the time the third initiation or soul merge is taken.

It is the organ for the distribution of the energy of the third aspect of divinity, which is called "active intelligence." The third chakra has a close connection with the throat chakra. The crown chakra has a correspondingly close connection with the first chakra.

The crown chakra relates the Monad and the personality. The third eye chakra relates the spiritual triad (spiritual will, intuition, higher mind—the vehicle of the Monad) to the personality.

In another diagram from the Alice Bailey book *Esoteric Healing*, Djwhal Khul gives a very interesting comparison between the third eye chakra, and the right eye and the left eye. As seen in the following diagram, the third eye is the eye of the monad, or Father, where the right eye is the eye of the soul.

The left eye is the eye of the personality. It is only when all three eyes are functioning and seeing simultaneously that a disciple and initiate has full in-sight into divine purpose. The diagram also shows the gland that is connected to each, and the level of spiritual attunement.

In most people you will find one of the eyes more developed than the other one. The right eye would probably relate to more right-brain development, the left eye to more left-brain development. This can be seen clairvoyantly when you look at each eye. Of course, the ideal is to develop all three. Any one of them is not better than the other. Integration and balance is forever the ideal.

The Third Eye   the head center   Will. Atma
  The eye of the Father, the Monad.
  The first aspect of will or power and purpose.
  Related to the *pineal gland.*

The Right Eye   the ajna center   Love. Buddhi
  The eye of the Son, the Soul.
  The second aspect of love/wisdom.
  Related to the *pituitary body.*

The Left Eye   the throat center   Active Intelligence
  The eye of the Mother, the personality.
  The third aspect of intelligence.
  Related to the *carotid gland.*

The third eye focused the intention to create. It is not the organ of creation, but rather embodies the idea lying behind active creativity. The throat center would be the chakra more connected with the actual act of creation.

The third eye's dense physical externalization is the pituitary gland. The two lobes of the pituitary gland correspond to the two petals of the third eye chakra. This chakra expresses imagination and desire in their two highest forms.

It is the organ of idealism and is connected to the sixth ray. The crown chakra is connected with the first ray. Although having only two petals, it is composed of 96 lesser or minor petals. The two petals spread out like wings of an airplane to the right and left of the head.

This is symbolic of the left-and right-hand path. The path of matter and the path of spirit. The third eye chakra only comes into creative activity when the antakarana has been built. In the earlier stages it is the throat center which is the creative agent.

In the earliest stage of all, it is the second chakra that is the creative agent. The building of the antakarana, or rainbow bridge, only becomes possible when the aspirant shifts from the sacral chakra into the throat chakra.

Throat Chakra

This chakra, according to Djwhal Khul, is found at the back of the neck reaching up into the medulla oblongata, involving the carotid gland, and down towards the shoulder blades. It is a very powerful and well-developed chakra of average humanity. It is ruled astrologically by Saturn.

The crown chakra is ruled by Uranus and Mercury rules the third eye chakra. Djwhal says that this is only where the disciple is concerned. The ruler ship changes after the third initiation or before the first initiation. These three planets form an interesting triangle or force in the disciple's consciousness.

This chakra is related to the first initiation and develops great activity and potency when this initiation is passed. When the initiate has achieved perfection the Shamballa energy of will and purpose will pour freely through the crown chakra. The love/wisdom energies of the Hierarchy will flow through the heart chakra. The energies of humanity will flow through the throat chakra. The third eye chakra will act as the agent of all three.

The throat chakra is the organ specifically of the creative word. It registers the intention or creative purpose of the soul, which has been transmitted to it from the third eye chakra. This process leads to some type of creative activity.

The dense physical externalization of the throat chakra is the thyroid gland. This gland symbolizes the third aspect of intelligence and of substance impregnated with mind. Djwhal says that it is connected to the Holy Ghost, which, again, is the third aspect of the Trinity.

The parathyroids are symbolic of Mary and Joseph and the relationship they hold to the overshadowing Holy Ghost (thyroid). The head center symbolizes the essential dualistic nature of God. The throat center symbolizes the triple nature of the divine expression.

The Heart Chakra

The heart chakra symbolically corresponds to the heart of the sun, and to the spiritual source of light and love. It begins to function effectively after the second initiation. The second initiation, of course, deals with mastery of the emotional body and control of desire.

It is at this stage the personal lower self is transmuted into love. The heart chakra is the organ for the distribution of Hierarchical energy poured out via the soul into the heart center of all aspirants, disciples and initiates. This brings about the regeneration of humanity, and firmly established the relationship between the Hierarchy and humanity.

The development of the heart chakra has to do with the aspirant's ability to learn to think with heart instead of thinking just with the mind. Another way of saying this would be the need of the aspirant to elevate the forces of the solar plexus or third chakra into the heart chakra.

The heart chakra is the medium through which the Hierarchy works and is also an agent for the soul. The heart chakra registers the energy of love, also esoterically called "Buddhi." The crown chakra is the point of contact for the spiritual will, or Atma.

The throat chakra is the point of expression of the Universal Mind, or manas. The heart chakra, according to Djwhal Khul, corresponds to the "solar fire" within the solar system.

The heart chakra is the chakra that brings about inclusiveness. Its dense physical externalization is the thymus gland. Since the thymus gland deals with one's immune system, the more loving one is, the better their immune system will work.

When the heart chakra becomes active the disciple is drawn into the ashram of the one of the Masters according to his soul ray. The Master is the heart center of the ashram. The opening of the heart chakra also leads the disciple into a consciousness of being of greater service to humanity.

Eventually the disciple becomes the heart of a group or organization just as the Master is the heart of the ashram. When the lower-self and personality are in charge the heart petals are inverted and face downwards.

As the polarization or identification back to the soul and Higher Self takes place the petals reverse their orientation and begin to reach upwards. This is also helped by the pull of the Master's ashram and the potency of the Hierarchical approach. The heart chakra is connected to the love/wisdom principle of the soul and the Christ consciousness.

The Solar Plexus or Third Chakra

The solar plexus chakra is an exceedingly active one. It was brought to high stage of collective development in the Atlantean period.

First two root races
Pre-Lemurian root race	First chakra
Lemurian root race	Second chakra
Atlantean root race	Third chakra
Aryan root race	Throat chakra
Meruvian root race	Third eye chakra
Paradisian last root race	Crown chakra

The third chakra is particularly related to the heart and third eye chakra. These three form a triangle of energies in the human body, according to Djwhal Khul. There is a down flow of energy from the soul to the third eye, to the heart, which affects the solar plexus, which again stimulates the heart chakra.

The solar plexus chakra is a reflection in the personality of the "heart of the sun." It is the central factor in the heart of the personality, for those below the probationary path. It is the astral body into the outer world. It is the chakra of desire. it is a chakra of great importance to the average man, and it is essential for the aspirant and disciple to learn to control it. Desire must be transmuted into fiery aspiration for self-realization.

The three lowest centers might be called centers of personality and must be under the control of the soul for beginning initiations to take place. The solar plexus, according to Djwhal Khul, is the great clearing-house for all energies below the diaphragm.

This refers to the major and minor chakras. The minor chakras consist of 21 lesser centers and 49 smaller centers. These minor centers are any-where in the etheric body where lines of energy (nadis) cross. The nadis are the etheric nervous system, which is the metaphysical correspondence to our physical nervous system.

The solar plexus chakra is very connected to the astral plane, and is the seat of the emotional body. It is the chakra in which average unenlightened humanity live. It is the center in which most mediums, channels and clairvoyants function. As these aspirants evolve their polarization will change from the astral identification to the third eye polarization. This will bring about a much higher level of spiritual work.

The great polarization of humanity in the solar plexus chakra is a basic cause of much of the stomach, liver, and digestive problems. This entire area below the diaphragm is in a constant state of turmoil in the average person. The solar plexus chakra is a center for collection, for a gathering in of all the lower energies, sending them to the receptive higher chakras.

Ideally, the solar plexus sends its energies to the heart chakra. The second chakra sends them to the throat chakra. The first chakra sends the energies to the crown chakra. Djwhal Khul has said in Alice Bailey's book *Esoteric Healing*, that after the third initiation the energies are controlled and raised by an act of will of the spiritual triad (spiritual will, intuition, and Higher Mind).

What happens then is the second chakra light and the solar plexus light dies out, and these two chakras will simply be recipients of spiri-tual energies from higher levels. They will no longer possess any direct inherent light of their own. it must be understood that Ascended Masters have transcended desire and the astral plane completely.

Esoteric Psychology and the Science of the Rays and Chakras of God: A Compilation

The dense physical externalization of the solar plexus chakra is the pancreas, although this chakra does affect the stomach and liver also. The solar plexus chakra is an organ of synthesis at a certain point in the higher development of a person.

A solar plexus chakra is an organ of synthesis at a certain point in the higher development of a person. The solar plexus functions as an instrument of integration of the personality when rightly used.

When the petals of the heart chakra are turned upwards it means that the emotional energy, desire, and ambition are focused towards soul and spiritual realization rather than the path of materialistic identification.

The transfer of the solar plexus energy into the higher chakras is the task of all aspirants on the path. The three major transfers of energy that ideally take place are:

1. From the three chakras below the diaphragm into the heart, throat and third eye.
2. From the heart and throat chakra into the third eye chakra and crown.
3. From the third eye into the crown. This signifies the complete unification of all the energies through the entire etheric body (which is where the chakras exist) into one central focal point of distribution, under direct control of the spiritual triad. The spiritual triad being the three-fold triad (spiritual will, intuition, and Higher Mind) and vehicle for the Monad.

Very often when this transfer of energy from the solar plexus to the heart chakra first begins to take place, many aspirants think they are having a heart attack. It is really just the opening of the heart chakra.

The Second Chakra

The second chakra is a very powerful center in that it is connected with the sexual impulse. Djwhal said in the Alice Bailey book *Esoteric Healing* that this chakra will remain a powerful center until two-thirds of mankind have taken initiation.

As the collective humanity evolves, this chakra will be controlled and activities involving sexuality will be carried forward in a much more intelligent manner, rather than under control of the lower self and uncontrolled desire and passion.

The second chakra corresponds to the physical sun, the source of vitality and life giving agent of our planet. Most importantly, Djwhal says that it is the chakra through which the forces of "impersonality" must eventually express themselves.

It is also the chakra where the problem of dualism must be resolved. This involves an attitude of mind that deals with purpose rather than desire. When this occurs there is transference from second chakra to fifth chakra creation. The second chakra is closely related to matter. It is the chakra that was the center of focus in the Lemurian root race.

The combination of the second chakra and the third eye chakra create a functioning duality, which Djwhal has called "personality." The dense physical externalization of this chakra is the gonad glands.

The First Chakra

This chakra is at the very base of the spine and supports all the other chakras. Djwhal says that it is relatively quiet at this time. It is only put into full activity by an act of the will, which is directed and controlled by the initiate. It is responsive only to the will aspect, and the will-to-be incarnated is the factor which controls its life.

This is the chakra where spirit and matter meet. Where life is related to form. It is the chakra where the "serpent of God" undergoes transformations. Djwhal has explained this in the Alice Bailey book *Esoteric Healing* in the following manner:

1. The serpent of matter lies coiled.
2. The serpent is transformed into the serpent of wisdom.
3. The serpent of wisdom is translated and becomes the "dragon of living light."

The kundalini fire will be awakened and raised up through all the chakras and into the crown when the channels up the spine are cleared.

Each chakra has a circular disk or web found between each pair of chakras. There are four of them. These webs are dissipated as purity of life and discipline of emotions and the development of spiritual will are developed. This also occurs when the four-fold personality is highly developed and the third eye chakra is awakened.

The Etheric Body, Nadis, Nervous System and Endocrine System

The chakras reside within the etheric body. The nadis (etheric nervous system), determine the nature and quality of the physical nervous system. The incoming and outgoing energies through the chakras greatly affect the flow of energy through the nadis and hence, the physical nervous system.

Esoterically the etheric body is considered a physical body even though it is made up of finer physical substance. The nadis and nervous system is also related to the spinal column. When these relationships are understood by the medical and psychiatric fields there will be a great revolution in their methods of healing.

It is the functioning of the chakras, the etheric body, the nervous system, and the endocrine system (whose health is a byproduct of the functioning or lack of functioning of the chakras) that determines the entire health of the physical body.

Traditional Western medicine and psychiatry have absolutely no understanding of the chakras, nadis, and the etheric body and the causative role they play in the health and disease of the physical and psychological self for that matter. To add to this, they have no understanding of the soul and its role. This is the revolution that is soon to take place.

The nadis in the physical body correspond to the spirit aspect of life. The nerves correspond to the soul aspect, esoterically speaking. When the chakras are open and awakened the disciple will have a highly electric nervous system. The nadis will be freely carrying an enormous flow of energy that will help to create a well-balanced endocrine system. This large and open flow of energy will cause the physical body to automatically be resistant to disease.

The problem with most people is an uneven development. Some chakras are unawakened, and others are over-stimulated. This causes whole areas of the body where the nadis are in an embryonic state and other areas where the nadis are highly energized.

This causes the flow of energy through the body to be blocked at certain areas. This greatly affects the functioning of the glands, and the functioning of the nervous system. This is the precursor to disease in all its multifaceted manifestations.

In summary, all disease can be traced to the condition of the chakras, for they determine the activity of non-activity of the nadis. These, in turn, affect the nervous system, which affects the endocrine system, which affects the blood stream, which affects the entire physical body.

The three chakras in supreme control today for the majority of the people on the planet are the third eye chakra, the solar plexus chakra and the second chakra. Djwhal says that as mankind evolves and "becomes that which he truly is," the chakras in control will be the crown, heart, and first chakra.

Low-grade humanity uses the solar plexus with a slight activity in the third eye. Average humanity works partly through the solar plexus but largely through the third eye and throat center. High-grade humanity uses the crown chakra, third eye, throat, heart, and solar plexus.

The soul pours its energy into the physical body through the etheric body. The etheric body is composed of the seven major chakras, and the 49 minor chakras, and the millions of infinitesimally small threads of energy or force fibers called nadis, that underlay the physical nervous system.

Mental Disease

Interestingly enough, in Atlantean times (emotionally centered) there was very little mental trouble because the mind nature was very quiescent. There was also very little eye trouble or nasal difficulties because the third eye was unawakened.

The third eye chakra is the organ of the integrated personality. In the Atlantean root race, personality integration was largely unknown, except for disciples and initiates, which was a very small fraction of the total population.

Because we are now in the Aryan root race, just the opposite will begin to happen. As you can see, whatever chakras are activated is where energy imbalances can occur.

In summary, the two main predisposing causes of physical health problems are the under-or over-stimulation of a given chakra. This causes the over-or the under-development of the glands within the endocrine system.

The hypo or hyper action of the glands affects the hormones that are secreted into the bloodstream. The clue to perfect health of an Ascended Master is the full control and self-mastery over the functioning of the chakras. The Master is balanced within the energy reception and distribution within each chakra. In no human being except a Master, are all the chakras properly awakened and functioning in a balanced manner, according to Djwhal Khul.

Just as the raising of the Kundalini can be dangerous if awakened prematurely, the same applies to the opening of the chakras. The evolution of the chakras, if understood properly, is a low and gradual thing, and proceeds in ordered cycle according to the ray of the aspirants monad.

The aspirant should, hence, focus on the following spiritual practices to ensure the proper opening and balance of all his chakras:

1. Purify, discipline, and transmute his three-fold lower nature.
2. Know thyself, and develop the mental body with good thoughts and good deeds.
3. Selfless service to humanity.
4. A life of high altruism, mastery, and purification of the three lower vehicles (physical, emotional, mental).
5. Master and subjugate the dweller on the threshold (glamour, maya, illusion, negative ego).
6. Remain disciplined with your spiritual practices, whatever they may be.
7. Learn to meditate.

Planetary Etheric Chakras

Another fascinating correspondence is how the chakras relate to the planetary energy centers. The diagram is self-explanatory.

Chakra	Planetary Etheric Center	Ray	Quality of Energy
Crown	Shamballa	First	Will energy
Heart	Hierarchy	Second	Love/Wisdom
Throat	Humanity	Fifth	Active Intelligence

Cities as Spiritual Centers

Djwhal Khul, in the Alice Bailey books, has stated that there are five major spiritual centers for energy distribution on the planet. These five centers will serve as centers of focus for future Hierarchical manifestation and externalization on earth.

The five cities are:
1. London—For countries under British influence.
2. New York—For the American continents and sphere of influence.
3. Geneva—For Europe and the former Soviet Union countries.
4. Tokyo—For the Far East.
5. Darjeeling—For Central Asia and India.

These five spiritual centers apparently form a five-pointed star of interlocking energies. Each city, in the process of the externalization of the Hierarchy, will form a headquarters for a Spiritual Master and his group of disciples. The Hierarchy as a whole will use these focal points for the distribution of spiritual energies.

18

The Destiny of Nations

Djwhal Khul, though Alice Bailey, wrote a fascinating book called *The Destiny of Nations*. It is a master thesis sharing the forces and energies that are affecting our world as a whole, and the individual countries that make up the earth.

Nations, in a sense, are a lot like individual people but much larger. Just as people have a personality ray and a soul ray, so do nations. My attempt in this chapter is to bring forth the essential teachings from this work so as to give you an introduction to the subject.

To begin with, there are five great rays of energy manifesting in our world as a whole today.

1. The sixth ray of devotion and idealism.
2. The seventh ray of ceremonial ritual.
3. The second ray of love/wisdom, which, in a sense, is always in manifestation because our solar system is a second ray solar system.
4. The third ray of active intelligence.
5. The first ray of Divine Will.

These five rays have an enormously powerful effect on this planet, just as they do when we have these rays manifesting within our monad, soul, personality, mind, emotional body, and physical body.

The Five Major Ideas Manifesting in the World Today

Djwhal Khul has delineated five major ideas manifesting in the world today. These are:

1. The ancient and inherited ideas which have controlled the racial life for centuries.
2. Ideas that are relatively new such as Nazism, Fascism, Communism.
3. The idea of democracy which is not particularly old or new, that people govern and the government represents the will of the people ideally.
4. The idea of the world state, divided into various sections.
5. The idea of the Spiritual Hierarchy which will govern the people through the world through the best elements of all these above-mentioned systems.

The First Ray Influence in the World

The first ray influence in the world as a whole has only occurred two other times. Once, in Lemurian times at the individualization of man. The second time, during the Atlantean root race during the battle between those who served the Law of One and the Lords of Materialism, also known as the Sons of Belial.

This ray has a destructive quality within it in a positive sense of destroying that old form. This ray, in conjunction with the second ray, is part of the reason for the tremendous crisis in the world today.

This destructive force can also be misused by man. An example of this is how, in the name of science, we have killed many of the forms in the animal kingdom. This is the destroying force manipulated by man's negative ego.

This ray also manifests as dominating first ray personalities coming into the world picture. These figures are usually in the political arena. This force, depending on the individual, can manifest as a dictator or a supremely powerful loving spiritual leader who has the good of the people enshrined in his heart.

This first ray also makes itself felt through the voice of the masses of the people throughout the world. This is manifesting in our world today as a mass voice crying out for values that focus on human betterment, peace, and good will between people

The Second Ray Influence in the World Today

This ray is coming from the Spiritual Hierarchy, just as the first ray was coming from Shamballa. This second ray energy of love is seeking to blend its energy with the first ray. The first ray, in a sense, prepares the way for the second ray. The second ray energy is primarily concentrated in the New Group of World Servers. This group has been chosen by the Hierarchy as its main channel of expression.

The Third Ray Affecting Humanity

The third ray of intelligent activity finds its expression through the third major center of the planet, which is humanity itself. This ray calls forth a loving intelligent response to the Shamballa and Hierarchical rays. According to Djwhal, this response is occurring in the world today.

The following diagram from the Alice Bailey book *Destiny of Nations*, summarizes what has been said so far.

I. Shamballa	Will or Power	Planetary head center,
The Holy City	Purpose…Plan	Spiritual pineal gland
	Life Aspect.	
	Ruler: Sanat Kumara, the Lord of the World.	
	The Ancient of Days	
	Melchizedek	
II. The Hierarchy	Love/Wisdom	Planetary heart center
The New Jerusalem	Consciousness	
	Group unity	
	Ruler: The Christ	
	The World Savior.	

III. Humanity The city, standing foursquare	Active Intelligence	Planetary throat center
	Creativity Self-consciousness	
Ruler:	Lucifer Son of the Morning The Prodigal Son	

Now this next piece of occult information, I think you will find absolutely fascinating. The ideology of the totalitarian government, although deluded by man, is a response to the first ray force from Shamballa. The ideology of democracy, as a form of government is a response to the second ray influence from the Hierarchy.

The ideology of communism as a form of government, although deluded by man, is a response to the third ray influence of humanity itself The three aspects of God's nature are manifested as forms of government. In their essential nature they are all divine, however, man's negative ego has misinterpreted the true nature of all three of them, in truth.

The Sixth and Seventh Rays' Influence in the World Today

The sixth ray began to pass out of manifestation in the world in 1625 after a long period of influence. The seventh ray of ceremonial order and magic began to manifest in 1675. The sixth ray is the most powerful ray in manifestation at this time. It is the line of least resistance for most people who constitute the Aryan race.

These great rays affect groups more than they do individuals. Once these groups organize under its influence a great momentum is created over a long period of time. It is for this reason that a great many people on a mass scale are having a hard time releasing this energy as it is in the process of going out of manifestation.

The sixth ray people are the reactionaries, conservatives, fanatics who hold onto the past, and inhibit progress of humanity as it is moving towards the new age. Even though this is the case, they do provide a needed balance and steadying process which is needed in the world at this time.

The seventh ray has steadily been gaining momentum since it came into manifestation. One of the major effects of the seventh ray energy is to integrate spirit and matter. The sixth ray stops at the astral or emotional plane. The seventh ray has the wonderful effect of grounding and physicalizing things into manifestation.

There are a large number of seventh ray souls who have incarnated into the world at this time. Their mission is to organize the activities of the age and end the old methods and crystallized outdated attitudes of the sixth ray and the Piscean Age. Part of the world crisis we are now in is because of the decreased influx of the sixth ray energy and the increasing flow of seventh ray energy.

Humanity is on a kind of bridge between two realities, however, not firmly anchored in either. This is also true of the transition between the Piscean Age and the Aquarian Age. The sixth and seventh ray energies are, in actuality, clashing. We see this in the political arena and in actuality all aspects of life.

The sixth ray controls the solar plexus chakra and the seventh ray controls the second chakra. This is why there is so much emotion, idealism, and desire mixed all together in the world conflict and transformation.

Every ray has a higher and lower form. It is like the ray can be used by the Higher Self or the lower-self. The higher expression of the sixth ray was found in Christianity as demonstrated by the Master Jesus. Jesus and the Lord Maitreya set the ideal for the 2000 year Piscean cycle. The word "ideal" is the key word of the sixth ray.

Djwhal Khul, in his writings, said that there were three great Masters who most perfectly manifested the ideal for humanity. One of these, I think, is going to surprise you. The first two are Christ and the Buddha.

The third was Hercules, who was the perfect disciple but not yet the perfect Son of God.

Buddha was the perfect initiate. He achieved illumination by perfection in all His attributes of Divinity. Christ was the absolute perfect expression of divinity for this cycle. Lord Maitreya's coming again at the beginning of the Aquarian Age will manifest even a higher perfection than manifested 2000 years ago.

In these three, we have examples of perfection that lie far ahead of the majority of the human race. In all three of them the sixth, second, and first rays were the controlling factors.

Hercules has a first ray soul. A second ray personality, and a sixth ray astral body. Buddha had a second ray soul, a first ray personality, and a sixth ray mind. Christ has a second ray soul, sixth ray personality, and a first ray mind.

The lower aspect of the sixth ray is the dogmatic, authoritative religion of the organized fundamentalist and orthodox churches of our time. This manifests within the church as formulated theologies, hatreds, bigotries, separativeness, self-righteousness, ego, pomp, luxurious outer appeal. This applies to all religions.

The seventh ray is a little harder to differentiate between the higher and lower aspect than the sixth ray. One way that can clearly be seen is in the difference between the white and black magician. The work of "white magic" is to integrate and synthesize the following aspects:

1. The within and the without.
2. That which is above and that which is below.
3. Spirit and matter.
4. Life and form.
5. Soul and the personality.
6. The soul and its outer expression.

7. The higher worlds of spiritual will, intuition, and higher abstract mind, with that of its lower reflection mind, emotion, and physical beingness.
8. Integrating the head and the heart, or the third chakra and the heart chakra.
9. The etheric and astral planes with the dense physical plane.
10. Intangible subjective reality with outer tangible reality.

The work of the black magician, of course, is just the opposite. Disintegration is its motto, and worship of the form side of life. This would be one aspect of the lower manifestation of this ray.

Spiritualism was the dominant religion of the old Atlantis and the seventh ray dominated that civilization, especially during its first half. The fifth ray of "concrete science" (the mind) dominates our Aryan age and we see how science and the mind has dominated our culture, to the eradicating of the soul of things in a great many ways.

The masses of people in the world today are still Atlantean (emotional) and are only emerging to the Aryan viewpoint (mind). The future Meruvian root race that is coming into manifestation now and is overlapping with the Aryan root race carries the **soul** of things. The higher aspect of the seventh ray, according to Djwhal Khul, is most active at this time.

The Nations and Their Rays

As mentioned earlier, every nation has a personality ray and a soul ray. Most nations of the earth are identified with their personality ray. The soul ray is only sensed by the aspirants, disciples, and initiates of any given nation. One of the main objectives of the New Group of World Servers is to invoke the soul ray for the nation in which they live.

The following diagram from the Alice Bailey book *Destiny of Nations*, gives the personality and soul rays of some of the most influential nations in this period of history.

Nation	Personality Ray	Soul Ray	National Motto
India	4th Ray. Harmony	1st Ray of Power through Conflict	I hide the Light.
China	3rd Ray of Intelligence	1st Ray of Power	I indicate the Way.
Germany	1st Ray of Power	4th Ray of Harmony through Conflict	I preserve.
France	3rd Ray of Intelligence	5th Ray of Knowledge	I release the Light.
Great Britain	1st Ray of Power	2nd Ray of Love	I serve.
Italy	4th Ray of Harmony	6th Ray of Idealism through Conflict	I carve the Paths.
U.S.A	6th Ray of Idealism	2nd Ray of Love	I light the Way.
Russia	6th Ray of Idealism	7th Ray of Order	I link two Ways.
Austria	5th Ray of Knowledge	4th Ray of Harmony through Conflict	I serve the Lighted Way
Spain	7th Ray of Order	6th Ray of Idealism	I disperse the Clouds.
Brazil	2nd Ray of Love	4th Ray of Harmony through Conflict.	I hide the seed.

If you study this diagram it is amazing how much sense it makes. For instance, Germany is a first ray personality which, of course, has to do with power, and look how they misused power in World War II. France is the third ray of intelligence and intellect, which, of course, makes total sense. The lower aspect being that of arrogance.

Great Britain is a first ray also and that again makes total sense. Look at Margaret Thatcher when she was in office and the whole psychology of the British government. Italy is the fourth ray, and look at the great art and sculpting that has been produced there. Do you see how perfect the science of the rays is in even describing countries, let alone incarnated personalities?

The United States is a 6th ray, which is idealism, which again is perfect for describing our country. Russia is the same, which totally fits. As these countries evolve you look on the diagram and see their soul ray and what they will be evolving into.

It is also very interesting to study the national motto or affirmation of each country. The United States is, "I light the way." The sixth ray in both the United States and Russia has manifested as fanatical adherence to an ideal. India's motto is "I hide the Light." This, again, perfectly describes India in terms of how they are so inwardly developed but not outwardly developed.

The seventh ray soul of the former Soviet Union, or Russia, led her to impose an enforced, ordered ideal. The United States' second ray soul guided her to idealism based on love.

Great Britain is the custodian of the wisdom aspect of the second ray. The United States will fulfill this same office in the immediate future. Brazil will then take over this job many thousands of years hence, according to Djwhal Khul.

These three countries with their second ray souls will demonstrate wisdom and right government based on true idealism and love. I, myself, being a second ray soul and Monad, know why I am so comfortable and happy to be living in the United States.

It is no accident why the Lord Maitreya is living in London England, being a second ray Master. Great Britain represents the aspect of mind that expresses itself in "intelligent government" based on loving understanding. This is the ideal for this government, although not fully fulfilled yet.

The United States represents the intuitive faculty, expressed as illumination. Brazil will represent, in the future, "Abstract consciousness," which is a blend of intellect and intuition.

Another interesting aspect to study in dealing with nations is whether they are feminine or masculine. India, France, the United States, Russia, and Brazil are all feminine nations. China, Germany, Great Britain, and Italy are all masculine. If you tune into these countries this really fits. Some more mental, others more nurturing and mothering.

The Effect of the Incoming Rays

The incoming seventh ray is slowly, but surely, imposing a new order and rhythm on mankind. When a new ray comes in at any given time it is felt in a sequential order. The following list gives this sequential order for any new incoming ray.

1. The sensing of an ideal.
2. The formulation of a theory.
3. The growth of public opinion.
4. The imposition of the new and developing pattern upon evolving life.
5. The production of a form based upon that pattern.
6. The stabilized functioning of the life within the new form.

Each ray embodies an idea that can be sensed as an ideal. Every ray produces three major patterns that are imposed upon the form nature of either man, a nation, or a planet. These three major patterns are the emotional pattern, mental pattern, and soul pattern.

The following diagram shows the rays that govern humanity as a whole and includes humanity's mind, astral and physical ray.

a. The Soul ray	2nd	humanity must express love.
b. The Personality ray	3rd	developing intelligence for transmutation into love/wisdom.
c. Mind ray	5th	scientific achievement.
d. Astral ray	6th	idealistic development.
e. Physical ray	7th	organization. business.

The following diagram is garnished from Benjamin Creme books. It shows the personality and soul ray of some of the other countries on the planet.

The Rays of Nations

	Soul	Personality
Afghanistan	6	4
Albania	2	7
Argentina	1	6
Austria	4	5
Australia	2	7
Bangladesh	7	6
Belgium	5	7
Bhutan	6	2
Burma	4	6
Brazil	4	2
China	1	3
Cambodia	6	2
Canada	2	1
Czechoslovakia	4	6
Denmark	3	2
Egypt	1	7
Finland	3	2
France	5	3
Germany	4	1
Great Britain	2	1
Greece	1	3
Hungary	6	4
Iceland	3	4
India	1	4
Indonesia	6	2
Ireland	6	6

Italy	6	4
Japan	6	4
Korea	6	4
Laos	4	6
Malaysia	3	3
Mongolia	3	6
Nepal	6	3
Netherlands	5	7
Norway	2	4
Pakistan	6	4
Philippines	6	2
Poland	6	6
Portugal	6	7
Romania	6	7
Russia	7	6
Spain	6	7
Sri Lanka	6	4
Sweden	3	2
Switzerland	2	3
Thailand	7	6
Tibet	7	4
Turkey	3	6
U.S.A.	2	6
Vietnam	4	6
Yugoslavia	6	7
Africa (the continent)	6	7
Asia as a whole	6	4
Europe as a whole	4	3
Scandinavia (4 nations)	3	2

The next diagram, from the Alice Bailey book *Esoteric Psychology*, shows the seven rays and the exact dates when the rays came in and out of manifestation.

Rays in and out of manifestation

Ray I	Not in manifestation.
Ray II	In manifestation since 1575 AD.
Ray III	In manifestation since 1425 AD.
Ray IV	To come slowly into manifestation around 2025 AD.
Ray V	In manifestation since 1775 AD.
Ray VI	Passing rapidly out of manifestation. Began to pass out in 1625 AD.
Ray VII	In manifestation since 1675 AD.

Major Cities and Their Rays

You may be surprised to understand that every city has a personality and soul ray also. In a previous chapter I spoke of the five major cities which will be serving as centers of spiritual transmission. These are London, New York, Tokyo, Geneva, and Darjeeling.

Djwhal has said that two more cities will be added in the future to make seven. The following diagram, from the Alice Bailey book *Destiny of Nations*, shows the soul, personality ray, and astrological sign governing these five major spiritual centers for distribution of spiritual energy.

City	Soul	Personality	Sign
London	5th ray	7th ray	Gemini
New York	2nd ray	3rd ray	Cancer
Tokyo	6th ray	4th ray	Cancer
Geneva	1st ray	2nd ray	Leo
Darjeeling	2nd ray	5th ray	Scorpio

The fact that the United Nations Headquarters is in New York and New York is one of these spiritual centers is no accident. The two future cities, which will make the number seven just like the seven chakras, will be located in Africa and Australia.

The centers have some relationship to the fact that we are in the fifth root race. These five cities through which the Hierarchy and Shamballa are working, correspond esoterically to the four chakras up the spine and the third eye center in the body of humanity and of individual man.

Los Angeles, Djwhal Khul has told us, in terms of its psychological age is just now coming out of its teenage years and is moving into the beginning years of maturity. It is a very spiritual city which its name, "City of the Angels" indicates. It does not have the same maturity as a city like London, however.

If you look at a lot of what is being taught in Los Angeles on a mass scale I think you can see the truth of this statement. I say this in no way as a criticism, for I happen to like Los Angeles and have benefited greatly from being here. It is interesting to think of the spiritual maturity level of the different cities around the globe.

The Seventh Ray and Its Effects on the Four Kingdoms

One of the effects of the seventh ray energy will be to create a closer integration and synthesis of the four kingdoms (human, animal, plant, and mineral). Part of humanity's job, which most people on this planet don't realize, is to be a distributing agent of spiritual energy to these lower kingdoms. The seventh ray will steadily refine both human and animal bodies to a more specialized state of development. This will allow the soul to have far better instruments to work through.

Another effect of the seventh ray will be to create a special closeness between the human and animal kingdom. One other side effect will be the extinction of certain types of animal bodies and very low-grade human bodies. One of the major qualities of the seventh ray disciple will be that of intense practicality.

The sixth ray disciple was much more abstract and mystical, had little understanding of the right relationship between spirit and matter. The sixth ray disciple tended to disregard matter and was only interested in the soul of things. This didn't help the creation of heaven on earth. This has caused a type of "split personality." The separation between science and religion is just one example of this.

One of the current tasks of the New Age lightworker is to heal this separation, and to spiritualize matter. The sixth ray disciple carried their work down to the astral plane and stopped. The sixth ray produced the Eastern school of occultism and the seventh ray will produce the Western school of occultism.

Now one very important point to understand in regard to all the incoming rays is that their effect varies according to the ray type of the disciple involved. Each person, of course, has a Monadic, soul, personality, mental, emotional, and physical ray. These more personal rays and the level of spiritual evolution of the disciple will have a great affect on how the more planetary rays affect the individual.

This diagram from the Alice Bailey book *Destiny of Nations*, gives a summation of the rays and the quality of energy they embody.

Ray I   Force–Energy–Action–The Occultist.
Ray II   Consciousness–Expansion–Initiation–The true Psychic
Ray III   Adaptation–Development/Evolution—The Magician.
Ray IV   Vibration–Response–Expression–The Artist
Ray V   Mentation–Knowledge–Science–The Scientist
Ray VI   Devotion–Abstraction–Idealism–The Devotee
Ray VII   Incantation–Magic–Ritual–The Ritualist

What Causes the Differences Among Disciples

Djwhal Khul, in the Alice Bailey book *White Magic,* listed the six main reasons that cause disciples to be different and hence to be affected by the great planetary rays differently. These six differences between people are:

1. Their ray type (physical, emotional, mental, personality, soul and Monad wise).
2. Their approach to truth, in terms of whether they follow the mystic or occult path.
3. Whether they are polarized physically, mentally, or emotionally.
4. Their level of evolution and initiation status.
5. Their astrological sign.
6. Their race (only because each race has a particular racial thoughtform).
7. I would add to this their past life experiences that have brought them to this current incarnation.

19

Ultimate Cosmic Ray Ascension Activation Meditation

Close Eyes–Let us begin by having everyone take a deep breath–Exhale.

We call all the Masters of the Planetary and Cosmic Hierarchy to help in this meditation.

We call forth a Planetary and Cosmic Axiatonal Alignment.

We call to Melchizedek, Mahatma and Metatron for the anchoring of the Platinum Net, to clear away any and all unwanted energies.

We call to Archangel Michael for the establishment of a Dome of Protection.

We call forth the establishment of a Pillar of Light, and a Planetary and Cosmic Ascension Column.

We now begin the process of fully anchoring and activating the Planetary and Cosmic rays.

We begin by calling forth the Ascended Master El Morya, the Chohan of the First Ray, to now fully anchor and activate the First Ray, representing the Will aspect of GOD, which is Red in color…

Bathe in the positive effects of this Red Ray now.

We call forth Master Kuthumi, and the Ascended Master Djwhal Khul, to now fully anchor and activate the Second Ray of Love/Wisdom, which is Blue in color….

Bathe in the positive effects of this Blue Ray now.

We call forth Master Serapis Bey, who is the Chohan of the Third Ray, to now fully anchor and activate the Third Ray of Active Intelligence, which is Yellow in color…

Bathe in the positive effects of this Yellow Ray now.

We call forth Master Paul the Venetian, who is the Chohan of the Fourth Ray, to now fully anchor and activate the Fourth Ray of Harmony, which is Emerald-Green in color…

Bathe in the positive effects of this Emerald-Green Ray now.

We call forth Master Hilarion, who is the Chohan of the Fifth Ray, to now fully anchor and activate the Fifth Ray of New Age Science, which is Orange in color…

Bathe in the positive effects of this Orange Ray now.

We call forth Sananda, the Chohan of the Sixth Ray, who in one of His past lives was known as the Master Jesus, to now fully anchor and activate the Sixth Ray of Devotion, which is Indigo in color…

Bathe in the positive effects of this Indigo Ray now.

We call forth St. Germain, the Chohan of the Seventh Ray, who also now just recently has taken over the position in the spiritual government known as the Mahachohan. We now request from St. Germain, the full anchoring and activation of the Seventh Ray of Ceremonial Order and Magic, which is Violet in color…

Bathe in the positive effects of this Violet Transmuting Flame.

We call forth the Seven Ray Masters, and the Ascended Master Djwhal Khul, to clear all lower and/or negative attributes from these first Seven

Rays, and replace them with the higher and positive attributes of the Christ/Buddha Archetype and Imprint.

We call forth the Ascended Master Lady Nada, to now fully anchor and activate the Eighth Ray of Higher Cleansing, which is Seafoam-Green in color…

Bathe in the positive effects of this Seafoam-Green Ray now.

We call forth Mother Mary, to now fully anchor and activate the Ninth Ray of Joy, and Attracting the Light Body, which is Blue-Green in color…

Bathe in the positive effects of this Blue-Green Ray now.

We call forth Allah Gobi, who holds the position in the spiritual government known as the Manu, which is a higher governmental position of the First Ray.

He has volunteered this evening to officially activate the Tenth Ray, which has to do with fully Anchoring the Light Body, and this Ray is Pearlescent in color…

Bathe in the positive effects of this Pearlescent Ray now.

We call forth Quan Yin, the Bodhisattva of Compassion, to now fully anchor and activate the Eleventh Ray, which serves as a Bridge to the New Age, and is Pink-Orange in color…

Bathe in the positive effects of this Pink-Orange Ray now.

We call forth the Ascended Master Pallas Athena, to now fully anchor and activate the Twelfth Ray, which embodies the full anchoring of the New Age, and the Christ Consciousness, which is Gold in color…

Bathe in the positive effects of this Gold Ray now.

We now move from the Planetary Rays to the Cosmic Rays.

We begin by calling forth Lord Buddha, our new Planetary Logos, to fully anchor and activate the Shamballic Ray, of Pure White Light…

Bathe in the profundity and glory of this Pure White Light, from Lord Buddha Himself.

We call forth Helios and Vesta, our Solar Logos, to now fully anchor and activate the Cosmic Solar Ray, from the Solar Core, which is Copper-Gold in color...

Bathe in the wonderful positive effects of this Copper-Gold Cosmic Ray now.

We call forth Melchior, our Galactic Logos, to now fully anchor and activate the Galactic Ray, which is Silver-Gold in color...

Bathe and soak in this exquisite Silver-Gold Ray.

We call forth Lord Melchizedek, our Universal Logos, for the full anchoring and activation of the Universal Ray, which is the purest and most refined Golden vibration available to Earth...

Bathe and absorb into every cell of your being, this Golden Radiation from Melchizedek.

We call forth Archangel Metatron, to fully anchor and activate the Ten Lost Cosmic Rays of the Yod Spectrum, which are all Hues of Platinum...

Bathe now and fully absorb these Ten Lost Cosmic Platinum Hues.

We call forth the Multiuniversal Logos, to now fully anchor and activate the Pure Core Platinum Ray Itself.

Become like a sponge and soak in this Pure Core Platinum Ray.

We call forth the Mahatma, who is a Cosmic Group Consciousness Being, that embodies all 352 levels of the GODHEAD, to fully anchor and activate the Mahatma Ray, which is a Cosmic White Light containing all colors of the spectrum.

Soak in this Rainbow colored Cosmic White Light, into the very core and essence of your being.

We call forth the Cosmic Council of Twelve, who are the Twelve Cosmic Beings that surround the Throne of Grace, to now fully anchor and activate Their Twelve Cosmic Rays.

These Twelve Cosmic Rays are so refined in nature, that they are translucent and beyond all color.

Soak in these exquisite Rays and translucent vibrations, into the very core essence of your heart and soul.

Last but not least, as a special dispensation, we call forth the Presence of GOD, and request an anchoring and activation of the "Clear Light, of the Ray of GOD."

Let us enter the silence now…

Let us now come back into our bodies, while continuing to absorb and enjoy these most refined Cosmic Rays.

20

The Seven Sacred Flames
Interdimensional Prayer Altar Progam

My Beloved Readers, following in this chapter is an overview of the Seven Sacred Flames Interdimensional Prayer Altar Program! This is a service we provide at the Melchizedek Synthesis Light Academy that I highly recommend joining. The following write-up is self-explanatory as to how the project works! Enjoy!

I, Dr. Joshua David Stone, and the Melchizedek Synthesis Light Academy, in conjunction with the Planetary and Cosmic Hierarchy, have physically and etherically anchored and activated in the Academy a "Seven Sacred Flames Altar." This altar, as designed by the inner plane Ascended Masters, has been set up to serve as a service vehicle for light-workers around the globe. Lightworkers are invited to fill out the simple prayer request at the end of this chapter, and this request will be placed under the sacred flame or flames of your choosing. The Seven Sacred Flames correspond to the Seven Sacred Rays governed by the seven Chohans (El Morya, Kuthumi, Serapis Bey, Paul the Venetian, Hilarion, Sananda and Lady Nada, and St. Germain). This altar is also being overlighted by Melchizedek, Archangel Metatron, the Mahatma, Djwhal Khul and the Holy Spirit.

Adding to the power and force of each Sacred Flame are, on the Red Sacred Flame, Melchior, the Manu Allah Gobi, Commander Ashtar, Archangels Michael and Faith, the Elohim Hercules and Amazonia, and Pallas Athena. Helping build the power and force on the Blue Sacred Flame are Helios and Vesta, Vywamus, the Lord and Lady of Sirius, Lord Maitreya, Lord Buddha, Isis, Archangels Jophiel and Christine, the Elohim Apollo and Lumina, and Master Lanto. Adding power and force to the Yellow Sacred Flame are Archangels Chamuel and Charity, the Elohim Heros and Amora, and the Maha Chohan. Adding to the Green Sacred Flame are Archangels Gabriel and Hope, the Elohim Purity and Astrea, the Lord and Lady of Arcturus, and Lakshmi, the Goddess of Prosperity. Adding power and force to the Orange Sacred Flame are Archangels Raphael and Mother Mary, and the Elohim Cyclopia and Virginia. Adding power and force to the Indigo Sacred Flame are Archangels Uriel and Aurora, the Elohim Peace and Aloha, the Goddess of Compassion Quan Yin, and Lady Nada. Adding power and force to the Violet Sacred Flame are Archangels Zadkiel and Amethyst, Lady Pontia, and the Elohim Arcturus and Victoria.

The concept of this new program is that all requests sent to the Academy will be placed physically and etherically under the flame of your choosing. This will keep you bathed for a one-month period under this Sacred Flame energy and influence on a continual basis. It will also mean that each night while you sleep you will be taken to the overlighting ashram of that particular influence for ascension activation, healing and training. It will also mean that the Masters overlighting the Sacred Flame of your choosing will be especially attentive and interactive with your consciousness during not only sleeping hours, but waking hours as well. Because of this fact, it is suggested that you consciously call to these Masters for help and guidance in all areas of your life.

You can send in as many requests as you want for the rest of this lifetime, however, not more than one a month. This will give each group of Masters the opportunity to work with you in a focused and direct manner.

There is also available an eighth rainbow-colored Sacred Flame under the auspices of Lord Melchizedek, Archangel Metatron, the Mahatma and the beloved Ascended Master Djwhal Khul, which is for the purpose of helping you to synthesize the seven rays.

I, Dr. Stone, recommend that you consider going through a training for seven months through each of the Seven Sacred Flames, in whichever order you want, and then in the eighth month apply for a five month training program in "Synthesis." This will give you a full year of training in each of the Seven Sacred Rays. During your training under the Eighth Sacred Flame of Synthesis, whenever you choose to utilize it, I highly recommend my book *Integrated Ascension: Revelation for the Next Millennium.* I consider this to be one of the most important books of the entire series and an essential adjunct to the training you will receive under the Eighth Sacred Flame influence.

The following chart can help you make your choices as to which Sacred Flame and group of Masters you wish to be trained under. This training does not pull you from your "God ordained ray blueprint," but, rather, is training you to become a full-fledged Ascended Master in all ray energies, which is the ideal for all masters. It is also not required to do a yearlong training program. If you would just like to do it for one month to develop a certain Sacred Flame and ray quality, that is perfectly fine. You can also request to remain under a certain ray influence for as long as you want, by sending in another request for the same Sacred Flame the following month. An example of this might be a person who is a little weak in their personal power and attuning to God's Will. This type of person might benefit from spending three months under the influence of the First Ray masters, in order to fully develop and blossom this quality. Again, the ideal is to fully integrate all Seven Rays and Sacred Flames fully and completely. After the first year program, you might want to spend longer periods of time in certain rays where you feel you need extra training and development.

My beloved readers, choose the Sacred Flame you wish to be placed under by looking at the Masters you wish to train with, the qualities you wish to develop, professional training you wish to expand, and the color flame frequency you wish to be energized by for the purpose of full ascension realization and planetary world service.

The cost of this program is by donation only and no one will ever be turned away for lack of funds, no matter how many times they use the service. Suggested donation is $3.00 a month, or a lifetime usage of the program for $25.00. Again, no one will be turned away for lack of funds, so do not let this be an issue. All are welcome to use this service. You do not have to be a member of the Academy to utilize this service. All Sacred Flame requests will be kept completely confidential. To make your request, please fill out the following form.

The Flames	Quality	Color	Profession
Sacred Flame Ray One	personal will, God's will	red	political training
Sacred Flame Ray Two	love/wisdom	blue	spiritual education spiritual teacher training
Sacred Flame Ray Three	active intelligence	yellow	business
Sacred Flame Ray Four	harmony	green	the arts, the art of healing
Sacred Flame Ray Five	concrete mind	orange	the science of anchoring the New Age, the science of healing
Sacred Flame Ray Six	devotion	indigo	the oneness of all religions
Sacred Flame Ray Seven	alchemy	violet	the violet transmuting flame, ceremonial order and magic

Sacred Flame Request Form

Name_____

Address_____

_____

Sacred Flame Selection_____

21

Ray Sessions available from the Academy

My Beloved Readers, also available from the Academy are channeled "Ray, Initiation and Light Quotient" sessions that Wistancia is in charge of doing. I highly recommend receiving a Ray Reading! I consider knowing one's rays to be even more important than having an astrological reading!

To receive a Ray Reading you can e-mail my Spiritual Partner, Wistancia, at wistancia@drjoshuadavidstone.com or call her at 818 706 8533. The readings can be done by audio cassette tape or over the phone! The cost of the session is $100 and I guarantee you, this will be one of the best investments you have ever made. Very few people on the planet can give accurate ray, initiation, and light quotient readings, so take advantage of this service!

22

My Spiritual Mission and Purpose by Dr Joshua David Stone

My Spiritual mission and purpose is a multifaceted process. Spirit and the inner plane Ascended Masters have asked myself and Wistancia (married since 1998), to anchor onto the Earth an inner plane Ashram and Spiritual/Psychological/Physical/Earthly Teaching and Healing Academy! This Academy is called the Melchizedek Synthesis Light Academy! We are overlighted in this mission by Melchizedek, the Mahatma, Archangel Metatron, the Inner Plane Ascended Master Djwhal Khul, and a large group of Ascended Masters and Angels such as the Divine Mother, Archangel Michael, Archangel Gabriel, Sai Baba, Vywamus, the Lord of Arcturus, Lord Buddha, Lord Maitreya, Mother Mary, Quan Yin, El Morya, Kuthumi, Serapis Bey, Paul the Venetian, Master Hilarion, Sananda, Lady Portia and Saint Germain, and a great many others who we like to call the "Core Group"!

I have also been asked by the inner plane Ascended Master Djwhal Khul, who again wrote the Alice Bailey books, and was also involved in the Theosophical Movement, to take over his inner plane Ashram when he moves on to his next Cosmic Position, in the not too distant future.

Djwhal holds Spiritual Leadership over what is called the inner plane Second Ray Synthesis Ashram. On the inner plane the Second Ray Department is a gigantic three story building complex with vast gardens.

The Ascended Master Djwhal Khul runs the first floor of the Second Ray Department in the Spiritual Hierarchy. Master Kuthumi, the Chohan of the Second Ray, runs the second floor. Lord Maitreya the Planetary Christ runs the third floor! When Djwhal Khul leaves for his next Cosmic Position, I will be taking over this first floor Department. The Second Ray Department is focused on the "Spiritual Education" of all lightworkers on Earth and is the Planetary Ray of the Love/Wisdom of God. What is unique, however, about the Synthesis Ashram is that it has a unique mission and purpose which is to help lightworkers perfectly master and integrate all 12 Planetary Rays which is one of the reasons I love this particular Spiritual leadership position and assignment so much! For this has been a great mission and focus of all my work!

Wistancia's and my mission has been to anchor the Synthesis Ashram and Teaching Academy onto the physical Earth, which we have done and are continuing to do in an ever increasing manner on a global level. Currently there are 40 branches of the Academy that have been set up around the world! The Academy actually first came into existence in 1996! This we have been guided to call the Melchizedek Synthesis Light Academy for the following reasons. It is called this because of the Overlighting Presence of Melchizedek (Our Universal Logos), the Mahatma (Avatar of Synthesis), and the Light which is the embodiment of Archangel Metatron, who created all outer light in our Universe and is the creator of the electron! These three beings, Djwhal Khul, and a very large Core Group of inner plane Planetary and Cosmic Masters help us in all this work.

I have also been asked by the inner plane Ascended Masters to be one of the main "High Priest Spokespersons for the Planetary Ascension Movement on Earth." I have been asked to do this because of the cutting-edge, yet easy to understand nature of all my books and work, as well as certain Spiritual Leadership qualities I humbly possess. In this regard, I represent all the Masters, which works out perfectly given the

Synthesis nature of my work. I function as kind of a "Point Man" for the Ascended Masters on Earth, as they have described it to me.

The Masters, under the guidance of Lord Buddha our Planetary Logos, have also guided us as part of our mission to bring Wesak to the West! So, for the last seven years we have held a Global Festival and Conference at Mt. Shasta, California for 2000 people. This, of course, honors the Wesak Festival, which is the holiest day of the year to the inner plane Ascended Masters, and the high point of incoming Spiritual energies to the Earth on the Taurus full moon each year! We invite all lightworkers to join us each year from all over the world for this momentous celebration, which is considered to be one of the premiere Spiritual Events in the New Age Movement!

The fourth part of my mission and purpose is the 40 volume "Easy to Read Encyclopedia of the Spiritual Path" that I have written. So far, I have completed 31 volumes in this Ascension Book Series. The Ascended Master Djwhal Khul prophesized in the 1940's that there would be a third dispensation of Ascended Master teachings what would appear at the turn of the century. The first dispensation of Ascended Master teachings was the Theosophical Movement, channeled by Madam Blavatsky. The second dispensation of Ascended Master teachings was the Alice Bailey books, channeled by Djwhal Khul, and *The I AM Discourses*, channeled by Saint Germain. My 40 volume series of books is by the grace of GOD and the Masters, the third dispensation of Ascended Master teachings as prophesized by Djwhal Khul. These books are co-creative channeled writings of myself and the inner plane Ascended Masters. What is unique about my work is how easy to read and understand it is, how practical, comprehensive, cutting-edge, as well as integrated and synthesized. Wistancia has added to this work with her wonderful book *Invocations to the Light*.

The fifth aspect of our work and mission, which is extremely unique, is the emphasis of "Synthesis." My books and all my work integrate in a very beautiful way all religions, all Spiritual paths, all mystery schools, all Spiritual teachings, and all forms of psychology! Everyone feels at home in this work because of its incredible inclusive nature! This synthesis ideal is also seen at the Wesak Celebrations, for people come from all religions, Spiritual paths, mystery schools, and teachings. The event is overlighted by over one million inner plane Ascended Masters, Archangels and Angels, Elohim Masters, and Christed Extraterrestrials. Wesak, the books, the Academy, and all our work embody this synthesis principle. This is part of why I and we have been given Spiritual Leadership of the Synthesis Ashram on Earth, and soon on the Inner Plane as well. This also explains our unique relationship to Melchizedek who holds responsibility for the "synthesis development" of all beings in our universe. Our connection to the Mahatma is explained by the fact that the Mahatma is the Cosmic embodiment of "synthesis" in the infinite Universe. This is also why the Mahatma also goes by the name, "The Avatar of Synthesis." Archangel Metatron who holds the position in the Cosmic Tree of Life of Kether, or the Crown, hence has a "Synthesis Overview" of all of the Sephiroth or Centers of the Cosmic Tree of Life! Djwhal Khul holds Spiritual leadership of the "Synthesis Ashram" on the Planetary, Solar, and Galactic levels for the Earth! The Core Group of Masters that overlight our mission are, again, the embodiment of the synthesis understanding!

The unique thing about our work is that it teaches some of the most cutting-edge co-created channeled work on the planet, in the realm of Ascension and Ascended Master Teachings. This can be seen in my books *The Complete Ascension Manual, Beyond Ascension, Cosmic Ascension, Revelations of a Melchizedek Initiate,* and *How to Teach Ascension Classes.* Because of my background as a Psychologist and licensed Marriage, Family and Child Counselor, I also specialize in some of the most advanced cutting-edge work on the planet in the field of Spiritual psychology. In this regard, I would guide you to my books, *Soul Psychology, Integrated Ascension, How to Clear the Negative Ego,* and *Ascension and Romantic Relationships*! Thirdly, I also have humbly brought forth some extremely cutting-edge work on the physical/earthly level in the field of healing, Spirituality and society, politics, social issues, Extraterrestrials, Spiritual leadership, Spirituality and business, Goddess work with Wistancia, and of course the annual Wesak Celebrations. This can be found in my books: *The Golden Keys to Ascension and Healing, Hidden Mysteries, Manual for Planetary Leadership, Your Ascension Mission: Embracing Your Puzzle Piece, How to be Successful in your Business from a Spiritual and Financial Perspective,* and *Empowerment and Integration Through The Goddess*—written by Wistancia and myself.

Adding to this, the 11 new books I have just completed and am completing. *The Golden Book of Melchizedek: How to Become an Integrated Christ/Buddha in this Lifetime, How to Release Fear-Based Thinking and Feeling: An In-depth Study of Spiritual Psychology, The Little Flame and Big Flame* (my first children's book), *Letters of Guidance to Students and Friends, Ascension Names and Terms Glossary, Ascension Activation Meditations of the Spiritual Hierarchy, The Divine Blueprint for the Seventh Golden Age, How to do Psychological and Spiritual Counseling for Self and Others, God and His Team of Super Heroes* (my second children's book) and *How to Achieve Perfect Radiant Health from the Soul's Perspective*!

Currently I have completed 31 volumes in my Ascension Book Series. Fourteen of these books are published by Light Technology Publishers. A newer version of *Soul Psychology* is published by Ballantine Publishers, owned by Random House, which I am quite excited about as well! The other books are in manuscript form and I am currently negotiating with various publishers for publishing rights! My books have also been translated and published in Germany, Brazil, Japan, Holland, Israel and this process continues to expand.

Spirit and the inner plane Ascended Masters have told me that because of this unique focus, that what I have actually done in a co-creative way and manner with them, is open a new Portal to God. This new portal opening stems out of all the cutting-edge Ascension Activations and Ascended Master Teachings, the totally cutting-edge Spiritual Psychology work because of my background as a Psychologist and licensed Marriage, Family and Child Counselor, and the unique ability to ground all the work into the physical/earthly world in a balanced and integrated manner. Spirit and the Masters have told me that this new Portal to God is on an inner and outer plane level, and continues to be built in a co-creative way with Spirit, the Masters, myself, and certain other Masters and High Level Initiates who are helping me on the inner and outer planes! I have Spiritual leadership, however, in spearheading this project, and it is one of the most exciting projects I am involved in.

In terms of my Spiritual initiation process as I have spoken of in my books, I have currently now taken my 16th major initiation. These are not the minor initiations that some groups work with, but are the major initiations that embody all the minor initiations within them. The Seventh Initiation is the achieving of Liberation and Ascension. The 10th Initiation is the completion of Planetary Ascension and the beginning of Solar Initiation. The 11th Initiation, being the first Galactic Initiation. The 12th Initiation, being the first Universal Initiation from an Earthly perspective. Having taken my 16th initiation, what is most important to me is that these initiations have been taken in an "integrated manner," for, in truth, the Masters told me that they are not really into Ascension, which may surprise a great many lightworkers. The Masters are into "*Integrated* Ascension"! There are many lightworkers taking initiations, but many are not doing so in an integrated and balanced manner! They are taking them on a Spiritual level, but they are not being properly integrated into the mental and emotional bodies or psychological level properly. They are also not transcending negative ego fear-based thinking and feeling and properly balancing their four-body system. They are also not integrating their initiations fully into the Physical/Earthly level, addressing such things as: Healing, Grounding their Missions, Finding their Puzzle Piece Mission and Purpose,

Prosperity Consciousness and Financial and Earthly Success, Integrating the God/Goddess, Embracing the Earth Mother and the Nature Kingdom, Properly Integrating into Third-Dimensional Society and Civilization in terms of the focus of their Service Mission. This is just mentioned as a very loving reminder of the importance of an integrated and balanced approach to one's Spiritual Path. The grace to have been able to take these 16 major initiations and be able to have completed my Planetary Ascension process and to have moved deeply into my Cosmic Ascension process, I give to GOD, Christ, the Holy Spirit, Melchizedek, the Mahatma, Archangel Metatron, and the Core Group of Masters I work with. I have dedicated myself and my life to GOD and the Masters' service, and I have humbly attempted to share everything I know, have used, and have done in my Spiritual path and Ascension process with all of you, my Beloved Readers!

Melchizedek, the Universal Logos, has also inwardly told me, that because of the Cosmic work I am involved with, that I have taken on the Spiritual assignment of being one of the "12 Prophets of Melchizedek on Earth." I am very humbled to serve in this capacity. For Melchizedek is the Universal Logos, who is like the President of our entire Universe. In truth, all Religions and Spiritual teachings have their source in Melchizedek and in the Great Ancient Order of Melchizedek. It is my great honor and privilege to serve GOD and Melchizedek in this capacity. This is something I have never spoken of before, although I have known of this for many, many years. I have been guided after all this time to share a little more deeply about my Spiritual mission on Earth at this time.

The Academy Website is one of the most profound Spiritual Websites you will ever explore because it embodies this "synthesis nature" and is an ever-expanding, living, easy-to-read Spiritual "encyclopedia" that fully integrates all 12 Rays in design and creation! This is also embodied in the free 140-page information packet that we send out to all who ask who wish to get involved and know more about our work! The information in the information packet is also available by just exploring the Academy Website!

We have also set up a wonderful Ministers Ordination and Training Program, which we invite all interested to read about. I am also very excited about a relatively recent book I have written called *How to Teach Ascension Classes*. Because I have become so busy with my Spiritual leadership and global world service work, I really do not have the time to teach weekly classes, as I have in the past. I firmly believe in the motto "Why *give* a person a fish, when you can *teach* them to fish!" In this vein, the Masters guided me to write a book on how to teach people to teach Ascension classes based on my work. I humbly suggest it is a most wonderful channeled book that can teach you in the easiest way and manner on every level to teach Ascension classes in your home or on a larger level if you choose. These classes are springing up now all over the globe and have been successful beyond my wildest dreams and expectations. When I wrote the book I was so involved with the process of writing it, I never fully envisioned the tremendous success it would have on a planetary and global level. Using this book and my other books, I have really done the initial homework for you, which can and will allow you to immediately begin teaching Ascension classes yourself. I humbly suggest that you look into the possibility of doing this yourself if you are so guided!

One other very interesting aspect of our Spiritual mission is something the Masters have been speaking to us about for over 10 years which is what they described as being "Ambassadors for the Christed Extraterrestrials"! We have always known this to be true! This was part of the reason I wrote the book *Hidden Mysteries*, which I humbly suggest is one of the best overviews in an easy to read and understand manner, of the entire Extraterrestrial Movement as it has affected our planet. If you have not read this book, I highly recommend that you do so. It is truly fascinating reading! My strongest personal connection to the Extraterrestrials is with the Arcturians! The Arcturians are the most advanced Christed Extraterrestrial race in our galaxy. They hold the future blueprint for the unfoldment of this planet. The Arcturians are like our future planet and future selves on a collective level. Part of my work, along with the Ascended Master Teachings I have been asked to bring through, has been to bring through a more conscious and personal connection to the Arcturians, the Ashtar Command, and other such Christed Extraterrestrial races. I also encourage you to read my book *Beyond Ascension* where I explore some of my personal experiences with the Arcturians, and how you may do so as well!

Currently, behind the scenes, we are working on some further expansions of this aspect of our mission, which we will share at a later time! Wistancia has also been involved with "White Time Healing," which is another most wonderful Extraterrestrial healing modality that she offers to the public!

One other aspect of our mission deals with having developed, with help from the inner plane Ascended Masters, some of the most advanced Ascension activation processes to accelerate Spiritual evolution that has ever been brought forth to this planet. In this co-creative process with the Masters, we have discovered the "keys" to how to accelerate Spiritual evolution at a rate of speed that in past years and centuries would have been unimaginable! This is why I call working with the Ascended Masters "The Rocketship to GOD Method of Spiritual Growth." There is no faster path to God Realization than working with the Ascended Masters, Archangels and Angels, Elohim Masters and Christed Extraterrestrials! What is wonderful about this process is that you do not have to leave your current Spiritual practice, religion, or Spiritual path. Stay on the path you are and just integrate this work into what you are currently doing! All paths as you know, lead to GOD, my friends! This is the profundity of following an eclectic path, and path of synthesis! I humbly suggest I have found some shortcuts! I share this with all lightworkers on earth, for I love GOD with all my heart and soul and mind and might, and I recognize that we are all incarnations of GOD, and Sons and Daughters of this same GOD, regardless of what religion, Spiritual path, or mystery school we are on. We are all, in truth, the Eternal Self and are all God! There is, in truth, only GOD, so what I share with you, I share with you, GOD, and myself for in the highest sense we are all one! What we each hold back from each other, we hold back from ourselves and from GOD. This is why I give freely all that I am, have learned and have, to you, my Beloved Readers, giving everything and holding back nothing! In my books and audiotapes, I have literally shared every single one of these ideas, tools, and Ascension activation methods for accelerating evolution that I have used and come to understand. My Beloved Readers, these tools and methods found in my books and on the audiotapes will "blow your mind as to their effectiveness," in terms of how profound, and easy to use they are! I would highly recommend that all lightworkers obtain the 13 Ascension Activation Meditation tapes I have put together for this purpose. Most of them were taped at the Wesak Celebrations with 1500 to 2000 people in attendance, with over one million inner plane Ascended Masters, Archangels and Angels, Elohim Masters, and Christed Extraterrestrials in attendance, under the Wesak full moon and the mountain of Mt Shasta. You can only imagine the power, love, and effectiveness of these Ascension activation audiotapes. I recommend getting all 13 tapes and working with one tape every day or every other day! I personally guarantee you that these tapes will accelerate your Spiritual evolution a thousandfold! You can find them in the information packets and on our Website. They are only available from the Academy! Trust me on this, the combination of reading my books, Wistancia's book, and working with these audio ascension activation tapes, will accelerate your Spiritual evolution beyond your wildest dreams and imagination!

One other extremely important part of my mission, which is a tremendous Spiritual passion of mine, is the training of lightworkers on earth in the area of Spiritual/Christ/Buddha thinking and negative ego/separative/fear-based thinking! These are the only two ways of thinking in the world, and each person thinks with one, the other, or a combination of both. If a person does not learn how to transcend negative ego thinking and feeling, it will end up, over time, corrupting every aspect of their lives including all channeling work, Spiritual teaching, and even healing work! One cannot be wrong with self and right with GOD. This is because our thoughts create our reality, as we all know! I cannot recommend more highly that every person reading this book, read my other books: *Soul Psychology*, *The Golden Book of Melchizedek: How to Become an Integrated Christ/Buddha in this Lifetime*, and *How to Release Fear-Based Thinking and Feeling: An In-depth Study of Spiritual Psychology*! I humbly suggest that these three books will be three of the most extraordinary self-help books in the area of mastering this psychological area of life. They are extremely easy to read, very practical and filled with tools that will help you in untold ways. Being a channel for the Ascended Masters and being uniquely trained as a Spiritual Psychologist and Marriage, Family and Child Counselor, as well as being raised in a family of psychologists, has given me an extraordinary ability to teach this material through my books in a most effective manner. The combination of my books on Ascension, and these books on Spiritual Psychology, along with Wistancia's book on the art of invocation, will literally revolutionize your consciousness in the comfort of your own home! The most extraordinary thing about all this work is how incredibly easy to read, and easy to understand it is. It is also incredibly comprehensive, completely cutting-edge, and totally integrated, balanced, and synthesized. It contains the best of all schools of thought in the past, present, and channeled cutting-edge future understanding that is available now! I humbly ask you to trust me in this regard and just read one of these books and you will immediately want to buy the others!

One other aspect of our work and mission is our involvement with the "Water of Life" and the Perfect Science products for the healing of our own physical bodies and the physical body of Mother Earth of all pollution in the air, water and earth. This is the miracle Mother Earth has been waiting for to bring her back to her "original edenic state" after so much abuse. This is not the time or the place to get into this subject in detail; however, I invite you to check out the "Water of Life" and the Perfect Science information in the Information Packet and on the Academy Website! It is truly the miracle we have all been waiting for to help heal the Earth!

One other aspect of our work and mission is a project that the Ascended Masters have asked us to put together on behalf of lightworkers and people around the globe. It is called the "Interdimensional Prayer Altar Program"! that the Masters have guided us to set up in the Academy in Agoura Hills, California on the property we live on. We have set up a "Physical Interdimensional Prayer Altar" where people can send in their prayers on any subject and we will place them on this Altar. In consultation with the Masters, Archangels and Angels, Elohim Masters, and Christed Extraterrestrials, we have set up an arrangement with them that all physical letters placed upon this Altar will be immediately worked upon by these Masters. We have been guided by the inner plane Ascended Masters to create 15 Prayer Altar Programs in different areas of life that people can sign up for. For example, there is one for health and one for financial help in your Spiritual mission. Two-thirds of these programs are totally free. There are five or six that are more advanced Spiritual acceleration programs where written material is sent to you to work with in conjunction with these programs so as to accelerate your Spiritual growth. All letters we receive by e-mail, fax, or letter are placed on the Altar by myself or my personal assistant. It is kept 100% confidential and is an extremely special service provided by the inner plane Ascended Masters and Angels to help all lightworkers and people on Earth with immediate help for whatever they need, should they desire assistance. Other examples of Prayer Altars are: Building your Higher Light Body, Extra Protection, Relationship Help, World Service Prayers, Help for your Animals, Prayer Altar for the Children, Integrating the Goddess, Integrating your Archetypes, Integrating the Seven Rays and working with the Seven Inner Plane Ashrams of the Christ, Integrating the Mantle of the Christ, Ascension Seat Integration, and Light, Love, and Power Body Building Program! These Prayer Altar Programs have been co-created with the inner plane Ascended Masters as another tool for not only helping all lightworkers with whatever they need help with, but also as another cutting-edge tool to accelerate Spiritual evolution!

In a similar regard, the Masters have guided us to set up a Melchizedek Synthesis Light Academy Membership Program which is based on three levels of involvement. Stage One, Stage Two, and Stage Three! Stage One and Stage Three are totally free. Stage Two costs only $20 for a Lifetime Membership with no other fees required. You also receive free large colored pictures of Melchizedek, the Mahatma, Archangel Metatron, and Djwhal Khul for joining. It is not necessary to join to get involved in the work; however, it has been set up by the inner plane Ascended Masters as another service and tool of the Academy to help lightworkers accelerate their Spiritual evolution! When joining the different Stages, the Masters take you under their wing, so to speak, and accelerate your evolution by working with you much more closely on the inner plane while you sleep at night and during your conscious waking hours. The joining is nothing more than a process that gives them the permission to work with you in this more intensive fashion! Again, it is not necessary to join to get involved in the work, and is really just another one of the many fantastic tools and services the Academy has made available to you to accelerate your Spiritual, psychological, and earthly/physical evolution in an integrated and balanced manner!

I had a dream shortly after completing my two new books, *The Golden Book of Melchizedek: How to Become an Integrated Christ/Buddha in This Lifetime,* and my book *How to Release Fear-Based Thinking and Feeling: An In-depth Study of Spiritual Psychology.* In the dream, I was being shown the different Spiritual missions people had. My Spiritual mission was the embodiment of the Holy Spirit. I clearly was shown how other people within GOD, Christ, and the Holy Spirit had missions of being more detached off-shoots of the Holy Spirit, and continuing outward from there, had all kinds of different Spiritual missions. However, mine was the embodiment of the Holy Spirit on Earth.

My Beloved Readers, I want to be very clear here that in sharing this I am in no way, shape, or form claiming to be the Holy Spirit. There is enough glamour in the New Age Movement and I am not interested in adding any more to it. What I am sharing here, which is being given to more clearly and precisely share my Spiritual mission and purpose, is that which I am here to strive to embody and demonstrate. The Holy Spirit is the third aspect of the Trinity of GOD. I have always greatly loved the Holy Spirit, for the Holy Spirit is like the "Voice of GOD"! It is the "Still, Small Voice Within"! When one prays to GOD, the Holy Spirit answers for GOD. The Holy Spirit is the answer to all questions, challenges, and problems. The Holy Spirit speaks for the Atonement or the At-one-ment! It teaches the Sons and Daughters of GOD how to recognize their true identity as God, Christ, the Buddha, and the Eternal Self! In truth, there are only two voices in life! There is the voice of the negative ego and the "Voice of the Holy Spirit"! There is the voice of negative ego/fear-based/separative thinking and feeling, and there is the Voice of God/Spiritual/Christ/Buddha thinking and feeling! There is the "Voice of Love" and the voice of fear! There is the "Voice of Oneness" and the voice of separation!

I was given this dream after completing these two books because, I humbly suggest, this is the energy I was embodying in writing them and that I am striving to embody at all times in my Spiritual mission and purpose on Earth. This is not surprising in the sense that this has always been my Spiritual ideal and the dream was just an inward confirmation in that moment that I was embodying and demonstrating that Spiritual Ideal in the energy flow I was in. This is what I strive to do in all my work, be it my Ascension Book Series, Wesak Celebrations, Teaching, Counseling, Videotapes, Audiotapes, and all my work, which is to strive to be the embodiment of a "Voice for God"! By the grace of GOD, Christ, the Holy Spirit, and the Masters, I provide a lot of the "answers" people and lightworkers are seeking! I teach people how to "undo" negative ego/fear-based/separative thinking and feeling, and show then how to fully realize God/Christ/Buddha thinking and feeling! I show them how to release and undo glamour, illusion, and maya, and instead seek "Truth, as GOD, Christ, the Holy Spirit, and the Masters would have you seek it!"

My real purpose, however, is not to just be the embodiment of the Holy Spirit on Earth, for I would not be embodying the Voice and Vision of the Holy Spirit if I just focused on this. The Voice and Vision of GOD, Christ, the Holy Spirit, and Melchizedek is that of synthesis! This is the other thing I feel in the deepest part of my heart and soul that I am here to embody! So my "truest and highest Spiritual ideal" that I am here to strive to embody, is GOD, Christ, the Holy Spirit, the inner plane Ascended Masters, the Archangels and Angels of the Light of GOD, the Elohim Councils of the Light of GOD, and the Christed Extraterrestrials of the Light of GOD. I feel in the deepest part of my heart and soul, and what I try to embody every moment of my life is "All that is of GOD and the Godforce on Earth!" In this regard, it is my Spiritual mission and purpose to strive to be the embodiment of the "synthesis nature of God on Earth"! This is why I have been given Spiritual leadership of the Synthesis Ashram and Academy on Earth and future leadership of the inner plane Synthesis Ashram that governs our planet.

I was also told by the Masters that I had achieved my Ascension in the fullest sense of the term and that I did not need to physically die anymore!

I have also been living on Light the last four years; however, this is not something I would recommend everyone do, for the Masters have told me they would actually prefer that almost all lightworkers live on what they call a partial light diet, which is a good healthy physical diet, and also absorb as well. Because of certain factors that are connected with my particular Spiritual Mission and purpose, living on Light has been appropriate for the Spiritual Mission, Spiritual blueprint, puzzle piece, Spiritual contract and Service mission that I came to fulfill!

The other thing I strive to do in my Spiritual mission is to embody Spiritual mastery on a Spiritual, psychological, and physical/earthly level. What most people and lightworkers do not realize is that there are three distinct levels to God Realization. There is a Spiritual level, a psychological level, and a physical/earthly level! To achieve true God Realization, all three levels must be equally mastered! Another way of saying this is that there are "Four Faces of GOD"! There is a Spiritual Face, a Mental Face, an Emotional Face, and a Material Face! To truly realize God, all four must be equally mastered, loved, honored, sanctified, integrated, and balanced! The "Mental and Emotional Faces of GOD" make up the psychological level of GOD. So, my Spiritual mission and purpose is to fully embody Spiritual mastery and unconditional love on all three of these levels and in all Four Faces of GOD! In a similar vein, my Spiritual mission and purpose is to embody self-mastery and proper integration of all "Seven Rays of GOD," not just one or a few. For the "Seven Rays of GOD" are, in truth, the true "Personality of GOD"! My Spiritual mission and purpose is to not only strive to embody all levels of GOD, but to also try and develop all my God-given abilities and Spiritual gifts, on a Spiritual, Psychological, and Physical/Earthly level, and in all Four Faces of GOD!

My Beloved Readers, all these things that I have written about in this chapter are what I strive to fully embody and demonstrate on the Earth every moment of my life, and is what I strive with all my heart and soul and mind and might to teach others to do as well!

As the Founder and Director of the Melchizedek Synthesis Light Academy along with Wistancia, with great humbleness and humility, it has been my great honor and privilege to share "my Spiritual mission and purpose" in a deeper and more profound manner at this time. I do so in the hopes that all who feel a resonance and attunement with this work will get involved with the Academy's "Teachings" and all that it has to offer. I also share this so that all who choose to get involved might join this vast group of lightworkers around the globe, to help spread the teachings and work of the inner plane Ascended Masters. The inner plane Ascended Masters and I, along with the Archangels and Angels, Elohim Councils, and Christed Extraterrestrials, put forth the Clarion Call to lightworkers around the world to first explore this work, then integrate this work, and then become Ambassadors of the Ascended Masters so we may at this time in Beloved Earth's history bring in fully now the Seventh Golden Age in all its Glory!

About the Author

Dr. Joshua David Stone has a Ph.D. in Transpersonal Psychology and is a licensed Marriage, Family and Child Counselor, in Agoura Hills, California. On a Spiritual level he anchors *The Melchizedek Synthesis Light Academy and Ashram*, which is an integrated inner and outer plane ashram that seeks to represent all paths to God! He serves as one of the leading spokespersons for the Planetary Ascension Movement. Through his books, tapes, workshops, lectures, and annual Wesak Celebrations, Dr. Stone is known as one of the leading Spiritual Teachers and Channels in the world on the teachings of the Ascended Masters, Spiritual Psychology, and Ascension! He has currently written over 31 volumes in his Ascension Book Series, which he also likes to call "The Easy to Read Encyclopedia of the Spiritual Path"!

For a free information packet of all Dr. Stone's workshops, books, audiotapes, Academy membership program, and global outreach program, please call or write to the following address:

Dr. Joshua David Stone
Melchizedek Synthesis Light Academy
28951 Malibu Rancho Rd.
Agoura Hills, CA 91301

Phone: 818-706-8458
Fax: 818-706-8540
e-mail: drstone@best.com

Please come visit my Website at:
http://www.drjoshuadavidstone.com

CPSIA information can be obtained at www.ICGtesting.com
Printed in the USA
LVOW13s1734040614

388620LV00001B/359/P